Railway Travel in World War Two

Front cover: One of the Southern Railway's wartime 'mixed traffic' Merchant Navy class locomotives, 21C9 "Shaw Savill" in its wartime black livery at Waterloo on 6 May 1943. (SR Official)

Rear cover: The iconic "Is Your Journey Really Necessary?" poster. (Railway Executive Committee 1942)

Inside flap: London & North Eastern Railway C1 class 4-4-2 number 4434 with a train on the fast line passes an unidentified 0-6-2T with a suburban train at Hatfield in May 1940. (Colour Rail)

Rear flap: London & North Eastern Railway C1 class 4-4-2 number 4411 arrives at a crowded Royston station in 1944. (Colour Rail)

Railway Travel in World War Two

Peter Steer

PEN & SWORD
TRANSPORT

AN IMPRINT OF PEN & SWORD BOOKS LTD
YORKSHIRE - PHILADELPHIA

First published in Great Britain in 2023 by
Pen and Sword Transport
An imprint of
Pen & Sword Books Ltd
Yorkshire - Philadelphia

ISBN 9781399063173

Typeset in INDIA by IMPEC eSolutions
Printed and bound in England by CPI Group (UK) Ltd, Croydon CR0 4YY

Pen & Sword Books Ltd incorporates the imprints of Pen & Sword Books
Archaeology, Atlas, Aviation, Battleground, Discovery, Family History, History,
Maritime, Military, Naval, Politics, Railways, Select, Transport, True Crime,
Fiction, Frontline Books, Leo Cooper, Praetorian Press, Seaforth Publishing,
Wharncliffe and White Owl.

For a complete list of Pen & Sword titles please contact

PEN & SWORD BOOKS LIMITED
47 Church Street, Barnsley, South Yorkshire, S70 2AS, England
E-mail: enquiries@pen-and-sword.co.uk
Website: www.pen-and-sword.co.uk

or

PEN AND SWORD BOOKS
1950 Lawrence Rd, Havertown, PA 19083, USA
E-mail: Uspen-and-sword@casematepublishers.com
Website: www.penandswordbooks.com

Contents

Introduction   6

Chapter 1   War is Declared   11
Chapter 2   Making Way for the Essential Traffic   41
Chapter 3   Is Your Journey Really Necessary?   63
Chapter 4   Visiting the Evacuated Children   81
Chapter 5   Government Departments Move to the Provinces   98
Chapter 6   Railway Travel in the Early Years of the War   112
Chapter 7   Surviving the Blitz   141
Chapter 8   The Government's Dilemma as
                 Passenger Numbers Rise   156
Chapter 9   Travel by Service Personnel   186
Chapter 10   Time to Take a Holiday   212
Chapter 11   Towards Victory   234

Bibliography   260
Index   266

Introduction

[Railway] travel was three times as expensive as before the war, yet it was probably three times as uncomfortable. Reservations were no longer permitted. There were usually no restaurant cars. If trains were not cancelled, they were likely to be late. Sometimes it was literally impossible for a grown man to force his way into corridors already jammed with weary war workers and servicemen on leave.

Angus Calder, *The People's War – Britain 1939 – 1945*, Jonathan Cape, 1969.

Angus Calder in the quotation above has concisely summarised the folk memory of railway travel during the Second World War. In his book *The People's War*, he acknowledges that the relocation of factories away from danger areas created the breakup of families and a new travel need, and he concurs with the widely accepted impression that during the war the reduced accommodation on the trains resulted in overcrowding. But was travelling by train always as bad as Calder describes? As for all such generalisations there is a wide range of 'truth' to be considered. Between the widely held view that every railway journey was an experience to be stoically endured and the extreme opposite possibility that it was generally 'business as usual', there is a spread of possible travelling experiences, all of which might be 'true' at different times and at different locations spread across the country. Calder later re-examined the public memory of the war. The historiographic thrust of his book *Myth of the Blitz* was that he did not deny the events in the same way that a holocaust denier might pervert facts but re-examined the freely available information to separate actuality from the public's understanding of events which were largely germinated by wartime propaganda and patriotic sentiment. He confronted the populist vision of a nation in which every loyal citizen gallantly contributed to the war effort and stoically accepted all the deprivations. In the same spirit of attempting to clear away any myths, this account reviews the mobility needs and travel experience of railway passengers during the war period. One well-remembered slogan adopted by the government and the hard-pressed railways was 'Is your journey really necessary?' The mythical totally patriotic population would surely not undertake any 'unnecessary' railway journey as this would be against the ethos of the all-out effort to win the war.

There has been very little research into the public's changing transport needs during the war and only a few references in literature. Some material from the Mass Observation (MO) programme has been published commercially and on-line but none that describes in depth railway travel. There have been overviews of British culture – cinema, radio, journalism, etc. and insights into the social history of the war period as well as accounts of everyday life during World War Two. These too do not give any insight into the part the railways played in providing mobility to the British public, but perhaps this is not surprising since the railways were such a familiar and reliable element of everyday life that they simply blended, unnoticed, into the public consciousness. Arguably this lack of reference to the railways indicates that overall, they provided a good service in the difficult circumstances.

There are many accounts attesting to the fact that the populace was not wholly united with degrees of disunity that included many dissenting politicians, trade unionists and the continuing IRA activity. Also, there were many social problems that were sadly generated by the war such as conflicts between those evacuated and their hosts, overcrowding, and complaints about the 'dirty habits' of the refugees.

Other examples of lack of national cooperation include reports of looting, profiteering and black-market activities. Compared to these anti-social activities, the use of the railways to make journeys that were not absolutely essential seems rather venal and as such a few extra journeys by train was likely to have been acceptable to many citizens.

While there is little academic literature specifically relating to railway travel during World War Two, Chris Sladen has written specifically about holiday travel during the war – which in the early twentieth century implied railway travel for any significantly distant holiday resort. A holiday journey might not be viewed by the government as 'necessary', so Sladen uses wartime holiday travel as an indicator that the public was not prepared to fall into line with the wartime passenger transport propaganda. Sladen quotes examples of the public's need for holidays based on the MO reports and he further illustrates his argument with a contemporary quotation from Vera Brittain's 1940 book *England's Hour* where she wrote, 'the British determination to celebrate a holiday is obvious to the most casual spectator'. Brittain, whose edited wartime diaries make no reference at all to railway travel, thereby contradicts the accepted view – the 'mythology of the blitz' – that everybody worked flat-out without holidays during the war. Sladen does however also quote Elizabeth Bowen who when writing retrospectively in 1949 offered the contrary and generally accepted opinion that everybody did work without breaks during the war.

There were some contemporary accounts published describing the railways' efforts during the war. Collie Knox wrote a book which was published towards the end of the war in 1944 when he provided an account which was ostensibly about the efforts of all the British railways as a whole but dealt almost exclusively with the activities of the Great Western Railway. In 1946, the Southern Railway published an account of its wartime struggles, *War on the Line*, written by Bernard Darwin. Neither book provides any details of the passengers' travel experience except for one short sentence in *War on the Line* when it is acknowledged that passengers were accustomed to and duly accepted delays in wartime. This short reference did however relate specifically to travel during the Blitz period.

This account will examine the travel experiences and the mobility needs of the railway passengers who travelled on the 'ordinary' services. To put these services into context some reference has to be made to the special services such as the trains provided for evacuees and the movement of troops. Also affecting the smooth running of the regular passenger trains was the operation of the freight trains which often had to take priority as they were carrying essential supplies of fuel and war materials. Sources have included reminiscences from those who remember the war years obtained either by direct personal conversation or from on-line resources. Also, contemporary newspaper and magazine accounts of travel by train have been a good source of contemporary opinion. The records of the Railway Executive Committee (REC) held at The National Archives at Kew have been searched to obtain information about the train services provided by the railways, the provision of facilities such as restaurant cars and passenger numbers information.

The files held at Kew also contained details about the friction between the REC and the government about limiting passenger numbers. The impression given when reading these files is that the railways never lost their sense of public service and that they would forever endeavour to provide a train service that would cater adequately for the 'traffic that presents itself'. The difficulty that the REC had to grapple with was that at the time the government wanted a reduction in passenger traffic the public had many new travel requirements which were as a direct result of the war. Much of this additional traffic the REC deemed to be 'government' traffic due to the dispersal of government departments to the safety of the provinces and the plethora of government approved discounted ticketing schemes such as help for parents visiting their evacuated children. The most significant of these schemes in respect to the total passenger numbers was a reduced price arrangement for service personnel partaking of leisure travel.

This book is an expansion of a dissertation entitled "Was Your Journey Really Necessary?", which formed part of my MA in railway studies at the University of York. I am grateful for the help and guidance provided by the course tutor, Dr David Turner, who would often send me details of potentially useful sources of information as well as providing invaluable advice. Much of the research was carried out during the Covid-19 lockdown in 2020. Due to the closing of the reading rooms so as to be able to complete the dissertation in the set time, I had to pivot the theme slightly to be able to use what I had already collected and other on-line material. I have since been able to fill in the gaps and what has struck me are the interesting parallels between the pandemic period and the wartime travel experience. Both events brought forth confusing government messaging, such as what is a 'necessary' reason to go outside your home or what is a 'necessary' railway journey? There has also been the 'one rule for us and one rule for them' syndrome, with parties during the lockdown at number ten Downing Street and during the war officials retaining reserved first-class accommodation for themselves for visits to evacuated government establishments in the provinces at a time when often the ordinary travellers were crammed into third class compartments or spilling out into the corridors. There were also the 'deniers' during the pandemic as there were during the war. During the pandemic these included those who believed that Covid was merely 'just a bit of flu' or that the vaccines were part of a sinister plot to control our minds. During the war when train services were cut, many passengers could not accept that this was really necessary while others rejected the need for a blackout on the trains – 'it is just done to annoy us' was a view espoused at a Southern Railway shareholders' meeting. Perhaps this shows that people have not changed very much during the last eighty years.

Chapter 1

War is Declared

Land services are not only essential links in the chains which ensure that our Forces are supplied … they must also play their part in maintaining the physical, social and moral well-being of the community.

Report on land transportation for the
Lord President's office, 1941

On 1 September 1939, with the international situation deteriorating and only two days before the British government declared war on Nazi Germany, the railways of Britain were once again brought 'under government control'. This was a repetition of what had happened a quarter of a century earlier at the outbreak of the Great War in 1914. The original Regulation of the Forces legislation used in 1914 had just been replaced with the new Emergency Powers (Defence) Act 1939 which had only received royal assent on 24 August. Defence regulation 69 of the Act empowered the Ministry of Transport to take control of the British railway undertakings by giving the ministry the legal ownership of all of the railway company assets.

In September 1939, the government may have been adamant that they had taken full control of the railways – and this would have been made possible within the terms of the Control Order – but, as in 1914, they placed themselves at arm's length from any of the day-to-day decisions. The nation's railways were not to be directly administered by the central government's Ministry of Transport – later to become the Ministry of War Transport – as responsibility for all the routine operational and management functions was to be entrusted to the

Railway Executive Committee (REC). This new committee became part of the national governance hierarchy as it was officially a wartime advisory body to the Minister of Transport, and was given the remit to coordinate the wartime operations of the London Passenger Transport Board (LPTB) and the four main line railways (often referred to as the 'big four'), which were the Southern Railway (SR), the Great Western Railway (GWR), the London Midland and Scottish Railway (LMSR), and the London and North Eastern Railway (LNER). Several minor undertakings such as the Kent and East Sussex Light Railway were also brought under the REC umbrella.

The British railway network in 1939 served almost all towns and larger villages across the land. The railways employed 580,000 staff of all grades. When the REC took charge, the combined railway route mileage operated by the four main-line companies was just short of 20,000 miles. The total amount of railway line that had been laid, taking account of the sections of multiple track lines and the sidings, etc. was 50,000 miles. To haul the trains over this extensive network the companies owned 20,000 steam locomotives with only a handful of diesel locomotives used for shunting duties. To carry the passengers there were 60,000 passenger vehicles and for the nation's goods traffic 1,250,000 wagons and vans. The railways owned 50 hotels situated at or very near to major stations and also had maritime links as they owned 76 docks, harbours and wharfs. The railways were also road hauliers, using 10,000 road vehicles for the short local trips between the station goods yards and their customers' premises. They owned 11,000 horses which were also used for local deliveries and as motive power when shunting wagons in the goods yards.

The railway system was still the main mode of transport for freight, most of which was in small consignments with relatively little 'bulk' traffic apart from minerals and coal. Although car ownership had increased rapidly during the 1930s, the lack of main roads avoiding congested town centres meant that the railways maintained their virtual monopoly on longer distance passenger travel. In an age when people lived close to their places of work, their daily, short distance journeys would have been made on foot, by bicycle or they may have used the buses. Many working people would only ever travel by train to reach the seaside resorts during their summer holidays.

In the late 1930s, with the prospect of another war in Europe, British national and local government departments had begun to make discrete preparations for a possible conflict. The threat of an impending war in 1912 had resulted in the first incarnation of the REC and at the time of the Munich crisis in September 1938 it was reformed. The committee was charged with preparing for a conflict which many at the time thought to be inevitable. The creation of this 'new' REC may not have been a 'state secret', but even the usually reliable and informative *Railway Gazette* failed to announce its revival. The committee's offices were placed below ground in the abandoned Down Street tube station. The location of this safe and secure subterranean accommodation was only later in 1944 to be made public. The committee's official notepaper was headed with the less than helpful address of 'London S.W.', and should you wish to contact the REC, their 'post box' was the address of the railways' trade body – the Railway Companies' Association. There was a discreet entrance at street level into what appeared to be a closed Piccadilly Line station, but for use during air raids there was also an alternative secret access. The former platform area at Down Street station had been partitioned off from the track and a single door provided to enable those arriving at the REC headquarters to step into the cramped offices from the driver's cab of a train. In September 1939 the LPTB issued twenty-two permits for named staff to travel in the driver's compartment from Piccadilly Circus station as far as the access door at the former Down Street station. A further eight permits were provided for 'female clerical staff'. Those wishing to arrive at Down Street by train had to first present their permit to the station master at Piccadilly Circus who would then escort the bearer to the train guard who would then be responsible for making the arrangements for the unadvertised stop.

The main railway executive committee was composed of senior railway managers – including all of the general managers from each of the railway companies, and after 1 September was to take precedence over the existing railway companies' boards of directors who were at that time mainly composed of bankers, lawyers and industrialists from other sectors of the economy and who were therefore not – apart from a few notable exceptions – professional railwaymen. The first chairman of the REC was Sir Ralph Wedgwood, who was at the time the chief general manager of the LNER. Several subcommittees were created including the mechanical and electrical engineer's subcommittee which had the recently knighted Sir Nigel Gresley as its first chairman. Thus, at first sight, this might indicate a formula for a well-run wartime operation but, as will be shown, there were to be many tensions between the REC and senior government ministers backed by their civil servants. From the very start of the war period, the main REC members were often slow to relinquish their traditional railway management instincts and would at times attempt to take 'commercial considerations' into account when planning the necessary restricted passenger services during the war. The REC was to be presented to the public as an organisation which had been established to harness the 'tremendous requirements of the forces and home defence' and at the same time 'continue to provide the public with the best service possible'. And, in fairness to the REC and the individual railway companies, during the war period they did strive to maintain the best service that was possible for their passengers in the very difficult circumstances.

Less than three weeks after the declaration of war on 25 September it was announced that one of the original REC members, the general manager of the SR, Gilbert Szlumper, was to be seconded to the War Office when he was appointed as the director general of transportation and movements. His seat on the committee was to be taken by the new SR general manager Eustace Missenden. Szlumper was to be based at Southampton and had an important role in arranging the embarkation of the British Expeditionary Force (BEF) to France.

The government was to guarantee the railways an income based on their performance averaged across the three years 1935, 1936 and 1937. The preceding year, 1938, was ignored as it was deemed to have been a 'bad year'. The original agreement made with the government was that each company would be guaranteed a share of £40million. If the railways were to earn an addition £3.5million they would be able to keep this additional income. If more than £43.5million was earned this surplus was to be shared with the government. It has been argued that the agreement between the REC and Chamberlain's government was flawed because the railways were guaranteed an income which was £6million above the combined total income in 1938, and furthermore the railways should not be entitled to such largesse since they had regularly not been able to pay dividends on the ordinary shares during the 1930s. Based on that premise, it has been asserted the railway administrations were incompetent. This standpoint ignores the effects of the recent Great Depression and the restrictions placed onto the railways as to the charges that they were able to levy for the transport of freight. While during the war some accusations were to be made that the railways lacked any incentive to provide a good service – but it must be stressed that the government did not align itself with this view – it is evident that on the whole that the 'public service' ethos ingrained in the professional managers' psyche was maintained despite the security of the income and this would often lead to conflict with the government when any reduction in services was necessary to make way for essential traffic.

Arguably, given the crucial strategic importance of the railways the companies should have been nationalised, and this was the wish of Attlee and Bevin who were the Labour Party members in the small wartime cabinet established later in May 1940 after Winston Churchill became prime minister. When railway nationalisation was discussed in 1940 at a cabinet meeting it was firmly rejected by Churchill who cited the uncertainties that he claimed to have witnessed within the railway administrations following the Great War when such a drastic change had been proposed. The prime minister opined that it would be a 'misfortune' if the railways were to be taken into full public ownership. Churchill had, as a Liberal MP, been an advocate of railway nationalisation, believing that the railways had become so essential to the running of the country that they should be treated as a public utility similar to gas and water and not be a source of profits for the railway owners whose charges effectively amounted to a tax on commerce. Times however had moved on; Churchill was now a Conservative and the regulations introduced when the railways were reorganised in 1923 had blunted much of the companies' powers in respect of charges. Furthermore, to embark on such a complicated process as nationalisation at a time of such grave crisis would have been foolhardy and very expensive in parliamentary time.

By 1938 with fears of an upcoming war, the first versions of evacuation schemes for the civilian population were prepared by the urban local authorities. Central to the planning was the presumption that the railways would be entrusted with the task of transporting evacuees away from the danger areas. The prospect of war had brought with it the threat of savage air raids on civilian targets. The Nazis had 'form' in this respect since Hitler had lent his friend Franco the German Condor Legion to support the nationalist cause during the Spanish civil war. The Legion, which remained under German command, included four bomber squadrons and is infamous for the devastation and huge loss of civilian life in the Basque town of Guernica in April 1937 as well as several lesser-known attacks on Barcelona. The contemporary newsreels shown in British cinemas that year featured the continuing civil war in Spain and the Sino-Japanese war which had broken out the previous year. The devastating effect of both these conflicts with indiscriminate attacks on non-military targets bore heavily on those entrusted to prepare for a possible mass evacuation intended to move much of the civilian population far away from any of the urban areas likely to be subjected to air raids. On 26 July 1938, the government appointed Anderson Committee reported to the home secretary who, after obtaining the necessary agreement of parliament, set out the fundamental principles to be followed should evacuation be necessary. It was declared that, except in exceptional circumstances, evacuation was not to be made compulsory, and this understandable and reasonable edict was to have unfortunate consequences as many vulnerable people were to remain in the danger areas. Anderson insisted that when groups of school children were evacuated, they should be kept together and accompanied by their usual teachers. While moving children away from the dangers of enemy air raids was important, the personal safety of the young and vulnerable was to be part of the government's aim, in strategic and practical terms their removal would mean that in the event of widescale bombing they would not be an additional burden on the hospitals and first aid posts. Also, with the reassurance that their children were far away and safe, their parents would be more likely to continue with essential wartime duties.

In 1937 when the Air-raid Precautions Bill was discussed in the House of Commons, consideration was given to the desirability or otherwise of the mass evacuation of the civilian population away from urban areas where indiscriminate bombing was likely. During the debate Somerset Maxwell who, despite being an MP for a rural location far removed from London, held strong views on the fate of the East End where the London Docks would be a prime target for enemy bombers. He cautioned against the mass evacuation of the population, maintaining that many residents had important work to do to maintain critical economic activities in the area. On this basis he reasoned that there was the stark choice to be made between either evacuating all residents living in the East End and consequently closing down an economically important area, or alternatively not have an evacuation scheme as everybody was needed to maintain the dockland facilities. He did argue however that the government must prepare to find accommodation for vulnerable people, including young children, in less dangerous areas and to move hospital patients into country districts to make room for the inevitable casualties.

Consequently, the ministry of health took overall charge of the evacuation of the school children, younger children with their mothers and expectant mothers together with the blind and other disabled people. With the assistance of the local authorities this ministry instigated the planning of this complex operation and to produce what they hoped would be workable plans to evacuate the vulnerable children and others away from the potentially dangerous areas. This was achieved even before Neville Chamberlain made his historic aeroplane journey to meet Adolf Hitler in Munich. To comply with the plan, the London County Council (LCC) had established its 'evacuation branch' of the education officer's department to take responsibility for the formulation of policy and the development of the welfare arrangements for evacuated adults and children when they reached their new wartime homes. Concerns began to be expressed about the desirability of separating children from their parents and these worries were later to prove to be completely justified. The LCC however claimed to be more attuned to public sentiment and were able to convince the government that the populace in fact favoured children being evacuated if, as Anderson had commanded, they were in the care of their teachers.

The LCC's initial proposals were to identify locations for what were soon to be known as the 'reception areas' to be ready to receive evacuees who would arrive by train from London. A line was drawn on a map from Bristol to the Wash and all the reception areas for London evacuees would be located below this line. Within this broad area any localities close to towns and cities such as Portsmouth, Gosport, Rochester, Chatham and Southampton (including the Isle of Wight) were excluded since these areas contained naval bases which were potential targets for bombers. In these areas, the local authorities had to arrange for the evacuation of school children and the other vulnerable people by train to pre-determined safe areas in rural Hampshire, Dorset and Wiltshire.

The early planning was vindicated when tensions rose in the days before the Munich conference. On Tuesday, 22 September 1938 there was the dramatic proposal that the pre-prepared plans should be set in motion on 30 September – a decision revoked only when the Munich agreement was signed on that very day. The evacuation may have been called off, but the general opinion was that the Munich agreement had only bought time as the likelihood of a war remained high and that the evacuation plans should be retained and modified as circumstances demanded.

In March 1939, the minister of health confirmed that should evacuation be necessary school parties of children in charge of their teachers were to be taken out separately from children who were under five – these would be evacuated accompanied by their mothers. Should the mothers also have children over five years old, these could be withdrawn from the school party and travel with their mother and younger siblings. It was also confirmed that evacuation would be by train, but any children with learning difficulties or were physically impaired for any reason were to go by road.

During August 1939 the tension had increased in the urban communities. In anticipation of imminent war, on 4 August key LCC staff were recalled from their holidays. Schools, which had been closed for the summer holidays, were ordered to reassemble. As the nation held its breath at 11.7am on Thursday 31 August, the order to commence the evacuation on 1 September was received by the local authorities. Children who were with their families on summer holiday away from the cities were advised to remain at their holiday residences. War was declared on the day the evacuation commenced.

One of the REC subcommittees was the operating and civil engineers' subcommittee which was tasked with the preparation of a schedule of emergency passenger train services to provide the additional paths for extra trains during any civilian evacuation scenario. Consequently, in line with the government's policy, during the first days of the war the REC instigated a severely curtailed passenger service based on the scheme drawn up by the subcommittee. Trains were run at reduced speeds to accommodate the anticipated extra military and civilian evacuation traffic which was originally expected to be hampered by disruptive air raids. The REC however disliked the prospect of limiting passenger travel and made this clear in a national press statement insisting that they had to give priority to traffic of an undefined 'urgent national character'. The REC was well prepared in August, as only days before the declaration of war, it duly issued posters forewarning the public of the anticipated travel restrictions.

It was decided that the special trains carrying evacuated children would be timetabled so that they did not affect the routines of the regular commuters. When possible, suburban services were run as normal before 8.00am and after 5.30pm, but only a skeleton service was provided during the day between these times to make way for the evacuation trains. On the main line routes, despite the troop and civilian evacuation trains, the railways hoped to maintain as near as normal a service as possible. The REC warned the travelling public that timetable changes might have to be made, and that any such changes would have to be implemented without any prior notice being given.

The evacuation programme swung into action, and the fully prepared steps taken to clear the railways for the necessary special trains. During the evacuation period, the REC initially held back from introducing the full draconian emergency timetables. Instead it delegated to its operations subcommittee the task of arranging for the cancellation of specific trains as and when it was thought necessary. Accordingly, the LNER announced that the high-speed streamlined expresses, Coronation, Silver Jubilee, West Riding Limited and the East Anglia express, were to be cancelled. On Monday, 4 September, the LMSR publicly announced that all of their excursion trains were to be cancelled and warned that cheap tickets on ordinary trains were under review. Later, on Wednesday, 6 September the LNER made changes to the Flying Scotsman timetable. The GWR, after hoping to be able to provide a 'business-as-usual' timetable, was soon to make severe reductions to its services. In addition to these reductions, the REC demanded an immediate reduction in the maximum speed of the trains. These hastily revised timetables could only be conveyed to the public by displaying posters at the stations and the companies hoped that passengers would refer to these and not overload their telephone enquiry services.

The children being evacuated from London and the other major cities were predominantly from the poorer families, since those who could afford it made their own 'private' evacuation arrangements. For many of the children evacuated by the LCC, travel by train was a new experience. They would have normally not have ventured far from their close-knit communities in the deprived areas of the capital; the possible exception being the annual hop-picking excursions into Kent which for many Londoners was their annual holiday, albeit a working break from their normal routine. The LCC initially assembled the evacuees at 1,389 pre-determined local locations who were then escorted to larger assembly points. These assembly points were used to regulate the flow of evacuees to avoid overcrowding at the railway stations as children with their teachers were either held back or hurried along to ensure a steady flow of evacuees to one or other of the 160 entraining stations. Eleven exchange stations were used in the transfer of parties from the LTPB to main line stations. On the first day of the evacuation the LCC used the railway network to transport a total of 286,918 people including the 50,000 children who departed from Ealing Broadway station to destinations in Somerset, Devon and Oxfordshire. It was this exercise which created the iconic photographic images which showed orderly groups of children each wearing a luggage label for identification and carrying their miniature gas masks and tiny suitcases. None of the children or evacuated adults were given any indication of their final destination. The parents were told to provide each of their children with food for the journey. The paternal LCC gave advice as to what should or should not be provided for the children's lunch. If possible, the children should be given sandwiches, biscuits and fruit, but not a drink as at the time this would have required the use of potentially dangerous glass bottles. Teachers would carry water for 'first aid' purposes only and given the modern thoughts on liquid intake the first aid most likely to have been required would have been to combat dehydration. The precise number of parents who arranged for their children to be evacuated without the assistance from the local authorities was never to be known to those arranging the mass evacuation.

The evacuees should not have had to travel in any discomfort; the SR, for example, timetabled 225 special trains spread over the four days. Every train ran to time, full or not, allowing, it was claimed, uncrowded travel for the 138,000 evacuees carried by the SR. The GWR for its part in the evacuation ran 163 special trains carrying a grand total of 112,894 passengers. The LCC's own account of the exercise does not indicate that much went amiss and this is confirmed by the 'official' railway histories, but probably due to gaps in the planning, inevitably some mistakes were made. A train scheduled to run from Paddington to Somerset travelled no further west than Wantage Road station in Berkshire when it was realised that the children could not be expected to travel such a long distance in a train of non-corridor stock without any lavatories. Plans were quickly changed, and the children were billeted in the Wantage locality. The ease by which such a change of plan could be made was in part due to the fact that only half of the number of potential evacuees were presented by their parents at the local assembly points. The number of evacuees carried by the SR for example was only 41 per cent of what the LCC had estimated. This resulted in Gilbert Szlumper, the former general manager of the SR who was at the time organising the embarkation of troops to France, to describe the evacuation as a 'waste of engine power' although he praised the railway managements for performing a smooth and punctual operation.

Away from London, the other local authorities' evacuation programmes were initiated, for example, children from Manchester were sent by train to the Lancashire Fylde coast. In North Wales, at Bangor, nearly 2,000 children and their teachers arrived by train and the nearby library was used to receive them and provide medical check-ups. The local authorities in Cornwall prepared to accept 20,000 children and those in Devon 34,350 women and children. The LNER evacuated over 81,000 children and mothers away from Tyneside, over 10,000 from Sunderland, over 4,500 from West Hartlepool, over 6,000 from Middlesbrough, 2,500 from Leeds, 22,000 from Hull, 22,500 from Edinburgh, 10,600 from Dundee and 47,000 from Glasgow and the surrounding River Clyde locality. Meanwhile the LMSR transported almost 104,000 from Manchester, over 25,000 from Birmingham, almost 12,000 from Bradford and over 100,000 from Liverpool.

At the end of their railway journey the LCC parties were welcomed at 271 stations in the various reception areas and placed in their new homes. Once safely billeted, the children were supervised in the task of writing their 'arrived safely' notes home and these had to include their new address. For this purpose, each child was given a pre-stamped post card. The children's new 'parents' were to receive a billeting allowance of 10/6 a week for a single child and a further 8/6 for each additional child. On 4 September 1939, the Ministry of Health announced that 'the operation of moving people and children in the priority classes out of London has come to an end'.

With hindsight, the efforts of the local authorities and the government fell well short of being described as a success. Despite the obvious dangers it was to prove difficult to separate parents from their children as the policy of evacuation was not universally accepted – many parents voiced the view that, 'if we die, we die together'. The number of evacuated London children might appear impressive but only about half the possible number were ever to be transported to the rural, 'safe' areas of the country. Other cities fared even worse – Edinburgh only 28 per cent and Sheffield only 15 per cent. Some cities did better, however; both Salford and Newcastle evacuated over 70 per cent of their school children.

Meanwhile, as well as the evacuation of children the railways also had to contend with the embarkation of overseas visitors – 5,000 foreign nationals who wished to be repatriated were conveyed to one port – not identified at the time but it was probably Dover – during a 48-hour period. On Monday, 4 September the Southern Railway announced that four of their boat trains to the continent would operate as usual. Trains leaving Victoria station for the SR's Channel ports carried almost exclusively non-British passengers. These returnees included young German girls who had worked as servants in English homes, Frenchmen who were joining the French army and London restaurant workers returning home to still neutral Italy.

In September 1939, while the evacuations of both young children and civil servants were underway, it was the intention that the 'normal' train services, despite the reduction in number, would be affected as little as possible. Nonetheless passengers were confronted with dramatic changes to their overall travelling experience on the railways. As they arrived at the station encumbered with their gas masks, they would have perceived that the railway landscape had changed with the appearance of armed soldiers guarding the major stations, sandbags at strategic locations, some railwaymen wearing tin-hats and the presence of Air Raid Precaution (ARP) wardens. The wardens have gained the reputation – most likely undeserved – for being officious and heavy handed. The blackout had to be strictly adhered to and enforced by ARP wardens who were often accused of being overzealous, insisting that lights close to the railway were extinguished while a passing Southern Electric train lit up the neighbourhood with the frequent dramatic blue arcs as the trains passed. The question of bright flashes caused by the arcing from the collector shoes on electric trains did give rise to concern. A letter writer to *The Times* of 15 September commented that should a German bomber arrive over Beachy Head, from his position high in the sky he would have a clearly guided route to London by following the line of bright blue flashes emanating from these trains. This issue did concern the REC, and its mechanical and electrical engineer (M&ME) subcommittee set up a group to investigate. Despite identifying some 'hot spots' such as at London Bridge and Waterloo no substantive conclusions were made. Frankly, this was a problem in the 'too difficult' box and, other than stopping trains during an air raid and thereby causing an obstruction to all railway operations, there was little that could be achieved to alleviate the problem.

The passengers would also have noticed that at the outbreak of war non-railway advertising posters were removed from display at the stations, although the posters depicting resort destinations remained as a delightful splash of colour contrasting with the grim aspect of blacked-out windows of the station buildings. Much of the space previously used for other companies' advertising was used for new posters issued by the REC. In the early days of the war frequent changes had to be made to railway timetables: first there was the original 'emergency timetable'; then subsequent amendments and variations to correct any chronic deficiencies in what had been first compiled; and then many service cancellations to make way for the 'secret' trains transporting troops on their way to France or for the later special leave trains. Therefore, at the LNER stations alongside its own artistic offerings and the REC posters there was the need to locally display timetable changes often at very short notice. The method for this task was to write in chalk on black paper creating temporary notices to be placed about the station where there had previously been commercial advertising. Unfortunately included in many of the wartime shortages was black paper after millions of households had used it to block off windows to meet the blackout rules policed by the ARP wardens. The LNER had to improvise and experimented with different inks on alternative paper before a practical solution was found – which probably to avoid a surge of demand they kept the precise details of their endeavours secret.

There might not at first have been any actual air raids in the early days of the war but there was the inconvenience of the air raid warnings. The Home Office and the ministry of transport made a joint statement giving instructions that trains should not be immediately stopped during an air raid. Goods trains were to proceed to the next signal box where they would be updated as to the air raid situation by the signalman and then continue their journey at no more than 10mph.

The REC gave instructions to the passengers as to what they should do in the event of an air raid. On hearing the alarm, they should pull down the blinds and close all carriage windows and ventilators. This should be done even in daylight raids to avoid injury from flying glass. Passengers were instructed to remain in the train if it should stop between stations during an air raid – unless advised otherwise by railway staff. Trains would continue to run but would be stopped at the next station. Here, as per the Home Office and Ministry of Transport directive, passengers were free to choose to alight and seek out the nearest public shelter should they so wish. The instructions continued with information as to what to do if the train had been subjected to a gas attack – something that fortunately was never to be necessary. There was obvious anxiety among railway passengers as to the dangers of being in a train during an air raid. One writer to *The Times* was concerned about the safety of those travelling in suburban trains to and from their workplaces. The trains he travelled on, he asserted, had wooden framed carriages with double bars across the drop lights on the doors. In the event of the train being bombed causing the doors to jam, he was fearful that the 'hapless occupants' would be trapped, unable to escape via the door window. The writer hoped that these bars would be immediately removed.

The first air-raid warnings in September 1939 created instant havoc at some main line stations. At the LNER's terminus at Liverpool Street following the arrival of several trains during an air-raid warning, large crowds of extremely nervous passengers were held within the station area by the police and air raid wardens. Many railwaymen going on duty were also prevented from entering the station by what was seen as over-zealous wardens. This was reported to the REC who argued that the wardens had no right to prevent passengers leaving the station or to prevent their staff from entering the premises to start work. REC member, Frank Pick (from the LPTB) told the committee that he understood that new regulations were being considered that would allow passengers and railway staff to proceed as normal unless there was evidence of actual hostilities around the station area. The REC duly recommended to the Ministry of Transport that instructions should be given to the police and ARP that passengers should be permitted to leave any station when an air raid was in progress and the government agreed to this suggestion. To ensure the safety of passengers during an actual air raid, notices were placed in stations directing passengers to the nearest air raid shelter.

Another issue that emerged concerned the validity of the much-used workmens tickets. On 6 September a warning was given at 6.45pm but the all-clear was not sounded until 9.15pm. Unfortunately, this resulted in those travelling on workmens tickets being told that the validity of their ticket had time expired. This was reported to the REC passenger superintendents subcommittee for resolution and consequently this issue was the subject of discussions between the REC and the Trades Union Congress on 18 September. Meanwhile on the same day the minister of transport gave notice in the House of Commons that the main-line railways would honour the workmens tickets until 20 minutes after the all-clear and this was reported in the *Railway Gazette* on 15 September. It was later to be agreed that those who had previously been forced to buy an 'ordinary' ticket to travel home would receive a refund. Also, at a later meeting, the REC agreed that workmens tickets should be available for travel on Sundays subject to confirmation from an employer that the ticket holder took part in Sunday shift working. This was a significant development, for this was the first time in British railway history that workmens tickets could be used on Sundays, and this was very distasteful to the many who held strong religious convictions.

The wartime passengers also had to cope with the imposition of the blackout. At the start of the war this was achieved by switching off all the station and carriage lights at night. Passengers were expected to travel in complete darkness, often having to rely only on station staff calling out the names of each station on arrival because only the smallest of signs denoting the station were permitted, and these had to be positioned in dark locations below awnings out of sight of any enemy aircraft. To help passengers navigate the dark stations, not only were the platform edges painted white but also white stripes were added to posts and any garden edging stones on the platforms.

For most passengers, the blackout rules made any winter evening or night-time journey unpleasant, and many, including parents whose older children had to travel by train during the winter months, feared the 'varied dangers' of travelling in unlit trains. The dark journeys were unpleasant at best but for many passengers – particularly unaccompanied women – they were often a terrifying experience. A female correspondent to *The Times* who had to endure a thirty-mile journey home every night on an SR train, was fearful because she could not see her fellow passengers in the complete darkness. It was 'trying', she claimed, to have to travel in an unlit train after a hard day's work as winter approached. There was a partial solution noted by the public, and this young lady also asked why, as on the buses, blue light bulbs were not provided within the compartments. The railways understood the problem and were already preparing to use the ARP acceptable blue filament light bulbs in all carriages. Unfortunately, due to insufficient 'blue' bulbs being manufactured, the change-over was to take a very long time. Not everybody resented the blackout however, in December 1939 the *Railway Gazette* printed a contribution from a serving officer who viewed the darkened railway carriage as '...a welcome sanctuary ... temporarily relaxed from the rigidity imposed during daylight hours by the wearing of a uniform...' – but he must be viewed as an exception; for most of the travellers it was a misery which had to be bravely accepted.

The staff magazine of the GWR printed a detailed account by Mr F.G. Richens of a night-time journey in blackout conditions from Swindon to Looe in Cornwall. The writer had been advised to 'make an early start,' but as a professional railwayman this was often a bonus because by arriving early at a station it usually meant that he would find some interesting activity to observe. When he arrived at the blacked-out Swindon station however he was confronted with total darkness and nothing to see. Swindon station was an eerie dark world but a low thin line of dim lights extending down the platform could just about be discerned. The use of hand-held torches was allowed provided they were shone down onto the feet, thereby making it possible to move about in the dark station with a degree of safety. All that could be seen by Mr Richens was feet attending to parcels, feet purposely progressing up and down the platform and feet belonging to a Welshman – well, who else, mused Mr Richens, would sing *Cwm Rhondda* at a blacked-out railway station as midnight approached? His attempt to purchase a cup of tea was fraught with difficulty – every door along the station looked the same, making finding the refreshment room a challenge. The entry of a train into the station was unheralded, only the sight of two newly arrived sailors bursting into the refreshment room gave any indication of its arrival. The writer had to check with a cheery member of the station staff if this was his train but was told that he had a little longer to wait.

From his account his train to the west of England was routed through Bristol and Bridgwater to Exeter. He does claim that the train also stopped at Frome and Yeovil – which is difficult to accept as this would have been a very zig-zag route. Perhaps he was not very familiar with the GWR lines and in the dark was quite unsure as to the route or the stations passed through. On boarding the train, he found himself sharing a compartment with five others. He thought that they looked rather odd in the newly installed dim blue light. He described his fellow travellers as looking somewhat 'bilious', but when he saw himself in the compartment mirror, he realised that he looked just as awful. He recalled the list of ARP instructions to travellers which he had seen advising railway passengers what to do during an air raid. Number three on the list of instructions proclaimed: 'if room is available lie down on the floor'. The size of his five large companions would have made this piece of advice somewhat impractical. He likened the train to a phantom, which flittered about from nowhere to nowhere. Every station looked the same as the one before – totally black. If the train really did take what seems to have been a somewhat complicated route from Swindon to Exeter, this would only have added to the passengers' general bewilderment as they popped their heads out of the windows at every stop attempting to see where they were. There were few clues to aid them, and it was probably only the shouts of the station staff that offered any certainty as to the train's exact location. The train arrived at Liskeard at 5.25am, but it was only there that Mr Richens was to discover that the wartime schedule did not include an early train to his final destination at Looe. Rather than wait two hours for a train down the branch, he decided to walk the eight miles to Looe and earn himself a good breakfast. An interesting feature of this contemporary account is that he travelled on a night service. Given that at the time train journeys took much longer than today and that generally people had much less free time, a long-distance journey at night was seen as a good use of that precious time. Such a nocturnal trip would save the cost of overnight accommodation and would often provide the traveller with a good night's sleep. The almost universal layout of the contemporary main line carriage at the time was to have a side corridor accessing compartments designed to sit up to eight passengers. Two rows of seats would face inwards. Typically, in a third-class compartment, three could sit either side and a fourth join them if the arm rests were raised. A nocturnal traveller might be assured of a good night's rest if he or she were fortunate enough to be able to lie down across the three seats on one side of a compartment.

With the reduced train services instigated at the beginning of the war, the luxury of being able to find half a compartment to oneself became much less likely. Mr Richens was faced with five other passengers which meant that any attempt that he might make to sleep had to be made sitting upright. He soon realised that any prospect of being able to sleep was unlikely. One fellow traveller had optimistically come with his carpet slippers to give him some comfort during the long night, but the others wriggled, rustled or tried to smoke.

In early 1939 the British military intelligence service's view was that the German high command's strategy would be to first attack and destroy all government buildings in an attempt to achieve a quick and decisive victory. That this was their intention was to prove to be correct when the centres of government were bombed and shelled to destruction by the Nazis when they crushed Poland in September 1939. On 6 September 1939 Sir John Anderson's committee demanded that urgent consideration must be given to the evacuation of a large proportion of government employed staff to safer areas away from the capital. It was acknowledged that such an evacuation would be difficult and dangerous during air attacks, therefore there was an urgent need to act during what appeared to be a lull before any hostilities commenced. Sir John's committee recommended that there must be an immediate implementation of the billeting and requisitioning powers provided in the Emergency Powers Act and that each government department should be charged with making its own *ad-hoc* plans in collaboration with the Ministry of Works and the Ministry of Transport. Fortunately, many of the government departments had already made contingency plans which had been prepared months earlier.

While a few of the civil servants were to be taken to their new places of work by car or bus, the majority travelled by special trains provided by the railway companies. The evacuation of civil servants away from London by train has not, unlike the original evacuation of school children, any place in the national folk-memory. Small children neatly labelled carrying their miniature suitcases and gas masks make appealing pictures, but adult civil servants with their heavy suitcases and – due to the shortage of bedding – bringing with them two blankets and possibly sheets struggling onto a train do not make such a memorable image. Premises used for the new office accommodation in the provinces included hotels and larger places of education such as private schools and larger colleges. Generally, hotels were the first choice as they were in the centre of the towns close to the railway stations, but as the war progressed and the number of outposted staff increased, premises such as schools which had outdoor space were seen as being suitable as temporary huts could be built to provide extra office accommodation. The hotels, despite the obvious advantage of having bedroom and restaurant facilities, were not used for accommodation, the billeting of staff in private houses was the norm, although as numbers increased (and particularly as more younger women arrived at their new place of employment) many public and private buildings were converted into hostels.

The largest of the early evacuations was to Bath where many important Admiralty departments were to be re-located. Bath might be some distance from London, but it had a good railway connection to the capital and acceptable connections to elsewhere in England. The main railway station at Bath was, and still is, Bath Spa which is 94 miles from London Paddington by the GWR main line via Swindon and Chippenham. During the war, the journey time by train was just under three hours. At the time there was the 'other' station in the city, Bath Green Park. This small terminus station was owned by the LMSR and provided connection with the Midlands via Gloucester and also via the railway line run by both the LMSR and the SR together, the Somerset and Dorset Joint Railway, providing access to the south coast. Any Royal Navy establishment which is not an actual floating vessel is colloquially referred to as a 'stone frigate'. Some of these were physical onshore buildings, others merely accountancy fictions – somewhere to 'book' a sailor's pay between postings. Giving the totality of the Admiralty's presence in the city, Bath might have been judged as something grander than a mere frigate, 'stone battleship' or 'stone aircraft carrier' might have been a more appropriate name for the extensive military complex that was to be quietly embedded within the ancient city. As if to hide their presence in plain sight, the Admiralty requested that no obvious air raid precautions such as barrage balloons were provided so as to suggest to any overflying enemy aircraft that Bath was nothing more than a Roman and Georgian heritage site and certainly not an important military target.

It was proposed to transfer 4,000 Admiralty staff to the beautiful Georgian city. It is interesting that one respondent for a request for wartime reminiscences recalled that at the very beginning of the war she and her mother had left the suburbs in West London to move to what they too perceived to be the safety of Bath. The mother was to be employed as a civilian clerk by the Admiralty. There was some important military production in the locality at the outbreak of war, but this was on a relatively small-scale such as the production of aircraft propellors, gun mountings and components for use in torpedoes. The enemy however had not in 1939 identified the historic city as a strategic target despite the importance of the Admiralty work in Bath, the Germans continued to regard Bath as a 'lesser town without specific aiming points'.

Today in our comprehensively 'connected' world of the internet, 24-hour news coverage and 'social media', it seems strange to us that there was apparently minimal secrecy within Bath as to the government's intentions. Plans for the evacuation of the Admiralty to Bath had leaked out to some of the Bath residents during the previous eight months so the sudden 'secret' arrival of what was to be described as 'a certain government department' would have not come as a surprise to most citizens in Bath. In December 1938, Alfred Sackett, the Headmaster of Kingswood School, had been confidentially forewarned that the government would need to take over the school buildings in the event of war. Furthermore, on 1 September the staff and residents in the Bath hotels were given 24 hours' notice that the

buildings were to be commandeered for war duty. The principal hotel
in Bath was the Empire, an impressive building situated at Orange
Grove. It was 102 feet tall with a distinctive and eccentric roofline
resembling a combination of cottage, house and castle architecture.
The location in the town known as Orange Grove commemorates the
visit of the Prince of Orange to take the healing waters at Bath in
1734. On 1 September there were 100 guests staying at the Empire
Hotel and this included ten who were long term residents and would
therefore have seen the fashionable hotel as being their home. All
the well-heeled clientele suddenly found themselves ejected onto
the pavement with their luggage waiting to be collected by a fleet of
taxis taking most of them to the GWR Bath Spa station. Other hotels
requisitioned included the Fernley Hotel situated at North Parade,
Pulteney Hotel in Great Pulteney Street, the Grand Pump Hotel
in Stall Street and the Spa Hotel in Sidney Street. It was intended
that all of these hotels would be used for office accommodation as
were other buildings in and around the town including the Technical
College at Lower Borough Walls, the Domestic Science Training
College at Broughton Hayes, the Royal school for Daughters of the
Officers of the Army in Landsdown Road and Brock Hall in Brock
Street. One local solicitor took exception to the proposals and wrote
a letter of complaint to Winston Churchill. The future war leader
was, at the beginning of the war, the First Lord of the Admiralty, a
political, not military appointment, but at the very centre of Royal
Navy policy making. The solicitor complained that due to both the
'known' number of the government sponsored evacuees such as school
children with some of their mothers and by the 'unknown' number of
what he termed 'voluntary evacuees' such as the mother and daughter
from West London who had made their own private arrangements
with Bath residents, there was now little scope to find billets for new
Admiralty arrivals.

This urgent need to find billets for the imminent influx of new
people from London to an already overcrowded Bath resulted in a

public appeal to all households in the city. A letter dated 9 September 1939 from the city mayor, Adrian Hopkins, was distributed to every household. The letter had a heading written in bold capital letters which stated that the contents were 'private and confidential to households of the City of Bath'. Upon reading the letter the patriotic citizens of Bath were instructed to burn the document 'after perusal'. The letter appealed not for 4,000 billets as had been Sir John Anderson's estimation, but a revised requirement for 4,700. As for the evacuation of children, some forethought and planning had been undertaken in the months before, and the mayor alluded to a discreet survey that had been conducted earlier in the year. He was to an extent in tune with the solicitor who had written to Churchill, as he appreciated that events had moved on and that the earlier survey was now out of date as many of the potential billets would now not be available. The mayor's letter stated that householders would be expected to make available their spare bedrooms and to provide breakfast and supper for their unexpected guests. If the provision of food was not possible, canteen facilities would be made available for some of the evacuated staff. He later made a statement to the local newspaper stressing that the householders must make every effort to provide at least a breakfast for each of their new guests. Each householder would receive a minimum of 21 shillings which was to be paid for by the evacuee. It was appreciated that this was a high cost for a low paid civil servant, but it was expected that those with higher salaries would pay more. For some poorer householders, the 21 shillings might not be sufficient, but for those who could accommodate more evacuees this would generate for them more income. It was suggested that if a household could accommodate, say, six evacuees for a total recompense of £6-6-0d, this would have been much more acceptable even for the poorest residents. Given this local publicity, it is strange that the enemy continued to view Bath as a 'lesser town without specific aiming points'.

Most of the evacuees arrived in Bath by train. Before Sunday, 17 September 1939, nearly 400 naval personnel had arrived in the city. On Sunday, 17 September three special trains were provided by the GWR to deliver a further 665 evacuated staff. The trains left Paddington at 11.45am, 1.45pm and 3.30pm. The intention had been to run seven trains to Bath that day but delays in completing the billeting arrangements at Bath resulted in four of the trains being cancelled. Following the resolution of the outstanding billeting issues, a further 961 Admiralty staff arrived between 18 and 23 September. On Sunday, 24 September, three more special trains were run conveying a further 1,696 personnel. Another 80 staff were expected to travel to Bath later.

The evacuation of Royal Navy staff away from London was carried out with such urgency and focus by those at the Admiralty in Whitehall that on the Saturday, 16 September, only a day before the majority of those to be moved to Bath were programmed to travel, nobody had found the time to either inform the fleet at sea or even the government that the evacuation was in progress. It was a simple matter to present the details to them of course, but it was much more problematic determining what should be revealed to the public via the press in the Monday newspapers. It was decided to release a statement giving minimal information only, confirming that some Admiralty departments had moved to the Bath locality – but not revealing which. The 'secret' information that was not to be made public knowledge was that those that were evacuated in September 1939 were to be employed in many very important and diverse roles within the Admiralty departments which were to be spread around Bath. These included those engaged in contract and purchase, electrical engineering, naval construction, hydrography, signals, stores, victualling, dockyard administration, exchequer and audit, and stores. The Royal Navy's scientific research and experiment department was evacuated to Bath and the city also hosted the Torpedo and Mining Department, the Admiralty Secretariat, the Chief Engineer, the Chief Inspector of Naval Ordnance, and the Inspector of Torpedoes and Mines.

While the Royal Navy relocated most of its administrative and design functions westward to Bath, the Royal Air Force made a similar move northward to another spa town, Harrogate. They were later to be joined by civil servants working for the new Ministry of Aircraft Production and the General Post Office (GPO). Set on the edge of the Yorkshire Dales, Harrogate, like Bath, was never considered to be a prime target for the Luftwaffe. This assumption proved correct as only one bomb was ever to be dropped on Harrogate throughout the whole war period despite it being a hub for important war work. The solitary bomb was delivered on 12 September 1940 when it landed on the Majestic Hotel. The hotel's winter garden and a house in Swan Road were both destroyed, and the blast succeeded in blowing out most of the shop windows in the town. The bomb was dropped from a lone enemy plane which appeared to have strayed from the main raiding party. Nonetheless the town was subjected to frequent air raid warnings, for example in October 1940 there was a total of nineteen.

In September 1939, staff from the Air Ministry Headquarters at Berkeley Square House in London were immediately evacuated to Harrogate. The Air Ministry had only taken occupation of Berkeley Square House during the previous year. It was at the time a controversial move and due to the growing risk of air raids questions were asked about the suitability of such a large and easily identifiable building for such an important national defence role. Sir Kingsley Wood, the secretary of state for air – the air force equivalent of the First Lord of the Admiralty – insisted that it was essential in the present circumstances that any new Air Ministry building should be within a reasonable distance from his department's headquarters in Kingsway. He insisted that Berkeley Square House was the only large building that met the ministry's requirements both in respect of space and location. Nonetheless despite the obvious practical benefits from the use of this modern new building in peacetime, at the outbreak of war there was a significant evacuation of staff to Harrogate from Berkeley Square House. The overall general increase in wartime staff however later resulted in a situation where Air Ministry space in London, including Berkeley Square House, was deemed to be 'full up'. Initially the air ministry staff evacuated included those from the supply branch, and the directorate of equipment. It had been proposed to move 3,000 staff, but this was later increased to 3,500. Most of these arrived at Harrogate by special trains from King's Cross. The LNER and the ministry organisers worked harmoniously together such that even when the train conveying the most civil servants arrived at Harrogate station, the well organised railway staff had all of the passengers and their luggage transferred to buses for onward travel to their billets within 25 minutes.

Harrogate's wartime history is complex. It was the home of the government department for managing the RAF which had also from 1919 taken on the responsibility for the meteorological office. Many RAF stations hosted weather data collection equipment. To add to the 'Air Ministry' presence, the closely related 'Ministry of Aircraft Production' was soon to arrive in the Yorkshire spa town. After the arrival of the ministry's signals services and general administration sections to Harrogate from October 1939 onwards, the establishment was renamed 'RAF Harrogate' on 1 December 1939. The term 'RAF Harrogate' also applied to several hotels dotted around the town centre which was denoted as the No. 7 Personnel Reception Centre. Only weeks after the start of the war the town became the home of the allied pilots training scheme when hundreds of pilots began arriving at Harrogate station to receive their tuition. These trainees were not just from Britain but also from Australia, Canada, New Zealand, India, France and Poland.

By May 1940 there was a grand total of 3,889 Air Ministry staff billeted at nine locations across Harrogate. Accommodation was provided at the Crown Hotel, the Grand Hotel, the Ladies College, the Harrogate Hydro Hotel, Harlow Manor, Beechwood Hotel and the White Hart Hotel. Part of the Prospect Hotel was also used for government staff. A month later this had increased to 4,137 after the addition of the Alexandra Hotel to the list of available accommodation. Other hotels continued to be used as office accommodation. Later in the war when there was a national government campaign for fuel economy, Harrogate residents complained that the lights in the government offices were always switched on – even at mid-day. The excuse for this apparent profligacy was that since the hotel rooms had originally been designed as bedrooms, there was not enough natural light to work during the daytime, particularly during mid-winter, as the *Harrogate Herald* of 28 January 1942 explained.

Later in 1940 RAF headquarters staff moved into the Harrogate Hydro Hotel and the staff then in residence were transferred to the Lancaster Hotel situated in the quaintly named Cold Bath Road. Working in the Lancaster Hotel in December 1940 were a total of 382 staff, of which ten were RAF officers, two were WAAF officers, plus a warrant officer and three flight sergeants. All of the others were classified as 'other ranks' and many of these would have been civilian auxiliary staff. In February 1940 the Air Ministry's communications unit was transferred from RAF Leighton Buzzard to RAF Harrogate.

The military activity in Harrogate and Bath created additional traffic on the railways. A significant change noticed by the regular railway passengers was the sudden appearance at the principal stations and on the trains of hordes of service personnel. This increase was first noted in the days preceding the declaration of war on 1 September. It was not only senior military staff – travelling in first-class compartments of course – but in the third-class compartments servicemen either travelling to or from home on leave, making their way to training establishments or journeying to join their regiments. This additional *ad-hoc* military travel was by the timetabled public services and not by the special troop trains provided by the railways at the time of the major mobilisations. As the nation awaited the onslaught of significant hostilities, travellers noticed that at the London termini such as King's Cross, servicemen were congregating late into the night awaiting their connecting trains. It was noticed that most of these servicemen were very young, boys really, and compared to their equivalents in the twenty-first century most of them – particularly those from rural areas

– had led a more sheltered life in relatively isolated communities and were unused to travel away from their immediate environment. To add to their discontent of negotiating what for them were strange parts of the country, they would also be likely to be suffering homesickness compounded with the natural anxiety generated by fears of what the future held for them as they anticipated having to fight for their country. Many middle-aged and older people had horrific memories of the carnage during the Great War, so a caring and compassionate public opened their hearts to these young men and a genuine concern developed for their wellbeing when it became apparent that no late-night catering facilities were being provided for them.

The REC too noticed the large number of service personnel travelling in mid-September 1939, and after making enquiries was informed by the Army, Navy and Air Force that it would be some time before any canteens for their troops in transit could be provided. The railways however were more helpful than the military appeared to have been, so to accommodate the needs of these servicemen it was arranged that railway owned refreshment rooms would be kept open longer for the benefit of any of them who were having to wait on the stations at times when the catering facilities would normally have been closed. Furthermore, the railways were prepared to offer meals at special reduced prices for members of HM forces on production of government vouchers. The railways then went even further by allowing empty carriages to be provided at important junction stations to provide a rest – and possibly a sleep – facility for service personnel awaiting connecting trains. Station staff were instructed to warn in good time anybody sleeping within these coaches that their connecting train was due. The REC also received requests for a special tariff for the more senior service personnel and their wives at the railway owned hotels. It was arranged that the LNER and LMSR should cooperate with each other and come to an agreement particularly in towns where both companies had hotels.

Chapter 2

Making Way for the Essential Traffic

On the eve of the Second World War ... the United Kingdom was still in the unique position of importing around half of its food and remained the largest exporter of energy [coal] and the largest importer of oil products.

David Edgerton, *The Rise and Fall of the British Nation*, Allen Lane, 2018

For the first weeks of the war, the travelling public endured a bewildering series of changes to their regular train services which were intended to clear the railways of any unnecessary traffic to accommodate the expected heavy evacuation and military traffic. The REC, who recognised the inconvenience and overcrowding that would be the result of the new timetables, produced a press statement clearly indicating that they disliked as much as the public the prospect of limiting passenger travel, but they had to give priority to what they described as traffic of 'an urgent national character'. The overarching aim of the emergency timetables was to provide the absolute minimum of service which would sustain the nation's commercial and industrial activities and at the same time enable the railways to have the capacity to provide for the conveyance of troops with their equipment and the evacuation of vulnerable civilians. To achieve these aims, initially drastic speed restrictions were imposed to ensure that the available locomotives could be used without any need to limit the train loadings.

The initial draconian passenger service reductions that had been hurriedly instigated in line with government policy were soon to be amended when on 5 September the REC conceded that each company should be free to run additional trains as required subject to the speed restriction of a maximum of 45 miles-per-hour between 'booked points'. This in practice resulted in trains not exceeding a maximum speed of 60 miles-per-hour. Given that speedometers were not fitted to locomotives, it must often have been difficult for the engine drivers to comply with this instruction. The chief engineer of the SR observed that trains seemed to be running as fast as ever, and he noted that some trains were travelling through Clapham Junction at over 55 miles-per-hour thereby exceeding the speed limit at that location. An instruction was issued to the drivers that the speed restrictions must be strictly adhered to even when trains were running late when time might otherwise be made up. Despite the newly imposed restrictions and the over exuberance of some drivers of express trains, the SR was running eighty per cent of its predominantly suburban stopping trains at 'normal' speeds which were below the wartime speed restriction. Of more concern to the railway's chief engineer was the inability to keep up with routine maintenance as many of his workforce had joined the armed forces and the impossibility of performing many of the maintenance tasks during the blackout conditions. To solve this difficulty, he requested a reduction in the Sunday services offered by the railway to allow his depleted staff access to the tracks.

During the unexpected calm of the 'phoney war' period, the REC, reported in the *Railway Gazette* on 20 September, conceded that 'commercial conditions' could dictate less restricted services. The railways had originally been instructed to plan for the worst, but it soon became obvious that the original timetable restrictions could be relaxed – although the term 'emergency' timetable would continue to be used. Achieving the desired balance between the competing military and commercial needs did however result in many short-notice timetable changes. After a brief period of confusion, the new printed wartime emergency timetables were soon to be published. The LNER, LMSR and SR introduced theirs on Monday, 11 September and the

GWR presented its new schedules to the public the following week on Monday, 18 September. In comparison to the peacetime timetables all four companies advertised significantly reduced passenger services. It was also confirmed that many of the reduced fare tickets would no longer be available. It might have been expected however that once these new printed timetables had been published, a degree of stability would ensure that was not to be the case.

The imposition of the emergency timetables resulted in considerable disruption to passenger traffic, but the public understood that military traffic must take precedence as the British Army was transported across the country to reach northern France. Railway passengers were requested to be patient and that extra trains would be provided when working conditions permitted. Most of the public seemed to patriotically accept a degree of discomfort and delay, even though many commuters had to endure what was effectively a longer working day often requiring an earlier start and a later return home after many of the suburban services had been cut by fifty per cent. The policy seems to have been successful as official public announcements reported that the troop trains from all parts of Great Britain 'followed each other with a punctuality that spoke highly for the railway management' and the *Railway Gazette* that September opined that this continuous day and night transportation could never have been achieved while normal passenger services were running.

While it was obvious to the regular railway passengers that troop trains and civilian evacuation trains would hinder normal traffic, it was perceived that the effect of both of these factors was soon reduced as the BEF arrived safely in France and the first wave of civilian evacuations had been completed. In fact, due to careful timetabling such as running the children's evacuation trains between the daily commuter services plus the scheduling of the government departments' evacuation trains on Sundays, the evacuation programme had not impacted as much as might have been expected on the 'ordinary' passenger train services. What could not be made public for fear of giving too much information to the enemy was that it was what might be termed the 'ordinary' freight traffic, not the increased military freight, that was the cause of severe disruption, and it was the non-military traffic which was often hindering the free movement of passenger traffic. In the 1930s, Britain's economy was based upon its empire connections with the nation relying on seaborne traffic for the importation of much of its food supply and essential raw materials. Shortages of important imported materials such as oil and rubber were to become a serious issue as these commodities were needed to fuel aircraft and tanks and in the manufacture of tyres for the fighting vehicles. Many of the ships carrying the imported goods that were sailing to Britain across the Mediterranean Sea or the Atlantic Ocean were bound for the Port of London and other important ports along the east coast. As had been predicted, with the threat from German U-boats, surface raiders and sea mines, the shipping routes through the English Channel and the North Sea became too dangerous for the passage of merchant vessels. Consequently, this important shipping had to be diverted to various west coast destinations such as Liverpool, Manchester and Glasgow.

The government had foreseen these difficulties and had begun planning for the war after the Munich crisis in 1938. Parliament had been made aware of the potential difficulties with the movement of essential supplies and that this would require the coordination of freight traffic. On 2 March 1939, the then Minister of Transport, Leslie Burgin, spoke in the House of Commons confirming that the government was diligently making preparations for such coordinated wartime freight operations. He acknowledged that there was likely to be congestion at the ports which would create storage and transport issues. The railways, the minister insisted, were the 'iron backbone of the country' and he was confident that they would be able to cope with the 'tremendous strain' that they would be subjected to at the outbreak of war. His remark was greeted with much derision from many of the MPs attending the House that afternoon since the railway companies were at the time claiming to be suffering from huge financial and operational difficulties. The railways' complaint was that due to the 1921 legislation they had to charge rigidly imposed fixed freight charges. The result of this was that they were not able to compete fairly with the burgeoning road traffic industry. Consequently, the railways had in 1939 been promoting their 'Square Deal' campaign demanding to be permitted to be set their own rates in order to compete on equal terms with the competition from the new and expanding road transport companies. Under pressure from MPs Burgin did concede that the railways were indeed financially 'not doing too well' and agreed that they were facing the prospect of having to spend 'millions of pounds' so as to be able to contribute towards the national effort should war break out. He also informed the MPs that a committee had been established to prepare for a possible war and that his officials were working closely with the railways. This 'committee' was of course the REC, but its deliberations were naturally being kept confidential. Burgin stated that he was satisfied that a 'tremendous amount of work' had been done to date and that he was in negotiations with the railways as to how they were to be financially compensated. He claimed that many measures had already been put in hand and cited examples – which in the context of the magnitude of the task seem with hindsight to be rather lame – such as the pooling of breakdown trains and the acquisition of necessary spare parts. By 3 September Leslie Burgin had been succeeded by Euan Wallace who then inherited the problem of transporting the nation's freight during the early war years using the 'iron backbone'.

The disruption to seaborne traffic had also been predicted early in 1939 by the government's Committee of Imperial Defence. It was anticipated that London and other east coast ports would soon come under heavy enemy aerial attack so at the outbreak of war ships should immediately be diverted to the relative safety of the west coast so as to either berth in the ports there or, if there was congestion, be held in safe anchorages along the coast. As a result of these pre-war warnings, one very important policy instigated by the Ministry of Transport was that any ship arriving in British waters should discharge all of its cargo at a single port and not continue on to several other ports partly unloading at each as had been the normal peace-time practice. This sensible and necessary course of action was not without consequences as inevitably there was congestion in the ports due to limited cranage and storage. In his earlier speech to the House of Commons the previous March, Leslie Burgin had commented that anybody with experience of ports would appreciate the problem of any congestion which was likely to occur following the diversion of traffic away from the southern and eastern ports. Congestion is like influenza, he opined, once it starts it spreads. Inland warehouses were to be used as intermediate stores for the diverted cargo and thus, as per Burgin's fears, this inevitably increased the requirement for land transport – much of which involved the railways. Consequently, following the diversion of seaborne traffic away from London, the nation's capital instead of receiving essential commodities directly into its own extensive docks was now receiving the majority of its imported food and other goods from already busy ports which were often over two hundred miles away. This diverted cargo was being transported south by rail resulting in many extra freight trains being run on the very busy routes south from Liverpool and other west coast ports to reach London.

For the first few months of the war, the nation held its breath anticipating the hostilities that would erupt after Germany conquered Poland. The cabinet was informed on 18 October 1939 that while there had been initially some disruption to seaborne traffic in the first weeks of the war following the effective closure of the Mediterranean routes, it was told that there was only a 'preliminary' delay while convoys were formed and that a 'greater flow' of incoming ships was promised.

After the railways had successfully completed the mass evacuation of children, the movement of civil servants to the provinces and dispatched the BEF off to France, many railway users seemed unable to understand why it was necessary for their railway services to continue to be so severely curtailed. The public which had originally accepted the need for reduced passenger services soon began to notice the lack of any obvious hostile activity, and this coupled to a sense of 'normality' in everyday life and not having to make any changes to their transport requirements due to wartime life, many regular railway travellers began to suspect that the cuts to their services were unnecessary. The public were aware of the railways' 'Square Deal' campaign which had claimed that more traffic could be carried by rail – if only parliament would allow them more commercial freedom. Thus, when passenger services were being curtailed due to the extra freight traffic, there were many detractors casting doubt on the whole 'Square Deal' rationale noting that now when the railways were given more traffic, they were apparently unable to adequately meet the demand. What these critics could not be told, as this information would be invaluable to the enemy and have a potentially negative effect on moral, was that in many parts of the country the railway system was being clogged-up with additional freight traffic – little of which was directly related to the wartime requirements of the military. Due to the necessity of secrecy concerning any information about both civilian and military traffic, the public could not be made privy to too much information such as details of the amounts and destinations of the essential food and fuel supplies that were required to feed and heat the nation which was having to be carried on extra goods trains.

Before the internet, social media and the plethora of broadcasting outlets, the government with the cooperation of a patriotic press were able to successfully damp down any sensitive information with a very light-touch approach to censorship. As has been noted, the very existence of the REC was not publicised even though many in the railway industry would have known of its existence and the role it was to play during the war. The government were keen to only tell the public what was absolutely necessary even if thoughtful and knowledgeable citizens could deduce for themselves what was the true situation.

It would have been difficult enough for the railways to suddenly have to accommodate the diverted imported goods from the northwest to the south in peacetime, but the war situation made it even more difficult. Before the motorways the railways carried most of the nation's long-distance freight traffic. It has been calculated that every night before September 1939, 678 overnight express goods trains ran criss-crossing the country. By operating these nocturnal services, the railways kept their main lines clear during the daytime for the fast, longer distance passenger services. These express goods trains had to be curtailed at the outbreak of war as it was not possible to run them efficiently during the newly imposed blackout conditions. This was because the railways' night workers had to be able to read all of the paper labels or chalked destination notices inscribed upon the various wagons. In normal times the goods sheds and marshalling yards at the city centre depots would have been fully lit during the hours of darkness. Even the use of hand-held torches was forbidden by the air raid precaution rules as these would have had to be raised to illuminate labels on wagons and would be likely to be spotted by any overflying enemy bomber crews. It would not have been sufficient to provide blinds or curtains over the windows in the goods sheds as much of the work was carried out in the extensive open-air yards and sealing off the massive entrances to the goods shed was problematic. Thus, there was the unexpected consequence (at least for the lay public and possibly many politicians), that the total blackout at the goods depots resulted in what had previously been the overnight express goods trains having to be marshalled and run during the daylight hours. These extra day trains were squeezing out the passenger trains on many heavily trafficked railway routes.

The fact that the railways' freight traffic was being disrupted by the blackout did however filter through into the consciousness of many members of the public, but most of them only grasped a partial understanding of the true situation. *The Times* newspaper did report on 15 September 1939 on the difficulties of running the express goods trains during daylight hours which had become necessary due to the blackout conditions. But many a frustrated *Times* newspaper reader when awaiting a delayed local train service operating to a much-reduced wartime timetable would observe that not only was his or her train nowhere to be seen, but there was also no evidence at all of the supposedly essential freight trains running through the station either. It was, of course, all about resources and the location of the frustrated passenger. Sleepy cross country or branch lines would not have been used for the important long-distance freight traffic, but the crews and locomotives would have been transferred away to be employed during daylight hours on the major trunk routes where they would be gallantly attempting to move the additional traffic. Such misunderstandings inevitably led to a climate of distrust and cynicism by those predisposed to be critical of anyone in authority, doubting any 'official' statements made by either the railway companies, the REC or the government.

The other significant railway freight traffic being interrupted by the war situation was coal. In 1939 coal was the nation's prime source of energy and was essential for both industry and for the heating of homes. The image of a railway system operating a succession of lengthy coal trains may be a reasonable impression, but before the war most coal destined for London and the south was not carried in what was even then antiquated four-wheel coal wagons on the railways but was being shipped down the east coast by coastal vessels. Two thirds of the coal consumed by the gas and electricity utilities in the south had been transported by this route which soon became endangered by enemy mines and submarines. The export of coal bound for the south from ports on the Tyne and Humber did not cease completely, but it did falter. In fact, due to the loss of traffic to Scandinavia, the Baltic and Russia the coastal coal vessels were often the *only* shipping to operate from these ports in stark contrast to the congestion at ports on the other side of the country. Nonetheless, in the first five months of the war the reduction in coal brought south by the sea route amounted to 2,500,000 tons and the railways struggled to make up the deficit by running extra coal trains.

The government pressured the REC to take steps to increase the amount of coal carried by rail in an attempt to make up the shortfall in coal supplies to the south of England. The Mines Department made requests to the various industrial concerns and to the gas and electricity companies to purchase their coal not from mines in the north but from those in the Midlands. The consequence of this would be shorter rail journeys to convey their coal to the south. Arrangements for 800,000 tons to be provided in this way were made but there was less than complete success as the final additional net total was only about 200,000 tons. From a coal supply standpoint, September had not been a good month to start a war. Winter was approaching and coal stocks had to be fully built up during the summer and autumn months as in peacetime the weekly consumption of the fuel in winter exceeded the weekly delivery rate of coal to the south. Stockpiling in preparation for the winter demand was essential, so if supplies were to be maintained passenger traffic was not to be allowed to obstruct the coal trains.

The first SR wartime timetable presented a considerable curtailment of both suburban and main-line services. The company warned the public that overcrowding on passenger trains might result especially at peak hours, but the promise was made that passenger loadings would be monitored, and adjustments made wherever possible. The result of this monitoring did result in the limited restoration of some services on 15 September, but this was to prove politically embarrassing when members of the REC read in their Sunday papers that SR services had reverted to 'normal'. The railway insisted that they had taken care on Friday, 15 September and Saturday, 16 September to avoid giving any impression that services were returning to normal, but reporters at stations seem to have inferred this for themselves after reading timetable posters displayed at stations. In October, the SR produced their winter timetable which now showed a reduction of between 16 and 17 per cent in the 'business hours' electrified services and a 35 per cent reduction on the steam operated main lines. Some late evening train services had been omitted.

It had been announced that all restaurant and buffet cars would be removed from trains so that extra carriages could be attached to the reduced number of trains. Following the REC's instructions, the SR did initially take out of service all of its restaurant cars but, unlike the other railways, this created a difficulty inasmuch as the majority of its catering vehicles were part of fixed formation electric trains, making the removal of a single carriage from the fixed formation problematic. The complete withdrawal of the new six-coach sets used on the Brighton and Eastbourne services which had a single Pullman vehicle serving food resulted in what was immediately perceived as a lower standard of train provided for the regular commuters. The withdrawn electric trains had been built to a high standard with side corridors and inter-coach connection. The replacement trains, even if the same age as the express sets – but some would have been much older – were almost exclusively non-corridor and were viewed as 'old' by the regular travellers who were not only having their breakfast service taken away from them, but they perceived that they also had to endure an old-fashioned train to travel to their work on. The SR immediately sought approval from the REC for the smart new electric trains with their catering vehicles to be fully reinstated. The possibility has to be considered that the SR was perhaps being disingenuous as the removal of a single vehicle from these sets would have been disagreeable but not impossible. It should be remembered however, and the SR would have pointed this out, that the reason for the withdrawal of catering vehicles was that additional carriages could be added to trains without overloading the locomotives. This logic was not applicable to the SR electric sets which were fixed units and did not require a locomotive. The removal of a catering vehicle would only reduce the set by one vehicle and the railway did not have readily available vehicles for replacements. Furthermore, the SR argued, if meals could be served on its trains on the short journeys to the south-east, how could the lack of restaurant cars be justified to those travelling on the much longer steam train journeys to the south-west? Rather than insisting that the SR remove the catering vehicles, the REC relented by permitting the reinstatement of these facilities and instructed its operating committee to review the whole issue of on-train catering. Furthermore the REC insisted that the SR must not in the future increase its provision of restaurant cars and that the other companies should adhere to the original decision pending a review of the whole issue of on-train catering. So fast was the reversal of the 'no catering' policy that the SR staff magazine was informing its subscribers that all catering vehicles *had* been withdrawn when all of them knew that this was definitely not so as all of the restaurant and buffet cars were back in service. The REC were not pleased about being seen to have been forced to change its mind, and in deference to the committee the SR decided not to publicly advertise the restoration of its restaurant cars immediately. This might not seem to make any commercial sense, but it was politically expedient at the time, and they judged that its affluent regular travellers would soon spread the good news by word of mouth. On 29 September, the REC conceded that the catering vehicles on all four railways could be reintroduced on 'limited lines', and its operating subcommittee were requested to produce a schedule of routes upon which the railways could operate restaurant and buffet cars.

In the first weeks of the war, the SR ran its longer distance trains to slower schedules making more intermediate stops to compensate for the reduction in the number of stopping trains on the main lines. For example, the 171.8 miles journey from Waterloo to Exeter Central had, on average, taken five hours and forty-five minutes in 1938 but this had increased to six hours twenty-two minutes, with a reduction in the number of trains from twelve to only seven. The *Railway Magazine* reported in December that the journey time for the 79.2 mile run from Waterloo to Southampton was extended from an average of one hour fifty minutes to two hours and three minutes with a reduction in the number of trains from twenty-eight to twenty. In comparison with 1938, on their mainly electrified suburban routes the number of SR services were reduced within the range 50 to 70 per cent less, but the journey times were not reduced. For example where there had been a 20 min service from Charing Cross to Caterham but this was reduced to an hourly service, and a *Times* reader complained that not only were the trains less frequent, but they were also frequently late – he cited the 7.24pm and 8.24pm from Charing Cross being delayed for over 40 minutes on most days. The 'business trains' however to London Bridge and Waterloo for the City at first ran to what was described as 'practically normal' schedules. The longer-distance electric train service from London to Portsmouth was reduced from forty-five trains a day to forty with a twenty per cent deceleration. The electrified Brighton route had a more substantial reduction in trains running – from 100 to 46, but with only a three per cent speed retardation. The SR did, at busy times, run 'duplicate' express trains, that is extra relief trains but nominally the same timetabled train service. Perhaps, not in the spirit of the REC's philosophy, the SR general manager, Eustace Missenden, attempting to rebalance the negative effect of the service restrictions, was of the opinion that if any duplicate express trains were run, a publicity advantage could be had if details were given to the press.

The Great Western Railway, after first giving the overly optimistic impression that it was to be 'business-as-usual' following the outbreak of war, were instructed to make severe reductions pending a new timetable to be published on 25 September. Its new published public timetable for the emergency service allowed comparison to the pre-war schedules. Compared to September 1938, the number of trains running between Paddington to Bristol was reduced from twenty to fourteen and the journey times indicated a thirty-two per cent deceleration. Despite the published timings, the GWR had to warn its passengers that it was 'unable to guarantee the punctuality of trains' according to the *Railway Gazette*. Nevertheless the GWR managed to provide what was described as a 'passable version' of the Cornish Riviera Express, restoring to the railway the distinction of operating the longest non-stop run in the country. The GWR however was to hold this honour for only two months, as from 4 December the LMSR began running the 5.40pm Euston to Manchester express non-stop for the 177 miles to Wilmslow and from 1 January 1940 its wartime Comet ran the 183 miles non-stop from Stockport to Euston. Later the LMSR was to claim to be running the longest non-stop run in the whole of Europe, the 9.30pm Glasgow to Euston – what had in peacetime been the Night Scot – which now ran non-stop from Carstairs to Crewe, a distance of 214 miles. The new GWR timetable also eliminated all of the GWR's many 'slip coaches', that is coaches detached from trains at speed and braked to a stop by the slip coach guard. Following the concessions given in respect to the SR's catering vehicles, the GWR too was permitted to reintroduce many restaurant car services. Also, as early as 15 September, the GWR announced that they would be restoring previously withdrawn sleeping cars on the Paddington to Plymouth route. This had been approved by the REC following a request from committee member Sir James Milne – the GWR General Manager. On 2 October, the GWR duly reinstated sleeping car accommodation on the Paddington and Plymouth service – but only for the privileged first-class passengers.

The LNER and LMSR also made drastic reductions to main-line and suburban services. The reduced wartime sleeping car services to Scotland were initially being shared by the LNER and the LMSR and were soon to be the subject of complaints from regular travellers about the inadequacy of the overall provision of sleeping accommodation on the Anglo-Scottish routes. One important and influential group of regular overnight passengers were MPs travelling to and from Westminster and their northern constituencies. Given this important clientele it is unsurprising that even at the start of the war in September 1939, again under pressure, the REC grudgingly agreed that extra sleeping cars could be run at the discretion of the companies provided that the extra capacity did not involve the running of any extra relief 'duplicate' trains. Accordingly, the LMSR reintroduced sleeping cars on their night service to Stranraer which would have been of benefit for MPs from Northern Ireland.

The first wartime emergency timetables provided for through services from London to Edinburgh to be provided only by the LNER – there was to be no LMSR service to the Scottish capital from Euston. The LNER mid-September Emergency Timetable reinstated restaurant cars on 29 services and buffet cars on 6 services but overall, the trimming down of the timetable resulted in the LNER suffering a 25 per cent reduction in traffic during the first two weeks of October.

The curtailed services on the LNER were judged to be more irksome than those on the LMS or the SR. Typical of the misery were the overcrowded commuter trains into London from stations beyond Hatfield and on 11 September chaos ensued on its north London suburban services. When one train bound for King's Cross arrived at Welwyn Garden City it was already full of passengers, every seat had been taken and there was very little standing space available. After the next stop at Hatfield every compartment had at least twenty commuters tightly packed into each full-width compartment. The train continued to King's Cross, stopping at every station, where a few more assertive commuters were able to squeeze themselves into the carriages, but many were left standing on the platforms. The new wartime timetable allowed an hour for the journey in place of the pre-war half an hour, but nonetheless the train arrived at King's Cross a quarter of an hour late. Similarly at Liverpool Street LNER trains were also crowded and running late with as many as twenty-two passengers crammed into each compartment. The LNER were forced on 12 September to increase its suburban emergency services by eighteen more trains.

On the LMS the conditions were deemed to be not quite as bad as on the LNER. Travellers from St Albans to St Pancras were fortunate as there was at least one fast train during the peak period in the morning. On Tuesday, 19 September, the press announced that the LMS were to run more express trains.

Members of the public, as might be expected, had their own ideas on the emergency. One writer to *The Times* denigrated the continued availability of first-class travel in wartime, branding the users as 'selfish'; another proposed that season tickets could be assigned to a company not an individual. Many others were critical and deeply suspicious of the rationale behind the preparation of the emergency timetables. A Birmingham businessman wrote to *The Times* complaining that the reduced services were working against the national interest and were adding to the difficulties in keeping industry moving during the war. He noted that long distance journeys were about 50 per cent longer than in peacetime and that there were 30 per cent fewer trains on the London to Birmingham route. Worse, it was often necessary to change trains more often than before and this added even more to his journey time. His extra travel difficulties were on top of the other problems that he and others had when trying to run industry with depleted staff numbers and petrol rationing. Travel restrictions worked against the business culture which existed before modern telephone systems, emails and on-line conference facilities. The way business operated in 1939 was predominantly for suppliers to meet their customers face-to-face, shake hands on a deal and have a drink or lunch together afterwards. The new railway timetables, the writer to *The Times* claimed, resulted in any business engagement at a location more than 30 miles from his office effectively taking up a full day.

The most severe reductions did not last for long. After the emergency evacuation and troop movement period had passed the LMSR introduced its revised 'emergency' timetable on 25 September. This continued to show considerable reductions in service compared to 1938, for example between Euston and Liverpool, the number of trains each day was reduced from 14 to 12 with an average deceleration of 38 per cent. The Birmingham businessman, should he need to have a meeting in London, would have seen the number of daily trains to the capital recover to fifteen trains a day but when compared to the 1938 service this was still five less than before and the average journey time had increased by over an hour from two hours five minutes to three hours ten minutes. Nonetheless, on a positive note the LMSR considered that it was now possible to introduce several new train services with restaurant cars both from their London termini and on northern routes such as from Manchester to Leeds.

The premier LNER Coronation express which had been scheduled to take six hours between King's Cross and Edinburgh now ambled along taking 9 hours 25 minutes. On the LNER's former Great Central routes from Marylebone to Manchester, services were reduced to only two daytime trains and one train at night with the journey time extended on the fastest train from 3 hours 6 minutes to 4 hours 27 minutes. Through services from the LNER to the GWR and SR were all withdrawn except for one passenger train which ran at night between York and Swindon via Banbury.

By November 1939 however it became clear to all who studied the situation that the REC's timetable policy had been over cautious. The LNER agreed and were telling this to its staff through the medium of their magazine. Perhaps it was a piece of wartime propaganda issued to keep up sagging staff morale, but the railway claimed that by October the '…goods traffic has been regulated [such] that the "restrictions" do not fill a single sheet of foolscap…'. There had been an initial reduction in passenger demand at the beginning of the war when there appears to have been the quite natural desire to stay close to home but as the weeks went by passengers started to return to the railways and it was agreed that some service improvements could be made. A significant change agreed with the REC was an increase in the permitted average speed to be raised from 45 to 50 miles-per-hour – but the maximum speed was not to exceed 60mph and engine crews were forbidden to travel any faster in order to make up lost time. In November both the LNER and the LMSR printed another new edition of their timetables which included many service restorations. Advertisements placed by the railways in many local newspapers announced the service improvements as 'Good News' for the travelling public. The LNER did provide some additional main-line trains and restored some of its suburban services such as between Hatfield and St Albans. In December, the LMSR produced a further 44-page leaflet advertising an accelerated and augmented service of trains taking advantage of the relaxed speed restriction. These improved services included refreshment facilities and were given descriptions such as an 8.15 am 'breakfast train' from Liverpool to Euston calling at Mossley Hill, Crewe and Bletchley. Meanwhile, the LNER announced that many of the suburban trains on the Great Northern lines into Broad Street station would be restored.

The withdrawal of the cheap day return tickets in September had caused hardship to those wishing to visit relatives who lived some distance from London, so on Thursday, 5 October there was more good news when it was announced that these day tickets would soon be made available on the GWR, LMS, LNER and SR. Cheap tickets had already been made available to on-duty members of the Metropolitan Police Force travelling to and from sports grounds and for blind persons who were either former servicemen or travelling on business with their companions. These tickets however could not at first be used to and from any 'London' destination, that is any station within the London Transport Passenger Board geographical area. Consideration was being given to the possibility of the reinstatement of the cheap day ticket facility for travel within the London area but due to concerns about overcrowding during the 'rush-hour', time restrictions would continue to be applied. When the cheaper day ticket option was restored, new restrictions were made as to the use of these tickets – they could not be used until after 10am or for return journeys Mondays to Fridays inclusive or between 4pm and 7pm to avoid additional congestion during rush hours. It had been accepted that the aim of these unpopular ticketing restrictions had been intended to inhibit 'non-essential' travel, but their reintroduction was appreciated by many. With cheap day tickets once again available in London and throughout the country, it was observed by *The Times* that despite the wet weather 'there was a noticeable increase in the number of housewives travelling from the suburbs to do their shopping'. Not all 'housewives' were pleased however for whilst these tickets were again available, the overall reduction in the number of trains being run when added to the time-of-day restrictions meant this concession was seriously devalued. A *Times* reader from Cranleigh in Surrey – a station on the rural byway between Guildford and Horsham which only had a sparse service – complained that to get to London the earliest train that she could use with an 'off-peak' ticket left Cranleigh not conveniently in the morning but early in the afternoon at 1.08pm. The hapless lady (after a change at Guildford), arrived at Waterloo at 2.24pm leaving only 1½ hours shopping time in London before having to catch the 3.57pm departure from Waterloo.

In December 1939, the *Railway Gazette* was pleased to report that the passenger services on the LNER East Coast route service were as close as was possible to 'normal'. The schedules lacked the Pullman express trains and the streamlined trains, but the new 50mph average speed and the elimination of long 'refreshment' stops that were no longer required following the restoration of on-train catering considerably improved matters for the traveller. The Flying Scotsman now took 80 mins less for its revised 8 hour 25 minute journey from King's Cross to Edinburgh. This was an improvement from the previous timing of 9 hours and 32 minutes, a 61 per cent deceleration to a 40 per cent deceleration. It must be remembered however that in the summer of 1938, the Flying Scotsman took only six hours to reach Edinburgh. Less famous LNER express trains were also accelerated, for example the 170-mile journey to Hull by the fastest train now took four hours 35 minutes, whereas previously it had taken 5 hours 20 minutes, a reverse of the deceleration imposed in September from 50 per cent to 31 per cent. Even accepting the withdrawal of the high-speed streamlined 'flyers', the LNER's performance hardly rates the claimed 'normal', as *Railway Magazine* noted in March. Nonetheless, the LNER were claiming that the improved services were then less than twenty per cent below the 1938 level.

The SR also announced in December that from 1 January 1940 they too would augment their main-line services with additional trains, some with restaurant cars, but generally its trains did not run to higher speeds, as timings to Exeter and Portsmouth and Brighton remained the same. The SR's fastest train to Brighton however still took exactly one hour, representing almost uniquely the same scheduled time as before the war. A significant proportion of the SR's income was from the sale of season tickets to commuters working in London. Following the outbreak of war there was less demand for commuter travel – over 20,000 season tickets were surrendered, mostly for the London suburban services. A probable explanation for this might be the 'calling-up' of reservists into the services. In November, the SR partially restored some peak hour services providing an additional 95 trains. These included twenty-nine trains run between 3pm and 5pm to avoid the earlier blackout after the end of the British Summer Time and the return to Greenwich Mean Time. The SR also provided additional trains from Waterloo, Charing Cross and Holborn Viaduct for the benefit of newspaper and other workers who were leaving their place of work in central London at around midnight.

The first Christmas of the war proved to be a stressful period for the railways, aggravated by some of the worst winter weather of the century. The initial, difficult, task had been to estimate the potential volume of traffic to be carried during this atypical Christmas season. The railways noted what they described as 'the widespread disturbance of population' which was likely to generate additional traffic for Christmas reunions, but this had to be balanced against any reluctance the public might have to travel during wartime. Nonetheless the railways made detailed plans for augmentation of the current restricted timetable to cope with the potential holiday traffic over the 1939 Christmas period. The REC published a poster advising travellers that the railways were to operate a limited number of additional trains. The SR advised that they proposed to provide 200 extra trains to the south coast resorts but as far as possible these would only run during daylight hours so as to avoid the blackout. The SR expected to find the Christmas period particularly difficult as it would be necessary for all of the anticipated Christmas leave traffic from 'overseas' forces – that is the BEF in France – and a large proportion of leave for those stationed at home would pass through its territory. The LMSR advertised an extra 478 passenger trains of which 101 would leave London and 104 would terminate in London. The LNER provided 400 additional trains between 15 and 31 December to cater for Christmas traffic using 110 restaurant cars and 35 sleeping cars. The GWR meanwhile proposed to temporarily reinstate 'famous expresses' which had been suspended due to the war including the 12 noon Torbay Express. Christmas fare was to be served in the train's restaurant car.

This pre-planning of additional services was to be justified when any uncertainty that fewer people might travel on these Christmas extra trains evaporated as it became obvious that in December 1939 there was an increase in demand for families desperate to get together over the festive period. Despite the government's wish that railway travel should be avoided, the public were not going to let the phoney war disrupt their Christmas. The Christmas traffic peaked just before the holiday when further additional services were run. Of these, 41 well-patronised trains were run on the penultimate day before Christmas and an extra 51 on the last day before Christmas. On Boxing Day, 16 extra trains were run for those returning from Christmas visits and the next day a further 23 extra trains were run. As well as the extra services, many timetabled trains on the long-distance routes were run in two or more parts, effectively resulting in 174 extra trains. Unfortunately, the weather interfered with the smooth running of the railways' Christmas services. Nevertheless, despite the severe cold weather holding up steamer services and resulting in 16 train cancellations, the SR transported 40,019 Christmas holiday passengers between London and the south coast.

In addition to the increase in passenger traffic, there was also the extra Christmas parcels to be conveyed by the railways. The LMSR ran additional parcels trains which included 100 in each direction into and out of London. The GWR ran 31 parcel post trains between Paddington and western destinations conveying 92,000 bags – an increase of 4,000 bags carried during the Christmas period in 1938. In a January 1940 article for the *Railway Gazette*, the GWR claimed that it had been one of the most difficult periods for several years. The SR experienced an increase in the number of passengers to their seaside resorts, at Brighton station there were 2,000 more passenger arrivals than in 1938. At Bognor Regis there were an extra 1,125 visitors, and those that arrived between 8pm and 9pm on Christmas Saturday were greeted by carols performed by the local Free Church Choir on the station concourse. Their performance so impressed the station master that he immediately agreed that the choir could give a second performance later that evening.

As an extra Christmas present to the travelling public, the minister of transport, Euan Wallace, announced in mid-December that more cheap return tickets would be made available facilitating occasional visits to attend special events, including day tickets for anglers. He also promised that in the New Year special tickets would also be available for those travelling to convalescent homes, institutions catering for the blind or those with mental health issues either as patients, visitors or escorts.

Chapter 3

Is Your Journey Really Necessary?

The approach of the railway companies as indicated in these posters is considerably more promising, virile and realistic than in any of the efforts so far completed by the authorities. Official posters so far have had on the whole a very unsatisfactory effect.

Mass Observation Report 1939

The REC's rather vague call to the public to give priority to undefined traffic of national importance left many of the public having to interpret for themselves exactly what this urgent traffic was. Obviously in a war situation there had to be a 'need to know' policy, but in respect to many such sensitive issues a degree of secrecy was required to maintain national security and avoid any unnecessary panic within the population. Given that so far there were no obvious hostilities, the new wartime 'normal' – which was so unlike that which was to follow in only a few months' time – did not in late 1939 generate any obvious change in the mobility needs for much of the general public. The apparent pressing need to change the long-established travel patterns by the imposition of such severe reductions in railway services was never going to be fully understood or appreciated by many within the population. Once the major evacuations had taken place it became difficult to convince the public that these reductions in services were necessary, in part because the gloomy predictions of bombing at the outbreak of war had not been fulfilled and what followed was a period of relative calm. The government had declared war on Germany following its brutal invasion of Poland, but there was to be no immediate concerted attack on Britain when the German high command was concentrating on events to the east of their country with Warsaw suffering the savage air raids.

Railway publicity in the early weeks of the war had concentrated on showing that the railways, despite the war, were continuing to serve the nation. Publicity posters produced in the early months of the war by the REC emphasized this with wording such as – 'day-in day-out ... night-in night-out ... British railways are carrying on'. Another poster lauded the railways for their 'efficient distribution of the nation's essential supplies'. This publicity emphasized the need to move freight by rail, but the sub-text that the public should avoid travel by train to assist the railways with this crucial task was not made clear. 'British railways are carrying on' was never going to be easily construed as meaning that passenger traffic needed to be restricted.

The government, with the REC, reasoned that the present publicity was inadequate and that there was an urgent need for a new publicity campaign to persuade the public to limit their personal travel. Unfortunately for many people there is a thin line between sensible and helpful advice provided as government information and the more questionable and unreliable message given by anything that might be perceived as being simply propaganda. The public were likely to be uncertain as to whether they were being told the whole truth when any attempt to convince not to travel was made. Families and friends desperately wanted to travel to meet each other and have fun days in the country or go away for their annual holiday by the sea. For decades the railway companies' posters had encouraged the public to get on the trains to pursue such activities. To be successful in reducing passenger numbers any new poster or newspaper advertisement campaign would require careful planning.

Part of the government's difficulty was that the public knew that many important facts were being kept from them. This was despite the fact that unlike the totalitarian regimes, British censorship procedures strove to strike a balance between press freedom and national security. Press reports alluding to military activity were scrutinised by the

Ministry of Information before they were released for publication after any necessary redaction. There were other non-military subjects that required a degree of censorship and a good example of this was the full details of the exceptionally cold weather during the winter of 1939/40. It seems strange to us today that in 1940 the British weather was a state secret. Without the global weather data gathering that is available today, the mid-twentieth century weather forecasters had to rely on reports from the many meteorological office weather stations situated across the country and not from satellite images. Knowledge of the weather over the British Isles would be invaluable to the enemy planning bomber raids or a full invasion, thus any information about the current state of the weather had to remain secret. For this reason, the BBC had ceased their regular weather forecasts and on the railways the station announcers were not permitted to blame 'weather' as a reason for delayed or cancelled trains. It is therefore unsurprising that passengers would often not be told why their train was delayed and the railways had to keep quiet and bravely soak up the blame for events that were outside their control such as thick fog, deep snowdrifts or flooding on the line. Some relaxation to the rules was to be made later in 1941 when it was agreed that trains could be described as being late due to 'weather conditions' provided that no mention was made of 'snow, ice or fog'.

For passengers the very welcome provision of additional passenger services at the end of 1939 and into 1940 was marred by extreme delays due to the exceptionally bad weather. What sets this 'great freeze' apart from other similar events is that it has been largely forgotten and has not passed into the popular weather lore in the same way as have the similar cold weather events of 1947 and 1963. This is in part due to the extreme weather of the winter of 1939/40 not being reported in the national press or by the BBC due to the wartime censorship. Of course, the public knew the weather was exceptionally severe as they could see for themselves the local situation from their windows, but what they were not told – and what the government needed to keep secret from any German agents who were believed to be embedded in the UK – was just how widespread the appalling weather conditions were and how debilitating were the effects in respect of transport, communications and the availability of essential supplies. From the military point of view the freezing weather did fortuitously spread across the whole of Europe, effectively preventing the enemy from taking any advantage of Britain's state of paralysation.

The wintry weather started in the latter half of December 1939 with freezing fog and severe frosts. Many of the most welcome extra trains provided by the railways over the Christmas period were delayed by fog. The heavy snow accompanied by frost resulted in January 1940 being the coldest month since February 1895. Severity of any winter weather can be judged by reference to the Meteorological Office's Central England Temperature (CET) data. The mean temperature for any month is derived from all the daily temperature readings taken within the geographical triangle enclosing Lancashire, London and Bristol. The value for January 1940, was minus 1.4 degrees Centigrade which was the first sub-zero CET of the twentieth century. The heaviest snowfalls were in the north when the most dramatic weather of the winter began on the 26 January. A two-day snowstorm engulfing the British Isles resulted in up to two feet of snow being deposited on parts of central England. Over 1,500 miles of railway were out of service due to snowdrifts which were often as much as ten to fifteen feet high.

The West Coast Main line was blocked by snowdrifts and the Settle and Carlisle line was blocked by stranded trains. For a few days the only route to Scotland was by the LNER. Examples of stranded passenger trains filled with hungry passengers include two express trains with a total of 500 passengers on board (of which 150 were children) spending the night trapped in the carriages at Adlington near Chorley on the LMSR line between Bolton and Preston. Another 120 passengers were stranded on bleak moorland 1,000 feet above sea level at Beattock Summit. This train, an LMSR Glasgow to Manchester express, was stuck in the snow for twenty-six hours with minimal food available on the train and it would have been unlikely that the steam heating from the engine could have kept the carriages warm for very long. The passengers shared what provisions they had with them, and, in the age when all the affluent ladies in first-class would have fashionably worn fur coats, they generously loaned these to the small children on the train. The passengers were eventually rescued by a railway breakdown team and subsequently escorted to the village of Abingtan which is situated at the bottom of the Beattock incline.

Despite having less snow in the south, within the area served by the SR a temperature of minus 20 degrees Celsius was recorded in Canterbury; the Thames froze over between Sunbury and Teddington; and there was sea ice on the shore at Bognor Regis, Folkestone and Southampton. This caused severe difficulties for the SR due to the icing-up of the 'live' conductor rails powering the Southern Electric trains. After the thaw in the spring of 1940, *The Railway Magazine* was able to confirm in its March edition that conductor rail icing had been a problem during the winter, but the London Transport electric trains had coped better with the freezing weather. The magazine reported that the LPTB trains were fitted with steel brushes and that throughout the night they operated special 'sleet trains' fitted with steel scrapers which also squirted anti-freeze onto the conductor rails. On the SR, snow and ice up to two inches thick often surrounded the conductor rails and had to be chipped off by hand.

The January storm resulted in the precipitation on lower lying areas across southern England falling not as snow but as freezing rain. This was due to a rare meteorological event that occurs when a warm front enters an area of very cold air, creating a 'sandwich' when a layer of warm air has cold air above it as well as below. Snow falling from the higher cold region melts as it falls through the warm air but is then 'supercooled' as raindrops freeze instantly upon reaching the surface. This resulted in everything being covered by a sheet of ice as the air temperature at ground level never rose above minus two degrees Celsius. This was the *wrong sort of rain* and the weight of the ice that built up on the SR's telegraph lines broke and brought to the ground many wires, causing disruption to the telegraphic and signalling systems as well as public telephone links since the GPO also used the trackside route. Worse, the ice covered the conductor rails, often up to an inch thick, bringing all electric trains to a near halt and flashovers from the conductor rail to earth were also reported.

Any forward movement of the SR electric trains was accompanied by severe arcing (all thoughts of wartime 'blackout' conditions forgotten) as they could only advance at a slow walking pace at best. On the evening of Saturday, 27 January many electric trains on the Western and Central Sections were stalled and stranded, although suburban trains on the Eastern Section fared better. On the following Monday a few Western and Central Section suburban trains were running again but for three days some country and main line electric trains were assisted by steam locomotives. A variety of locomotives were used ranging from goods 0-6-0s to Atlantic 4-4-2s and 4-6-0s. This resulted in exhilarating performances when the collector shoes were able to make a good contact with the conductor rail and dramatic spectacles with blue-green arcs from the collector shoes and an eruption of exhaust steam from the locomotives when contact with the live rail became almost impossible due to the ice. The few electric services that were run were formed of either a single or a pair of the Brighton line six-car sets, or two of the four-car sets built for the Portsmouth lines. The intention was that the trains would draw current whenever possible with the steam locomotive assisting when ice was encountered. Where possible the electric current would be used to heat and light the trains and to drive the Westinghouse pumps for the brakes. On the SR's Western Section, where on at least one occasion it was recorded that a T9 4-4-0 locomotive was used to haul a train of Portsmouth electric stock, only the screw coupling connected the locomotive to the electric train as these were equipped for vacuuming breaking while the electric trains had air brakes. In this bizarre situation the steam locomotive driver took charge of the train, communicating with the motorman (who had control of the train brakes) by hand signals. The drivers of the steam locomotives were very keen to engage in rapid accelerations wherever possible to avoid the ignominy of being propelled by an electric train. Meanwhile on the SR Central Section, twelve-car trains were assisted by locomotives less regal than the T9s such as Billington 0-6-0 goods locomotives and 0-6-2 tank locomotives. These former London, Brighton and South Coast Railway locomotives were fitted with Westinghouse air brakes as had been the standard for that company. Also, in the south of England, the Somerset and Dorset Joint Railway suffered massive damage to the telegraph wires with over 200 poles brought to the ground due to the accumulation of ice and snow. *The Railway Magazine* reported that emergency posts were established along the line allowing permissive working at five-minute intervals and the weight of the trains was reduced to ensure that the locomotives had sufficient power for their task.

This now long forgotten event illustrates how during the war it was necessary to control news output, but it is of note that the weather censorship produced a bizarre situation when the *Manchester Guardian* was bold enough to report dramatic delays to trains – 'Train Journeys Last For Days' – without mentioning the cause; although they did mischievously append to their story a sentence stating that a radio broadcast the previous evening had reminded listeners to provide crumbs for the birds during severe weather. The previous day however the gallant *Daily Mirror* had reported that the Thames had frozen over due to the freezing weather which had 'begun a month ago'. The next day the same newspaper carried a front-page report which was headlined 'The Great Jam'. The public was belatedly informed that travel restrictions were to continue due to the severe weather that continued to isolate whole areas of the country. Once the security threat was over and censorship restrictions removed, the railways could boast of their achievements. In response to public criticism of the railways' performance during the bad weather, the Railway

Executive issued a poster with the slogan '…and still the Railwaymen carried on!' The poster showed four pictures – one from each of the Big Four – indicating the exceptional conditions, the SR contribution showing telegraph wires brought to the ground and some track with a layer of ice upon the conductor rail.

Earlier in January, to counter the increasing crisis developing due to a shortage of coal in the south, a difficult situation exacerbated by the exceptionally severe weather conditions, the government set up an emergency committee headed by Lord Hyndley, who was later to become the first Chairman of the National Coal Board when the industry was nationalised in 1947. This committee successfully instigated a programme of additional coal trains, resulting in a gradual increase in deliveries to the public utilities amounting to 18,000 tons a week. But progress was seriously hampered by the weather, resulting in a complete cessation of all coal traffic during the weekend of 27/29 January and this consequently resulted in an acute shortage of the fuel. On 29 January the President of the Board of Trade – who was at the time Sir Andrew Rae Duncan, a Scottish businessman who had been brought into the government during the war – formed another committee to oversee the situation. He reported that railway sidings in various parts of the country were filled with wagons containing coal 'owned' by various companies. It was estimated that these wagons, held captive due to the exceptional snow and fog conditions, equated to thirty coal trains. Before the war the local coal merchants not only owned the coal that they had bought from the mining companies but also the railway wagons to transport it, but as a wartime measure the REC instructed that all of these 'private owner' wagons had to be pooled. Furthermore, Sir Andrew's committee ordered that all of the coal must be requisitioned by the government for public use irrespective of its ownership or quality. As well as the trains in the sidings, similar arrangements were made relating to 70 more coal trains running direct from the mines.

But any thoughts of keeping the coal crisis a secret had to be abandoned as the public had to be involved in solving the problem.

The *Daily Mirror* on 30 January reported that the government had proclaimed that 'you must watch your coal'. While reassuring that there was only a 'temporary' shortage, the plea was for householders to 'go easy' with their coal – or they may find themselves without any. The cause of the shortage was given as transport disorganisation due to severe weather.

The apparent poor service provided by the railways during the exceptionally bad winter could be excused, but the more general dissatisfaction about the service reductions coming from the business community was more difficult to explain away. These may have had some merit, for many passengers believed that their journeys were 'necessary'. What is uncertain is the degree to which simple changes in working practices such as the grouping together of appointments in a locality to minimise trips to the provinces, or by using letter or telephone communication could, and should have been, seriously considered by the complainers. The railways now had a dilemma as now publicity material had to cease promoting their core businesses and potentially enter the darker world of propaganda, a place where they were in danger of encountering both cynicism and scepticism. The public might easily mistrust any 'government controlled' messages. It could be argued that many people were highly sceptical and cynical remembering the exaggerated propaganda circulated during the Great War – often quoted are the lurid accounts of rabid German soldiers bayoneting babies. This may have blunted any belief in the very early reports of the Nazi atrocities, particularly in respect to their gross anti-semitism. The REC in 1939 was producing many posters extolling the hard work of the railway companies, but these were not being well received. The SR's officers' committee was very disparaging of the REC's efforts, denigrating what was described as the posters' 'depressing' style. It was agreed that one particular REC poster should be restricted so that only six were to be displayed at the larger stations and only one at all the other stations.

To counter any public misconceptions or lack of belief in the need for restricted travel and to produce publicity material that would be effective, late in 1939 the REC had commissioned an urgent report from the MO unit to assess the public's reaction to a set of six sample posters. These six posters were proposals for publication; some of these were in draft form only but some were almost ready for publication. The railways may have gained a reputation for producing high-quality advertising posters which were displayed at stations and elsewhere, but to date there had not been any academic research into the effectiveness of this advertising medium. The MO organisation is best known for recording the everyday life of British people by collecting personal writings from members of the public between 1937 and the early 1950s. The organisation's usual method of acquiring data was through a panel of volunteers who had been recruited to reply to regular questionnaires and tasks, and this included the writing of diaries. In addition, a team of paid investigators were sent out to witness a variety of public situations to record people's behaviour and conversation in as much detail as possible.

For the REC's survey, the MO used a small team of researchers to carry out interviews at all of the main London termini and at three smaller London area stations – Uxbridge Road, Cricklewood and Kilburn. The MO unit, with a confidence based on previous travel surveys, were satisfied that this London-centric sample would accurately represent the views held country-wide. The MO reported that their researchers had been able to interview travellers using both long and shorter distance journeys and that only 'steam train' passengers were interviewed. The use of the term 'steam train' indicated that they concerned themselves only with main-line passengers and did not survey 'underground' passengers on the LPTB lines. By using this description, perhaps the MO had forgotten that hundreds of passengers using the Southern Electric main-line services to Brighton and Portsmouth would be found at Victoria and Waterloo stations. The principal task for the researchers was to test the immediate impact of the six sample posters. An early version of the iconic 'Is Your Journey Really Necessary' campaign poster was not included in the survey, but the report's conclusions appear to have guided its final design even though its publication was to be two years after the survey. In addition, more general and wider information was obtained during the interviews eliciting comments relating to the public's grumbles about the railway companies and their feelings and fears about railway travel during the nightly blackout. The MO's research also investigated the positioning of any posters in order to obtain maximum visibility and, more importantly, the impact of the poster. To achieve this secondary aim additional questions were asked about how passengers moved around the railway stations and to the degree to which they noticed any posters that were displayed thereabouts. In an age when social class was perhaps more important than it is today, MO produced tables which went beyond separating the opinions of men as distinct from those from women as the male and female respondents were further subdivided into four classes as they were tabulated as being either 'upper', 'middle', 'artisan' or 'working' class.

The fieldwork started on Saturday, 21 October 1939 and the completed report was delivered to the MO's REC contact Richmond Temple only six days later on Friday, 27 October. The total charge to the REC was a mere £50. Given the importance of the task, and the amount of detail the MO required, this was not only a quick and thorough endeavour but also a very cheap report.

The six draft posters were each shown in turn to the participants. The first was described in the report shorthand as 'Boy'. On the top of the picture there was a boy playing with a train set comprising a circle of track with a train filling all of the circle. On each of the toy carriages was a label, either 'passengers', 'war materials', 'shells', 'food', 'passengers' or 'troops.' Beneath the picture the text read 'could you FIT ANY MORE TRAINS IN HERE. TRAINS CARRYING SHELLS, TROOPS & WAR MATERIALS ARE USING THE TRACKS DAY AND NIGHT.' This poster tied for third place in the 'most liked' survey with fourteen per cent of those questioned stating that they liked it the best. There was however a divergence of opinion between the views of men and women. Twice as many women than men preferred this poster. The researchers – using stereotype logic possibly more prevalent in the 1930s than would be acceptable today – inferred that the cute small boy had appealed to the females' mothering instincts, or as they put it less directly, 'parent appeal'. On the other hand, there were those who at first misunderstood the message, and one person commented, 'Silly, I thought it was a toy advert at first.' The MO in its conclusions agreed that the interviewee had made a valid point as there was nothing that was immediately obvious to differentiate this poster from a Hornby or Meccano advert.

The second poster offered to the participants was the least finished in the design process. It was referred to as 'Blackout' and appeared somewhat less professional than the other posters. It displayed two photographs, one of which showed a clear vista of railway lines contrasting with the second which showed a similar image but was dark and blurred. The first photograph was labelled 'PEACE', the second 'WAR'. Written above the images was the wording: 'THE RAILWAYS IN WAR-TIME' followed by 'ACTON MARSHALLING YARDS'. Below the two contrasting photographs was the text 'GOODS TRAINS MUST STILL BE LOADED IN THE BLACK-OUT'. This was the least favoured of the six posters shown with only eight per cent of those surveyed deciding that it was the one they liked the best. Some however were complimentary, a forty-year-old man described as being upper-class commented 'Very striking. You can see without reading [that it] expressed the contrast between peace and war very well'. Based on the overall public response however, the MO report advised that this poster, or a variant of it, should not be used as it would be likely to 'do more harm than good'. A wise decision perhaps, for too much should not have been made about the railways' nocturnal freight handling difficulties.

The third poster showed a red box alongside a photograph of lines of open railway wagons filled with what appeared to most viewers as a load of stones. The accompanying words printed in bold type read

'FOOD, SHELLS and FUEL MUST HAVE PRIORITY. If your train is crowded – DO YOU MIND?'. This poster was identified by the researchers as the 'Trucks' design, and they identified this as the most popular of the six with twenty-eight per cent of those questioned liking it the best. One thirty-year-old upper-class man liked this design and described 'Trucks' as 'pictorial' and opining that 'it catches the attention'. A middle-class man said it was '… unusual. People will look at it and say "what's that picture? A lot of sheep or something?" And they will look again.' A fifty-year-old woman observed, 'well, it has a drawing on it. It's the sort of thing people will look at, I think'. A working man, aged thirty-five pointing to the drawing of the trucks said, 'Well, they've got those well. They must get there'. Another working man aged thirty commented that the poster was, 'to the point and really effective, even if you don't read it.'

The fourth poster was text only without any illustration, denoted as the 'Your Part' poster. The text was 'YOUR PART IN THE WAR. Many of your trains are now carrying the men who are fighting for you. Engines that used to pull passenger trains are now hauling the FOOD, FUEL, SHELLS, MINES and MATERIALS for war industry. SUCH TRAINS MUST COME FIRST. Every member of the railway staff is working his hardest – Every possible wheel is being moved in the interests of the nation's vital needs – NEVERTHELESS Passenger services have had to be cut and speeds reduced to make room on the tracks for these trains. This is YOUR PART IN THE WAR.' This poster was liked best by fourteen per cent of those questioned, making it a joint third place in the order of preference in a tie with 'Boy'.

At the top of the fifth poster, designated 'Blackpool', was a drawing of a passenger train crossing a high viaduct and embankment. Underneath the picture was written 'THIS BRITISH ENGINE USED TO PULL HOLIDAY TRAINS TO BLACKPOOL. LIKE HUNDREDS OF OTHERS IT IS NOW PULLING TROOP TRAINS OR AMMUNITION HERE OR TO THE FRONT. THIS IS AN EXAMPLE OF HOW THE RAILWAYS ARE HELPING

TO WIN THE WAR. MORE ENGINES ON THIS MEAN FEWER PASSENGER TRAINS BUT SOLDIERS' LIVES AND YOUR SAFETY DEPEND ON EVERY TRAIN BEING USED TO THE GREATEST POSSIBLE EXTENT.' Sixteen per cent of those taking part in the survey liked this poster the best, making it the second most popular. A working-class women aged forty commented on this poster, '… by the look of it it's nicer than the others, I like the picture.'

Apart from the few recipients who found the subject of Blackpool and the train interesting, there was generally little interest in the content shown in any of the posters that the MO saw fit to record. Based on the survey results a version of this poster was later produced for public display. The completed and published version of 'Blackpool' showed a photograph of a train emerging from a tunnel and not crossing a viaduct as on the draft version. The locomotive had a very 'LNER' appearance but its number, usually painted on the front buffer beam, had been obliterated and the letters 'BR' superimposed. A soldier standing guard with his rifle is shown beside the track. The words of the actual poster were not quite the same as the 1939 sample poster, but it offered to the viewer a similar sentiment and did start with the words 'This British engine used to pull holiday trains to Blackpool …'

The sixth poster ('Guns'), proclaimed a similar message to the fifth but was much bolder and more succinct. Huge capital letters widely spaced declared: 'FEWER TRAINS MORE GUNS. GUNS SAVE OUR SOLDIERS' LIVES. Despite its direct no-nonsense and straight to the message approach, this poster was not liked. Only thirteen per cent of those shown the posters deemed this the one they liked best. There was a prevalence for men to vote for this poster compared to the number of women interviewed. This gender disparity was also found in comments relating to the 'Your part in the war' poster. The MO suggested that the more war-like and to the point message was it was more likely to appeal directly to what they perceived as the more aggressive nature of the males who took part in the survey. The researchers concluded that this indicated that women were likely to show greater antagonism to war-like images and any text that had anything to do with war symbolism. But one person surveyed expressed the opinion that 'I like what it says, and it also clearly expresses opinions of the public – we don't matter as much as others.'

The MO researchers concluded after analysing their findings that while the 'Trucks' poster was the most popular in every social class group, it was the most popular with those in the upper and middle classes. Conversely the 'Blackpool' and the 'guns' posters were both less likely to meet the favour of those deemed to be upper classes. Nonetheless the 'Guns' poster elicited the most patriotic comments such as 'yes, our soldiers have to be saved' and 'it is in the interest of the country' and 'it's patriotic, you see'.

The 'Boy' poster was more favoured amongst the working class, and one thirty-five-year-old woman commented, 'I like the kid and it ain't too painful to read'. The interpretation made of the class divergence was that as two-thirds of the regular passengers' were probably from the upper and middle classes, the 'Trucks' poster, or a development of it, would have most effect on passengers' travelling habits. It was suggested that any overtly military sentiment was less likely to have impact on the more affluent regular travellers. Conversely the 'Blackpool' poster, by appealing to the less travelled lower classes, would be of less use to the REC when considering a publicity campaign. The 'Guns' poster due to its military nature would not appeal to the regular, more wealthy travellers and was bracketed with 'Blackout' as a poster that should not be used.

The MO researchers after collecting all the data did a, necessarily quick, analysis of what they had been able to record. To reach their conclusions they also tabulated the least liked posters and again split their findings into both gender and class categories.

The researchers' initial conclusions – which they had to admit were rather crude due to the urgency of their task – was that the six posters could be divided into three groups. The first contained 'Trucks' and 'Blackpool'. These posters, they concluded, had a wide appeal with a lower level of dislike. There were however important class differences which did negate some of the overall impact of the Blackpool poster since it had less appeal to the upper classes who were more likely to travel.

The second group was comprised of 'Boy' and 'Your part'. These were deemed 'middle-road' in overall appeal with 'Your Part' not being appreciated by a high proportion of upper- and middle-class people. The third group – 'Guns' and 'Blackout' – were deemed to be generally unpopular, the latter particularly with working-class women.

After examining the posters, the MO offered the REC general advice on advertising technique. In the wartime environment the REC now needed advertising posters to, if possible, reduce and not encourage passenger travel. The MO expressed some concern that the railway industry had a lack of understanding as to how the public related to its publicity material. An understanding of public perception of poster content was now critical as the REC ventured into unknown new territory. The railway companies may have been masters at persuading potential passengers but now the MO had to point out to the railway companies that they now had nothing tangible to 'sell'. Now, in wartime, railway posters had to generate something which was less easy to define – the obscure, personal and individual commodity of goodwill. To generate goodwill through an advertising poster the MO advised that the image on display must be able to induce in the viewer personal feelings and an emotional response. They had recently made a comprehensive study of Ministry of Information posters and leaflets and concluded that an emotional response could not be achieved by highlighting the second-person pronoun 'you' since it would not readily transfer to meaning 'me'. When used, it was argued, any second-person pronoun must be strengthened with a linkage such as the phrase 'your duty'. Also, if the pronoun was used carelessly 'you' might appear to be patronising. If 'you' or 'your' is used, the MO advised, it must be repeated to strengthen the message or alternatively there must be an illustration within the poster to reinforce that the text refers directly to 'me' or to 'us'. For example, the effective 'Trucks' poster had both 'you' and 'your' in the text and was reinforced with an illustration of the trucks carrying the necessary fuel for the home use of the viewer. (Although, perversely, many saw the trucks as conveying stone, not coal.) The other poster which received a high number of 'likes' was 'Blackpool' and importantly this used the wording 'your safety' and the reference to the popular seaside resort equated, according to the MO report writer, as to 'us'. The 'Boy' poster contained the pronoun 'you' with the illustration of the boy which, again in the opinion of the report writer, had the illustrative link to 'child', and was therefore given the approval of so many working-class women, that is it achieved 'parental appeal'. The less favoured 'Guns' had only 'our' in the text without any link, while 'Blackout' had no personal pronouns at all nor any illustrative linkage.

That the REC took due notice of the report can be determined from many examples of subsequently published posters which can be found in literature, museums and on the internet. The posters associated with the 'Is Your Journey Really Necessary' campaign are good examples of what was learnt from the MO's report. Two major versions of the poster were distributed throughout the REC's campaign which began later in 1942. Both showed the window to a booking office at a station, and both carried the slogan. Note that the personal pronoun 'your' was used and that it was duly coupled to 'journey' in line with the MO advice. The illustrative linkage to the text as recommended by the MO report showed figures standing in the booking office who were contemplating whether to travel or not hopefully would translate in the viewers' mind from 'you' to 'me'. To populate the booking office the REC took the MO's advice in two directions. One, later, version of the poster showed an armed soldier holding up his arm to bar the way of any person intending to buy a ticket. This would have chimed with the outwardly more patriotic working classes and militaristic men. This 'sentry' version would not have worked for the less militaristic upper classes and for many women; but it was the alternative version which was primarily aimed at this group – and particularly relevant to those embarking on casual travel – as it clearly showed a well-dressed and affluent middle-aged man and wife accompanied by their small dog.

The MO research team was very complimentary about the high standard of the sample railway posters that had been submitted by the REC for evaluation. They opined that the approach shown in the preparation of these posters, together with other railway posters they had seen, would potentially result in new wartime posters that would generate a positive public response.

Chapter 4

Visiting the Evacuated Children

[Evacuation was] one of the most extraordinary state interventions in family life…

James Heartfield, *Unpatriotic History of the Second World War*, Zero Books, 2012

The evacuation of children created an unexpected demand for wartime railway travel when parents visited their children who had been reluctantly dispersed across the country and, surprisingly, further additional passenger traffic in the opposite direction as thousands of children returned home much to the dismay of the local authorities. Many of the journeys made by parents and other close relatives to visit evacuated children were undertaken as part of a government approved programme and as such could be construed as being part of the 'government travel' which increased passenger numbers at a time when the government was insisting that the REC and the railways took steps to reduce passenger traffic to make way for freight trains carrying war materials. Many of the parents who travelled to distant locations were unfamiliar with train travel, particularly those from working-class areas in London who in normal circumstances would only take the train – if ever – to a known and trusted holiday destination.

After the four days of intense activity at the beginning of September 1940, the exhausted LCC staff sat back anticipating that their work was done, but it was not to be so as further 'management' of the evacuees was soon to follow. The dispersal of children away from the dangerous urban centres may have at least appeared to solve one problem for the government but the splitting-up of families resulted in a new demand for railway travel as parents made what might be deemed 'unnecessary' journeys to visit their dearly missed offspring. Worse from the government's point of view, many children became so homesick that they soon returned home, many of them travelling by train after collection by a parent. In Bath by December a thousand children, one third of those who had arrived in the city from London, had returned home, not in large groups but as a slow steady flow. Some assistance was given to evacuees who returned home but this would appear to have been unofficial as children often travelled using what was described as 'chits' written out by an official stating that the cost of travel would be borne by their local authority. The railway companies did not approve of this irregular arrangement and declared that no children were to be allowed onto trains without a paid-for ticket. One brother and sister evacuated from central London to a large country house deep in the Oxfordshire countryside were so homesick they wrote to their parents threatening that if they were not collected immediately, they would make their own way home.

Despite the much publicised 'successes' of the evacuation, the reality would have given most parents real concern had they been fully aware of the situation in the reception areas. Despite all the meticulous planning by both the central government and the local authorities there was much criticism about the handling of the evacuation. The LCC responded by in part blaming the local authorities in the reception areas who they alleged lacked any experience in the handling of urban social problems which they now suddenly had to confront as the evacuation scheme was rolled out. When many distressed children arrived at unfamiliar destinations, they were received by harassed local volunteers who were not child welfare specialists and had not even been given important information about the children about to arrive. They did not know the numbers to be expected – and neither did the sending authorities as not all eligible children were presented by their parents for evacuation. As the children arrived the harassed local staff lacked information such as the religion or social class of the evacuees. They had to take immediate charge of the children and unsurprisingly many unfortunate mistakes were made – such as billeting Jewish children with families unaware of the child's religious dietary requirements.

Furthermore, many working-class children were not to be fully accepted by their middle-class hosts and requests were soon made for transfers to other billets. The local authorities began receiving complaints from some of the more affluent households about the social habits of the poorer, working-class children relating to their ignorance of elementary hygiene and their uncleanliness. In many cases these criticisms were also aimed at the working-class mothers who accompanied the very young children. In Bath it was reported that the majority of mothers and children had settled well, but the city was awash with rumours that the evacuees, many of whom had come from the east London docklands and described as 'dirty' such that some, it was reported, needed a 'pretty drastic cleaning'. It was stressed however that these were in the minority. Much later in the war – in 1943 – these issues were investigated by a survey conducted by the National Federation of Women's Institutes on behalf of the LCC. The resulting report concurred that while many of these allegations had been true, there had been no attempt by the many very vocal critics to place the relatively few unfortunate incidents into perspective in relation to the total number of children and mothers evacuated. This contemporary conclusion by the LCC should be a warning to those who cite instances of any social problem – many recent books on the subject stress the clash of cultures between the mainly working-class evacuees and the better-off middle-class host families. While the image of dirty working-class children and mothers might have been exaggerated – even if supported by evidence from a contemporary Mass Observation survey – what was of importance to the railways in 1939 was that due to rumours filtering back to the parents that all was not well, a new travel demand was being created. In part as a consequence of wild rumours circulating, many of the worried parents wanted to visit their children to check that they really were happy and settled into their wartime homes. For many parents there was also a strong sense of guilt which became the main driving force as they had reluctantly coaxed their children into leaving the security of their family homes by giving them rather weak explanations such as, for example, 'you are going away for a nice holiday'.

There were concessionary fares available for those in the armed forces travelling when off-duty, so within days of the evacuation in early September 1939, the REC was vigorously lobbied to introduce a similar arrangement to enable concerned relatives to visit their evacuated children. The REC initially diverted such requests to the government department whom they saw as the appropriate source – that was those in charge of the evacuations at the Ministry of Health. The REC was however minded that some form of concessionary fare arrangement must be implemented for the poorer families who were desperate to see their children, particularly as the usual 'off-peak' return ticket facility had been temporarily suspended. The railway companies proved to be in tune with this need and several additional relief trains had already been provided from the cities to the reception areas specifically for relatives wishing to visit their children. These trains were not well patronised as the full fare had to be charged making such visits unaffordable for most parents. Sensing the public need, the REC passenger superintendents subcommittee invited representatives from the Ministry of Transport, the Ministry of Health and the LCC to attend their meeting to discuss better transport arrangements to facilitate visits to the evacuated children. The Ministry of Transport input into the debate was to inform the subcommittee that they considered the provision of cheap tickets for use of what they deemed to be unnecessary travel as unacceptable as this would make it difficult to defend the price restrictions then being imposed on what they considered to be the more important and nationally necessary business travel. The Ministry of Health was also unenthusiastic, wishing to discourage family visits as these would 'have a disquieting effect on the children and create difficulties for the people on whom the children were billeted'. The LCC concurred, agreeing that 'any encouragement given to parents would have an unsettling effect on the evacuation scheme'. Furthermore, only two weeks after the mass evacuation, the steady return home of evacuees was noticeable and often when parents who had travelled by train for visits to the safe areas, they subsequently made the journey home escorting their unhappy children. The REC however was aware of the hardship of those wishing to visit their wives and children and were in favour of issuing cheap–day tickets for those 'anxious to visit family'.

On 27 September, questions were asked in the House of Commons to the minister of transport, Captain Euan Wallace. Many MPs supported the poorer parents, and Wallace was to be reminded that owing to the withdrawal of cheap fares many parents now found it impossible to visit their children. These parents were very worried about their children's welfare, and that many of them were contemplating collecting their children to bring them back into the potentially dangerous home areas should they not be able to regularly visit them to be reassured of their continuing happiness. The minister was further urged to make representation to the railway companies to issue special cheap tickets at stated intervals. On 25 September it was announced that the provision of cheap fares to enable mothers and other family members to visit their evacuated children was 'under consideration'. The prospect of such a scheme was not universally popular; a letter to *The Times* from a vicarage at Hazelmere in Surrey expressed the view with less than full Christian charity that relatives visiting children would impose even more financial burden on the host families.

Meanwhile the local authorities were however becoming increasingly concerned about the number of children returning to their homes in the cities and how much of this was after parental visits was uncertain. As early as October, of the 60,000 children evacuated from Manchester, 13,000 had already returned home. Much to the concern of the education committee in Manchester as most teachers remained with the evacuated children, this exodus home to that city had the unfortunate effect of a total of 45,000 children not receiving any education in the city when the 32,000 children whose parents had not presented their children for evacuation was taken into account. Meanwhile, at Brechin in Scotland by mid-November, of the 643 children who had been evacuated only 240 remained and of the 133 adults only 40 remained in the town. In Montrose where 2,500 evacuees had arrived only 380 remained. An official government campaign pleaded with the parents, insisting that they should 'leave the children where they are' but it was to no avail. In January 1940 it was concluded that almost half of those evacuated in the well-remembered and iconic first evacuation of children had drifted back to home, and this figure included 90 per cent of the mothers with their younger children. The return of the mothers with young children was often blamed on the fathers who after concluding that it remained 'safe' at home they wanted their wives and children to come home. One nine-year-old boy named James, who had been evacuated to Luton in Bedfordshire with his older sister Kathleen, did not remain there for long. Eighty-three years later, James could not remember how he returned home – but it was probably by train as he lived in a house within walking distance of St Pancras station. He confirms that he was not alone in returning to central London, maintaining that his was a typical experience. During this mass return to home many working-class children probably made what was only their second railway journey of their short lives coming home into the 'danger' in the cities.

The government and local authorities were faced with a dilemma. If visits were encouraged, this would potentially result in more parents returning to the cities with their children. If visits were not allowed, many parents would fear the worst and travel to the reception areas to collect their children anyway. Both options therefore came with the risk of too many children returning to what might soon become a conflict zone where not only would their lives be endangered but they would become a distracting burden on those engaged in search and rescue after air raids and to those providing post-air raid welfare and medical services. It was finally decided, most probably based on the premise that it was better that the parents visited their children to be made aware of the true situation at their child's billet rather than to act on unsubstantiated speculative rumours, that some form of cheap fare should be made available. Accordingly, a conference was convened at the offices of the Ministry of Health on 13 November 1939. A scheme had been devised which would be operated by the main line railway companies on a 'commercial' basis – that is the fares had to cover the operational costs, as it was made clear that there was to be no government subsidy to finance the scheme.

It was proposed that cheap tickets would be issued on Sundays for travel by parents and relatives to visit evacuated children in the reception areas after the presentation of a voucher. The destinations would have to be greater than 40 miles distant but less than 160 miles. Tickets would be issued from main line stations to the nearest local station to the evacuated child's new home. Relatives would have to pay any additional bus fare to complete their journey. It was proposed that there was to be no limit to the number of vouchers issued to the parents and relatives. The railways would provide all of the publicity for the scheme, but the ministries of health and transport requested the assistance from the local authorities in the issuing of the vouchers and providing advice as to correct railway destinations, etc. The LCC gave a guarded approval to these proposals but insisted that it would not accept any responsibility for the scheme. The health ministry then requested that local authority staff issue the vouchers after they had initially interviewed applicants to confirm entitlement to a voucher – but it was stressed that those doing the questioning should do so with a light touch. Staff engaged in this work needed to be given sufficient information as to be able to advise on the best route and where to leave the train for a particular village. A representative of the LCC stated that while it would be happy to assist, it did not have the clerical staff with the competence to answer any of the applicants' questions. After some protracted discussion it was agreed that the LCC's teachers – the majority of whom – unlike in Manchester – remained in London at work in the still-open schools – were the best people to issue the vouchers to the parents.

The outline of this arrangement was announced by Euan Wallace in the House of Commons on 15 November. His public announcement made it clear that any concessions were only to be available to parents and relatives of children who had been evacuated and billeted as part of the government's evacuation scheme. What is not known is how many parents made journeys to visit the 'privately' evacuated children following arrangements being made for their children to reside with friends or family members in far-flung parts of the country well away from the bombing. This additional travel by train to visit these evacuees cannot be identified from the ticket sales, and probably they remained longer in their wartime homes than the working-class children who were often not happy away from their parents and their usual urban environment. Sadly, it seems that many poorer parents who, on the instruction from their local authority, had left their children at holiday locations when the evacuation was announced were also to be excluded from the scheme.

This task of issuing the vouchers in effect turned the LCC's education officer's department into a travel agency. The unfortunate teachers – who were without question intelligent and articulate people – now had the difficult task of having to determine which arrival station the voucher should be made out for. Not a straightforward task as the children's new billets were not necessarily within easy reach of any railway station. Furthermore, the task of issuing the vouchers had for the convenience of the working parents to take place in the early evenings, usually at the schools. Accurate voucher issuing was a complex task; there had to be liaison with both the parents and those now looking after the children at a time long before private homes and even a few of the schools in rural parts of the reception areas had a telephone connection. Further complications would arise when at short notice information about late timetable changes had somehow to be conveyed to the parents. The number of vouchers issued had to be given to the railway companies a week before the Sunday on which travel was to take place.

Initially in London a total of 136 schools and divisional offices opened their doors to issue vouchers to the parents. This number was soon to be reduced in part due to the difficulty in obtaining sufficient teachers to volunteer for this difficult work. The vouchers were headed 'Government Evacuation Scheme – visitors to evacuees'. Blank spaces on the form had to be filled in by the issuing teachers. To be written on the form was the date of the journey, the departure and arrival stations and the ultimate destination by bus if appropriate. In bold capital letters on the bottom of the voucher was the strict instruction that 'children and other evacuees should not be brought home on any of these trips'.

The first day of the scheme was on Sunday, 26 November. Chaos ensued resulting in the LCC receiving a letter the following day from the Ministry of Transport complaining about mistakes made when the vouchers were issued. The ministry had expected teething troubles, but the outcome was worse than it had anticipated due to the many mistakes made in the issuing of vouchers. The ministry letter complained that the errors during the previous week had exceeded '… the blackest fear we could ever have entertained.' The volunteer teachers had made multiple mistakes such as issuing vouchers to destinations for which there was not a Sunday service, or that there was no bus service available from the destination station to the evacuees' new home locality. Many errors were compounded by the lack of continuity of issuing staff, the volunteers would change every night at each issuing location. A two mile walk from Newbury station to the small village of Speen might not be too onerous (Speen had a station on the GWR Lambourn branch from Newbury but there were no trains on Sundays), but vouchers were issued for travel to Wolverton station for an ultimate destination of Lavendon, 12 miles away, and for Olney, 10 miles distance. Most bizarre was a voucher for Torquay which entitled the bearer to travel only as far as the SR station at Exeter Central – but the GWR station at Exeter St David's would have at least put the parent on the right railway, even if it was 24 miles short of the intended destination. Vouchers were issued for rail travel to Frome from where, somehow, the parents were expected to make their own way to Glastonbury, 22 miles distant, and even to Weymouth, which is 61 miles away.

The whole experience was very distressing for many of the poorer parents. They were unused to long-distance railway travel and were naturally upset when having bought their tickets for a challenging journey were only able to get close to, but not close enough, to their children to be able to see them and to be reassured that they were happy in their new surroundings. The Ministry of Transport was helpful, offering to display notices at the main departure stations declaring the destinations cited on vouchers for which there was no direct connection and warning potential travellers that unless they had made their own arrangements for onward travel from the railway stations named it was unlikely that they would be able to complete their journey. They also offered to provide representatives to be available at Waterloo and Paddington stations to give advice to confused parents with no experience of long-distance railway travel. The LCC in a letter to the Ministry of Transport shamefully passed the blame for the debacle on the first Sunday onto the inexperienced teachers, describing their failings as 'completely irresponsible' and that they had ignored the LCC's 'most lucid instructions'. The railways were more cooperative however, following a meeting of all the commercial managers, they offered to assist by conveying any passenger to their intended destination wherever this was possible, overriding any destination or date errors on the voucher.

After this unfortunate start, the scheme was soon modified so that relatives who had vouchers would be conveyed to the reception areas by special trains paying a ticket price equal to the cost of a one-way journey on the route. Many such special trains were run from London and the railways duly promoted these services with posters giving the times of the trains and the cost of the tickets. The posters provide evidence of the ticket prices and stations served by these trains and indicate the character of the locations which were selected to be reception areas. Many of the stations to which tickets were made available were local stations in very rural locations in small market towns and some in the larger villages. The posters also show how little time the parents would have had with their children on these day-return trips, particularly if a bus journey or a lengthy walk had to be fitted in between the train's arrival time and the returning train's departure time.

As an example, one of the destinations that London parents and relatives could travel to by GWR on 17 December was the delightful small market town of Bruton in Somerset which is situated on the GWR main line between Reading and Taunton for which a return third class ticket cost each parent 11/6 and allowed six hours to travel on to the child's billet, see him or her and then travel back to the station. The same train stopped at Langport East station. Langport is another small town in rural Somerset, a return ticket cost 12/- and allowed about five and a half hours to make a visit. A parent paying 9/3 could travel to and from another isolated station on the same line, Savernake (Low Level), which was at the time the junction for the Marlborough branch. A relatively long stay of about ten hours was possible for visitors here, but the station was in a very rural and isolated location in Wiltshire set in the beautiful countryside close to Wolf Hall, the former residence of Jane Seymour, one of Henry VIII's wives. More time was available to visit the child, but most parents would have been faced with a lengthy walk or bus ride from Savernake (Low Level) to their child's wartime home. This GWR service provided the relatives with a direct train from London to stations that would normally be reached only by changing to the slow local trains at an intermediate large station. Such journeys using the normal timetable would take much longer and, more importantly, make the necessary 'out-and-back' trip in a single day problematic.

The LNER also operated special trains from Liverpool Street and King's Cross. These included a train run on 10 December from King's Cross to Biggleswade, Sandy and St Neots terminating at Huntingdon (North). All these destinations are small market towns in Bedfordshire and Cambridgeshire. Passengers could also board the train at either Finsbury Park, Wood Green or New Barnet. The ticket prices ranged from 4/2d to 7/9d. The timetable allowed parents and other relatives over eight hours to visit children in Huntingdon, eight and three-quarters of an hour in St Neots and over nine hours in either Sandy or Biggleswade. Also, on 10 December the LMS also ran a special train from Euston (picking up passengers at several suburban stations) to Leighton Buzzard, Bletchley and Weedon. The price of tickets ranged between 4/8d and 9/1d. Those visiting Weedon, then still a small village, had less than six hours to visit their children.

Despite the apparent cheapness of the tickets, strangely, fewer were bought by the relatives than the number of vouchers that had been issued. An explanation for this might be that the schools would distribute vouchers to parents but on receiving them they elected not to travel deciding that even at 'half-price' the journey was unaffordable and allowed insufficient time to visit their children. For example, in respect of longer distant special trains, on Sunday, 19 December, a King's Cross to Grantham special train had a potential 1,477 passengers travelling with the vouchers but only 984 tickets were purchased and on the same day a Waterloo to Swanage train carried only 512 passengers despite 645 vouchers being issued.

In Scotland when similar arrangements were made for parents to travel from Edinburgh and Dundee by LMS and LNER excursion trains the take-up by parents was also very low. As had been the experience in London, the number of 'cheap' tickets issued fell far short of the number of vouchers issued. These failings were discussed at a meeting of the offices of the regional transport commissioner in Edinburgh. Attending the meeting were representatives from the Scottish department of health, local authorities, the LMSR, the LNER and the Ministry of Transport. The consensus was that the outcome had been very disappointing. It was agreed that as these trains were run on a commercial basis, it was obvious that several proposed excursions would have to be cancelled. Examples of poor take-up were given including the 110 vouchers that had been issued for an LNER train run on 10 December from Edinburgh to Harwich and Newcastleton when only 84 tickets were sold. For this excursion, the vouchers issued included some for advertised connections onward to Selkirk and Kelso, but due to the lack of tickets sold the rail connections were cancelled and a replacement bus provided. It was agreed at the meeting that, as had been found in England, the poor response was simply due to the fares being too expensive for working-class families and that the longer journeys did not provide sufficient time for the parents to spend with their children. No special trains had been run from Glasgow. The representative from that city at the meeting explained that, in their opinion, the excursions might induce the return home of children and that the arrival of parents might result in friction between them and householders. Much to the regret of the local authority representatives present, the Ministry of Transport representatives confirmed that further fare reductions could not be made. The meeting offered the suggestion that instead of excursion trains period tickets should be issued at the 'cheap-day' rate but would be valid for up to seven days. This would inevitably result in overnight stays, but the visitors, not the local authority or the government, would be responsible for the cost of any accommodation.

During January 1940, both the SR and the GWR instigated some private initiatives by offering tickets for excursions arranged for parents wishing to visit their children in the reception areas. On 24 January the SR conveyed 2,012 passengers in five special trains to the west of England and while this was the railway's own project, the Ministry of Transport assisted by distributing the advertising handbills. The

GWR also operated a two–day trip to the reception areas running as far west as Gileston which is a small village near West Aberthaw on the South Wales coast. This was a remote destination for a long-distance train, but this does indicate the spread of the London evacuees. The station has been closed since 1964 and today trains on the Vale of Glamorgan Line pass through the station site as they travel between Aberthaw High Level and St Athan stations. The excursion departed on a Saturday and returned to London on Sunday. The GWR insisted that those who wished to leave the train at any stopping point to travel on to other towns could do so but 'at their own risk'. To qualify for the excursion, parents and relatives had to produce evidence that they had a child billeted in the area and that they had pre-booked overnight accommodation.

With so many children returning and the expectation that there would be a new demand for evacuation should bombing raids on London commence, the LCC began preparations to re-evacuate children and to extend their evacuation offer to parents who had previously refused to release their children. There was a difficulty however as only 8,000 more children could be transported to locations in the reception areas where their schools had been evacuated. The huge task began with a plan to register children in preparation for a proposed second evacuation programme. By December 1939 only 25,000 children had been registered and of these only 7,500 had been medically examined. The medical examination was now deemed necessary to ensure that all of the children could be declared fit and clean to avoid any more of the earlier complaints about London children arriving at their new billets unclean and with unfortunate transmittable diseases. There was a reluctance by parents to register their children, excuses given included the lack of bombing in London and parents continually hearing adverse reports from children who had already evacuated. With hindsight and with the knowledge that London and other cities were soon to face the onslaught of the Blitz, the LCC's argument that children must be evacuated must now seem to have been overwhelming, but the reality was that, despite the dangers, many parents, quite naturally, wanted to hold on to their family group – even in such dangerous times. These parents were to be criticised by those who seemed to lack an understanding of the dynamics of urban family life when they alleged that the parents' apparent unreasonable obstructiveness was due to the fact that they regarded any official advice about their children's safety from either the government, local authorities or their schoolteachers as a form of personal insult. Most of the 'reasons' offered for keeping children in London were not likely to have any traction with the LCC's education officer and his evacuation branch, but rebellious parents had one good card to play. It was difficult for the LCC to argue against one 'reason' offered for not allowing their children to be evacuated. The parents had noticed that – due to the lack of school accommodation in the reception areas – the provisions of the Education Act of 1870 which made education compulsory for children between the ages of 5 and 13 had effectively been suspended, therefore the children, it was argued, should remain in London where they could be properly educated.

In February 1940 the Ministry of Health issued a circular proposing that the planned evacuation of more school children would only take place should bombing raids commence. It was understood that it would be necessary to re-evacuate the many children who had returned from what was termed 'safe' areas to the 'evacuation' areas. It was anticipated that there would soon be a demand for such evacuation should the expected bombing of cities commence. But this policy of 'wait until the bombing starts' caused some concern by many at both the Ministry of Health and at the local authorities. The main issue confronting the LCC was that it would take time to arrange sufficient destinations and recruit the additional volunteers. Also, there was a shortage of local medical staff to carry out the pre-evacuation medical checks on the children. The LCC told the Ministry of Health that it was concerned about child welfare issues in the reception areas and offered to assist. It was suggested that the children should receive their medicals when they arrived in the reception areas. The LCC recommended that there should be a publicity campaign to recruit up to 8,000 more billets for what seemed to be the inevitable second major evacuation of children. Most important, the LCC insisted that there should be another publicity campaign to encourage parents to allow their children to register for evacuation before any raids began.

The Ministry of Health however seemed to be less concerned than the LCC and responded by claiming that they had a list of destinations drawn up after consultation with the railway companies and that they would assist with the medical examinations. The officials at the ministry were confident that sufficient billets could be found for the extra children, but, as the LCC had predicted, these would be likely to be in areas away from where the schools that they had previously attended had been evacuated. The ministry also stated that it would be difficult to appeal for more children to register for evacuation until their parents perceived that they were in an imminent danger. Discussions continued during February and March 1940. Reacting to concerns about the evacuees' education, the ministry insisted that what it described as 'a second offer of evacuation' must guarantee compulsory education in the reception areas. The ministry asserted that in order to achieve a return to full education, metropolitan teachers should be transferred to the reception areas where they must be assured of a 'reasonably good billet'. In an attempt to encourage parents to allow their children to be evacuated, every household in London received a leaflet proclaiming, 'another chance to send your children away'. Despite these efforts, by the end of March 1940 only 10 per cent of eligible children had been registered for evacuation while unfortunately a further 10 per cent of the parents made it clear that they refused to allow their children to be evacuated. To the further dismay of the LCC there was also a very poor response to the plea for more billets for the evacuated children.

In his book *Unpatriotic History of the Second World War*, James Heartfield argues that the mass evacuation of children had been 'one of the most extraordinary state interventions in family life', and it is hard to disagree with this sentiment. The local authorities' often clumsy schemes predominantly evacuated working-class children from the poorer parts of their cities, and this resulted in the breaking up of families and often causing unnecessary stress and social tensions. It is reasonable to suggest that the private evacuations organised directly by the more affluent parents were less damaging and upsetting for the children. It is inconceivable that better-off parents who had family connections outside of the cities, and possibly even had 'town' and 'country' residences, would ever allow 'the council' to take charge of their children and were able and willing to make their own independent arrangements. Even some artisans would feel that it was an affront to their dignity to have strangers look after their children and would consequently organise for themselves safe locations for them and – even if the rules had allowed it – would have seen it to be demeaning to go through the process of obtaining vouchers from officious local authority staff.

These instances of these independent arrangements were spread across all social groups. The brother and sister who were so determined to return to London from deepest Berkshire were not evacuated by the LCC. Their evacuation had been arranged between their father, a retired soldier, who had been a faithful batman to a Major-General. The officer had died in the mid-1930s, but his widow had agreed that the two children could be sent to spend the war period as part of the household in her mansion. The ex-soldier was not rich, but he had a 'good connection'. At the other end of the social spectrum, Princess Elizabeth – the future Queen – and her younger sister Princess Margaret Rose were evacuated from Buckingham Palace to the relative safety of Windsor Castle. Most parents who made private arrangements however were probably middle-class; for them the cost of the occasional full-price return railway ticket would be no deterrent to them from making regular railway journeys to visit their children. Many of these families would have owned cars, but petrol rationing was in force, making railway travel more practical.

Chapter 5

Government Departments
Move to the Provinces

The 70 per cent more passengers carried by the railways during
the war years [included] billeted war workers returning home for
weekends ... snatching the chance ... to spend a few hours with
their family. It could never be enough and often the time spent
travelling would be as long as that spent with the family.

Robert Mackay, Half the Battle,
Manchester University Press, 2003

Following the evacuation from London of thousands of civil servants,
the overall net effect on the amount of travel by train nationally is
difficult to assess. There were many more 'business' journeys made
as many more senior staff criss-crossed the country to make visits to
the remote and secret production centres and offices. This involved
additional first–class travel by train particularly for officials who
remained London based. It is reasonable to assume that the majority
of the middle and lower graded civil servants would have made
journeys home whenever it was permissible and affordable, but their
'extra' wartime railway travel must be balanced against the probable
elimination of their peacetime daily commute into London.

An official government survey undertaken in 1943 provides some
indication as to how the lower graded civil servants might have
travelled to work each day had they remained in London. The survey
results showed that in London only nineteen per cent of the capital's
commuters travelled to work by train. Commuting by train was a low
proportion of the overall total (the equivalent for commuting by bus

in London was forty-two per cent) but it was the highest percentage in the country when compared with, for example, the mere four per cent travelling to work by train in the northeast of England. Breaking down the results into occupation, the survey indicated that fifteen per cent of all clerical staff travelled by train (the equivalent percentage for bus travel was forty-three per cent). These broad figures give an indication, but only an indication, as to how likely it was that junior staff who had been transferred away from London to the provinces might previously have commuted to their original workplaces. Given the prestige of a secure career in the civil service, it is not unreasonable to speculate that many of the younger civil servants who were evacuated from London were likely to be among the better educated and connected youngsters who would have been expecting to travel daily from their parents' homes in the leafy home counties suburbs to their offices by train.

The outposted government departments required large numbers of junior staff. To provide clerical services at the Admiralty offices scattered around Bath, the evacuees from London included about 900 women and girls, most of them under 21 years old (thus at the time not 'adults'). Very few of them were paid more than £3 a week with the majority being paid between 30 shillings and 50 shillings a week. The Admiralty assumed a paternal duty of care for these young women, noting that they would not have anticipated that they would live anywhere other than at home with their parents, consequently most of them were to be housed in hostels rather than private homes. Without financial assistance it is unlikely that they would have been able to afford the railway tickets to make frequent visits to their homes in the London area.

Staff at Bath would frequently be required to travel back to London for meetings and it was soon realised that compared to travel in an official car, rail travel provided by the regular fast GWR trains was both quicker and more comfortable. Nonetheless, what was described as a 'fast car' service was initially introduced to convey important messages and documents which required an urgent official signature in Whitehall, but this service appears to have been reduced in favour of couriers taking such items by train. In peacetime when all the Admiralty offices had been in Whitehall, lower grade messengers would provide a guaranteed 30 minutes delivery between offices within any building and an hour maximum delivery to another government office within London. The main courier route from Bath was by train to Paddington, but there was another important Royal Navy location at Plymouth. Bath to Plymouth documents were sent with a courier by car a distance of 16 miles to Westbury station in time for a fast train for the 106-mile GWR journey to Plymouth. There was a growing dissatisfaction amongst the civil servants tasked with these courier duties. Many minor and perhaps trivial complaints were raised by them but the real issue upsetting the rebellious couriers was that they considered it belittling that they, as relatively high-ranking civil servants, were having to perform the work of lowly messengers. What they should have been carrying were security sensitive items such as official files of various levels of secrecy, rolls of drawings – secret or otherwise, hydrographic charts and models. The couriers claimed that they had been repeatedly asked to carry private items – even a tennis racket on one occasion – but this particular allegation was vigorously denied. Another objection from the couriers was that due to the sensitive nature of their baggage they were carrying they could not be identified as being Admiralty staff, so when encountering GWR staff at the stations they had to masquerade as agents for Carter Paterson. This was a falsehood to which they strongly objected to as Carter Paterson was a lowly private road haulage company jointly owned by the four main line railway companies and not, in their eyes, the superior civil service organisation to which they had a proud allegiance.

Whilst all of the evacuated Admiralty staff at the Bath sites had non-combat roles, many of the male staff members joined the 6th (Bath Admiralty) Battalion of the Somerset Home Guard. These part-time soldiers wore the cap badge of the regiment to which they were affiliated – the Somerset Light Infantry. The Bath Admiralty

Home Guard was formed in 1940 and had within its ranks men who were Admiralty staff in reserved occupations and other local men who were either under-age or over-age for regular military service. Despite having navy connections, the brigade nonetheless wore the army khaki uniform. The brigade was made up of five patrols, number one at Kelston Park, number two at Langridge, number three at Warminster Road, number five at Prior Park and number six at Newton Park at Newton St. Loe which is four miles due west of the city. Due to the nature of the Admiralty war work in Bath, the time that any of these part-time soldiers spent in the battalion was often very short due to the high turnover of staff as the men were frequently posted elsewhere.

A feature of many of the Bath Admiralty sites was that they were close to the main line railway station but far enough away in the rural extremities of the city to be at a safe distance from any possible bombing raid on the centre. Before military intelligence services had the advantage of global satellite coverage it was unlikely that the enemy would ever be able to notice or evaluate the importance of a few 'extra' temporary huts that were progressively being added to expand the office accommodation at sites across the city. But Bath did not escape the air raids completely, there were a few bombs dropped on the city during 1940 and 1941, but in 1942 it became the target for a number of retaliatory raids by the Luftwaffe. These were part of the so-called Baedeker raids which were launched in retaliation for the RAF's attacks on Rostow and Lübeck. The Germans announced that their target list was now to be drawn from Baedeker's *Great Britain: A Handbook for Travellers* and threatened that they would bomb every building in Britain that had a three-star rating in the guide. Bath was therefore in grave danger; and the historic centre was to suffer air raid damage to many of the culturally important buildings such as the Royal Crescent and Bath Abbey. More humble residences also suffered, there was a direct hit on the edge at Second Avenue, Oldfield Park which destroyed twenty houses. At Bath Spa station a German bomb landed on one of the platforms. The explosion damaged both station buildings and all four tracks through the station. Damage to rolling stock was also reported – two wagons destroyed and others damaged. The station water supply also suffered damage. The death toll over the two nights of raids was four hundred and seventeen.

Many members of the Bath Admiralty Home Guard who had bravely played their part in the defence of Bath during the April 1942 raids received commendations and medals. Two of them, J.A. Leslie, a former sales representative on loan to the Bath Royal Navy Secretariat, and H.D. Rees, a draughtsman in the naval ordnance department, were both rewarded with gallantry medals for their rescue work at the Regina Hotel. Both men both worked tirelessly from the time that the hotel was bombed in the early hours of 27 April until the evening of the next day. They entered the hotel basement to rescue a trapped woman and in doing so put themselves at risk of being crushed by the unstable masonry which they had to move to dislodge her. Later Leslie climbed up the side of a shop to tear down a blind which was on fire, thereby preventing a further spread of the flames. During this brave action his clothes caught fire and he had to be doused with water. Leslie was awarded the George Medal and Rees the British Empire Medal. In the same platoon as Leslie and Rees was J.W. Martell who also took part in the rescue of many who had been trapped in the basement below the smouldering hotel building. R.K. Conner, a draughtsman in the department of naval construction together with R.M.B. Judson, an electrical engineering assistant, were part of a platoon which rescued forty people who had been buried under debris. Conner had also forced his entry into a house which was on fire.

As the war progressed, the Admiralty vacated most of the city hotels in Bath and moved to more suitable locations such as at Fox Hill, Ensleigh and Landsdown Road where purpose built military hutments were constructed to supplement the existing buildings. The exception was the Empire Hotel which was retained. The staff working in the relocated Admiralty offices continued to be billeted with local families or in hostels. The Ensleigh site was about three miles to the north of Bath. The establishment at Landsdown included Kingswood School which was also north of the city and just over two miles from the GWR station. Significantly there was a considerable amount of important design work carried out in Bath. For example Kingswood School which, after the boys and staff had all evacuated to Uppingham School in the East Midlands, became an important naval engineering establishment with its main claim to fame that it was within the school buildings that the final designs for the Mulberry Harbours were completed. This 'portable' harbour design was to prove critical to the success of the D-Day landings in 1944.

Harrogate, where the RAF, the Air Ministry and later the Ministry of Aircraft Production had been outposted, did not have as good a railway connection to London as had Bath, being 203 miles away from London, King's Cross. In peacetime using the fastest trains this journey had taken three hours and forty-two minutes. The drastic decelerations at the start of the war increased the schedule to five hours thirty minutes, but after the subsequent relaxations to the strict emergency timetable by November 1940 there was an improvement reducing the very best train journey to four hours fifty-one minutes. Mr Addison, a senior civil servant, was tasked to report on the working and billeting conditions at Harrogate and in his report, he opined that the railway connection to the town was less than satisfactory particularly for those Air Ministry staff with responsibilities for war production – such as for those who were involved with aircraft production who had a requirement to regularly visit factories around the country. When the staff from other government departments began to share Harrogate with the RAF, they too concurred with Addison, sharing his opinion that Harrogate was not a suitable location for such important war work due in part to its distance from London and the centres of manufacture. Nonetheless the main railway station at Harrogate was located in the centre of the town and was conveniently situated only minutes away from the main Air Ministry site in St Georges Street. With the constant churn of service and civilian personnel, the railway and its LNER station were kept very busy throughout the war. Despite complaints that Harrogate was remote from production centres, it had good connections southwards to Leeds where there were connections westwards into Lancashire. Other lines gave access to York and Hull in the east. A business trip to the Midlands however, to what was the very heart of manufacturing would, as feared by Addison, have been difficult as it was likely to have required many changes of train.

In response to Addison's criticisms about billeting arrangements, the Air Ministry responded by stating that they hoped that the overcrowding in the billets would soon be eased by the re-allocation of staff which was now possible after the requisitioning of the Hydro Hotel but had to concede that what they described as 'normal' comforts and facilities were lacking. The accommodation problem largely affected the younger staff who had been removed from the security of their parents' homes to live in Harrogate. Like the Admiralty staff at Bath, these younger civil servants were on comparatively low pay and after they had paid their billeting money (the standard £1-1s had been set as the minimum charge) and had other deductions from their salaries, they had little money left to meet the cost of transport or to buy themselves lunch and, furthermore, recreational facilities were totally inadequate. Acknowledgement of these problems resulted in a reduction in the billeting deduction from salaries and the implementation of concessionary travel on local public transport.

The more senior staff outposted to Harrogate often had the financial ability to bring their families to the town to reside locally, a win-win situation as this kept their wives and children safe from any future bombing and saved them the need to regularly travel back to London. This group of civil servants became a semi-permanent group within the community, taking advantages of the relative safety and security of living in the Yorkshire spa town. In this relatively relaxed atmosphere, they organised Christmas parties for their children and concert parties for the adults and to some locals they must have been perceived as an unwelcome 'invasion' into the settled social life within the refined Yorkshire town. Other, unmarried civil servants chose to make their own independent arrangements so as not to endure the 'communal' nature of the billets and were soon to be seeking out private accommodation. A great number of other men however, which Addison, after accounting for the most junior and most senior grades of staff, described as comprising a 'large residue', had families in London which, due to either financial reasons or because they had other personal commitments, by necessity had to maintain their family base in the capital. This large group of civil servants had to make the long train journey south for any personal contact with their families.

The difficulties for men who had to maintain families back in London was noted at other locations including the civil aviation authorities which had also moved away from London, taking over the Grand Spa Hotel in Bristol in September 1939. This move followed the passing of the Air Navigation (Restriction in Time of War) Order 1939. The Air Ministry brought together all of the civil aviation resources together to form the National Air Communications Service. In the 1930s British Airways operated the commercial flights to Europe and Imperial Airways operated services throughout the extensive British Empire. 1,600 staff working for both companies were evacuated from their usual bases at the London airports at Croydon and Heston to their new wartime bases in Bristol and Exeter. Amongst those relocated were administrative staff, flying and engineering staff and clerical staff. The government were paying as usual a guinea a week ($£1$-1s) to cover each evacuee's billeting costs. As had been noted by Addison at Harrogate, of those whose place of work had been relocated to the provinces away from the capital, many were men who had retained homes in and around London. They had to continue to pay rent and rates for any accommodation in which their wives and families were still resident or worse, their house or flat was now empty – but the financial liability remained.

The National Air Communications Service, noting this staffing issue, wrote a letter to the REC formally requesting that these evacuees be given the same reduced fare facility as those serving in the forces – that is a return ticket for the price of a single one-way fare. This was immediately rejected by the passenger superintendents' subcommittee of the REC on the basis that no such special arrangement was at the time given to civilian staff travelling home from their evacuated workplace. The subcommittee pointed out that as well as government departments, many private businesses had moved to the provinces and their staff had to pay the full fare, usually purchasing a monthly return ticket. Despite comparing the largesse shown to those serving in the armed forces with the inflexibility shown to civilians whose lives had been turned upside down by the changes brought about by the war, those pleading for fare concessions did not receive the same support as had the parents wishing to visit their children who had been evacuated. This was resented by men who wished to travel home to visit their wives and children but could not afford to pay the full return fare.

An early initiative by the new prime minister, Winston Churchill, was the creation of the Ministry of Aircraft Production. On 14 May 1940, Lord Beaverbrook was appointed as the first minister of this new ministry and charged with the task of increasing aircraft production to meet the RAF's growing requirements. During the war period the ministry oversaw the growth of the British aircraft industry into the largest in the country. Harrogate was one of the twelve regional offices reporting to the ministry's headquarters in London. Harrogate also became the home to a large contingent of GPO staff who had also been evacuated from London. Their accommodation included both the Cairn Hydro and the Grandby hotels.

In September 1940 there were more very important newcomers to Harrogate when the town became the headquarters of the new Women's Auxiliary Air Force (WAAF) which was to further increase rail travel to and from the spa town. The WAAF had been established in June 1939 in anticipation of war and had been at first based at West Drayton in Middlesex. Mobilisation of this new force occurred on 28 August 1939 and within a year thousands of volunteers had been trained. The main role of the WAAF was to replace male RAF personnel as far as was possible for tasks in which there were manpower shortages. This proved to be a moving target due to the ebb and flow of the RAF's requirements. In August 1940 the decision was made to transfer all of the WAAF training facilities to Harrogate. In August the RAF's Group Captain Blackburn and Flight Lieutenant Williams at Harrogate met Lady Daphne Barnes, a WAAF company assistant who had been appointed in November 1939 to make preliminary arrangements for the move. The Headquarters staff and the main body of the WAAF depot at West Drayton was transported by a special train to Harrogate on 18 September 1940. The train departed from West Drayton at 09.22hrs and travelled via Leicester to Harrogate arriving at 17.12hrs. From the station, the WAAFs marched to their new home at the Grand Hotel, a distance of just under half a mile. The notionally WAAF only unit included seventy male RAF personnel, 62 men with eight officers; and the WAAF number was 545 women with five officers. Also at the Grand Hotel was a single nursing sister. Later WAAF arrivals were to be installed at other locations in Harrogate such as Ashville College, the Ladies College and at Pannal Ash College. In July 1940, the Clovelly Hotel was requisitioned for use by the WAAF, and in November 1940 the WAAF left the Ladies College as it was deemed structurally unsound, transferring to the Alexandra Hotel. After repairs to the hotel carried out by the Ministry of Works, the building was reoccupied by staff working for the Ministry of Aircraft Production. Harrogate now became the enlistment centre for the WAAF, when hundreds of new recruits who had at first visited the various RAF recruitment centres across the country began to travel by train to Harrogate. During October 1940, a total of 1,669 potential new recruits were processed and of these 1,543 were successfully enrolled, 107 suffered rejection and seven 'refused to enrol' – obviously having second thoughts after their initial contact with the military.

Conscription for women was introduced in December 1941 which increased the WAAF ranks such that by July 1943 the force's peak strength of 182,000 had been achieved. With the broad remit of the WAAF, the training provided at Harrogate had to prepare the recruits for a wide range of duties which included administrative duties, maintaining and repairing aircraft, meteorology and cooking. The training of all new WAAF personnel took place in Harrogate during the time period when the depot was stationed in the town. The trainees were all billeted in the local hotels. One example of how the WAAFs could be used for tasks that might be perceived at the time as 'men's work' was reported in November 1942 when the first WAAF to be trained as a railway transport officer took up her duties at what was described in the *Harrogate Herald* as a 'railway station in the Midlands'.

The WAAF headquarters was not to remain in Harrogate for very long for as on 10 May 1941 the facilities were closed, and a new depot established at Stanmore which is just to the east of Bridgnorth in Shropshire. The establishment at Stanmore had previously been known as RAF Bridgnorth but was to become the 'No.1 Women's Auxiliary Air Force Depot'. The WAAFs stationed at Harrogate left the town in the same way that they had arrived – by special train. The fact that there were now more WAAFs in Harrogate than when they had arrived in 1940 is illustrated by the fact that for their departure two special trains had to be arranged, the first left Harrogate at 09.50hrs and arrived at Bridgnorth at 14.29hrs; the second left Harrogate 10 minutes later and took a little longer to complete its journey as it arrived at 15.11hrs.

Several government departments were evacuated to North Wales. The Ministry of Food (MOF) arrived at Colwyn Bay and other government departments soon established their wartime offices in the locality including the Inland Revenue which worked from several of Llandudno's hotels including the Imperial Hotel. Llandudno also hosted the Royal Artillery's Coast Gunnery School which had moved from Essex to the Great Orme. Further north, the Ministry of Works and Buildings took over the Palace Hotel and also the Exchange Buildings in Liverpool. As for all of the civil servants evacuated to distant parts of the country, across the northwest there were the usual difficulties in respect to the billeting arrangements.

The Admiralty and the Air Ministry evacuation of their staff to Bath and Harrogate was, given the exceptional circumstances, carried out in a reasonably organised manner. Not so the MOF relocation to Colwyn Bay which by comparison can be judged as a relatively disorganised and badly planned operation. In 1941, a treasury liaison officer, Mr Slater, was instructed to write a report on the failing administration at Colwyn Bay. He reported that by that time the bulk of the MOF staff had been evacuated to Colwyn Bay. There was a total of 4,360 staff in the Welsh seaside town of whom 1,189 worked in the trade and finance department. Only 322 MOF staff remained in London at Neville House, but 356 others had been outposted to Oxford to be responsible for the nation's fresh fruit and vegetable supplies and a few, forty-four trade and finance staff, were then based at Godstone in Surrey.

Slater's damning report reveals that the evacuation from London had been carried out in a hurried and shambolic fashion with little overall planning or control. He discovered that different groups of civil servants had located themselves in a total of thirty-three different buildings spread across the town. This fracturing of the traditional London order had led to the breaking up of the established MOF branches and different groups of civil servants had blatantly reorganised themselves into new autonomous groups which inevitably had led to an increase in staff as all of the pre-war control from the centre had been lost. Soon after the civil servants arrived in North Wales, Slater reported, it was not uncommon for a new 'adviser' – who was usually unpaid – to take up residence in one of the offices in Colwyn Bay and the establishment officers would not know of his presence for several weeks, and by that time additional paid clerical staff would be required and recruited. When a new special problem arose, the out-of-control civil servants' immediate reaction was to set up another section to work on it thereby creating a further increase in lower grade staff. The establishment management was under extreme pressure, the principal assistant secretary knew in a general way what was going on in his department and was able to co-ordinate such matters as grading and salaries for specialist staff brought in from trade and industry but, Slater concluded, it was 'manifestly impossible' for him to know if the staff were fully occupied in each of the many buildings or whether their work was fully justified.

Slater counted 130 staff engaged in establishment matters at Colwyn Bay, along with 475 typists, 260 cleaners, 80 night watchmen and 200 messengers. Both young girls and men were employed as messengers. When not delivering internal post between the thirty-three different buildings, at best they spent their time performing very menial tasks – such as stamping pre-printed forms to change the address from London to Colwyn Bay – and at worst he observed groups of 'bored looking girls, sitting in small ante-rooms'. This, he concluded, was bad training for the girls and, of course, if seen by members of the public it further tarnished the MOF's reputation. The male messengers were also used as door keepers, but increasingly girls who had been recruited locally were also being used.

It is no surprise therefore that there was low morale within the staff at MOF Colwyn Bay. This was in part blamed on the administration difficulties and also because the MOF was looked upon by town residents as 'an army of occupation'. Despite the war, Colwyn Bay continued to be a holiday destination and following the arrival of the regular summer visitors there was less accommodation available for the unhappy evacuees and the standards within the billets were such that it was not uncommon for as many as four persons having to share the same room.

This unfortunate situation proved to be particularly unpopular with the younger female staff. According to the welfare officer, staff sickness increased due to the prolonged periods that staff had been away from their parental homes. The removal from their homes in and around London was particularly hard for the younger, female staff. Colwyn Bay is almost 200 miles by train from London Euston and rail travel would have been the only practical way for evacuees to travel home for a well-earned and very short break from their duties at the MOF. The journey by train took about five hours and would thus have been very expensive for young civil servants, both in leave time and in money. It was not to be long before it was realised that the enforced evacuation of civil servants away from their families was having a detrimental effect on their mental and physical wellbeing, particularly for the younger and lower paid staff members. In November 1939 it was agreed that evacuated civil servants could claim two free return tickets a year, the first of which could be obtained in December to facilitate a return home for Christmas. On the more positive side, the staff surveyed approved of both the canteens and the social centre provided. Also appreciated was that the welfare staff were always at hand to assist the evacuees with their personal problems.

The senior managers at the Ministry of Food however were not sympathetic to the distress experienced by those working for them. Following the 2020 pandemic there was much concern about mental health issues caused by the stress of the lockdown. In 1940, attitudes were very different, the senior civil servants appearing ignorant of the feelings of the young women who were working hard over a hundred miles from home and isolated from their usual circle of family and friends. The view from the senior staff was that the constant complaints from the junior staff were merely petty grievances. Nonetheless they did get very concerned when the obvious low morale began to affect the work output of their departments.

Chapter 6

Railway Travel in the Early Years of the War

The emergency timetables were planned with the view of the possibility of severe dislocation of transport by air raids ... and were regarded as the minimum service which would keep the activities of the country alive.

'Mercury', *Railway Magazine* December 1939

Following the instigation of the revised timetables in September 1939, the LNER claimed a thirty-two per cent reduction in passengers during the first seven weeks of the war period, this percentage reduction roughly equated to the percentage reduction in the number of services the railway had been able to provide. Many electrification schemes had been proposed earlier in the twentieth century on the basis that more frequent trains would inevitably result in more passengers travelling on the improved services. It is tempting to speculate that the LNER's experience demonstrates the reverse of this well-proven theory, but it is uncertain as to whether the public's demand for travel had been damped down due to fewer trains being run or by the prospect of overcrowding in the blackout conditions, but it may have been simply due to an anxious desire to 'stay at home' in the disturbing and frightening times experienced by the population at the start of the war.

As early as 19 September the REC began to discuss ways of improving the railways' passenger comfort by relaxing the blackout regulations, which were particularly irksome for those travelling on the longer distance train services. To ensure that the railways complied fully with the Defence of the Realm regulations, the unpopular blackout restrictions had to be rigidly imposed. These restrictions were, as was claimed by one reader of *The Times*, creating 'unnecessary hinderance to commercial, government and military efficiency' because of the inability of passengers to be able to read and write during their train journey. In part due to the relatively longer journey times compared to today, those working in business, the military or government did not consider a long train journey as 'dead time', but an opportunity to perform tasks such as reading reports or completing any paperwork. The whole public however, not just the business community, were suffering the severely reduced lighting or non-existent lighting in the trains during the blackout hours and were craving a solution to the train lighting problem. This concern was expressed at the SR's March 1940 shareholders' annual general meeting – more than six months after the imposition of the new regulations – when the directors were given an insight into public sentiment in respect to the blackout. They were bluntly informed that many of their passengers seemed to believe that the blackout was not necessary and furthermore expressed the bizarre notion that the restrictions had been imposed just to annoy them. The provision of the disliked blue bulbs replacing the banned white bulbs was being carried out by the SR as speedily as was possible with priority being given to the long-distance trains initially, but with only the promise that the blue lighting would replace the total darkness on their commuter trains 'as soon as was possible'. The SR confirmed that blue bulbs had been ordered as per government's pre-war decree, but sufficient quantities had not arrived in time.

Any relaxation of the rules would of course require government approval. An early suggestion from the railway professionals at the REC was that they could provide near normal lighting in the carriages if this was to be extinguished immediately during an air raid. This simple proposal was duly contained in a letter signed by the chairman and sent to the government.

This plea resulted in the announcement in October by the minister of transport, Captain Euan Wallace, that normal lighting would be available on long-distance trains provided that the lights were switched off by a member of the railway staff operating a 'master switch' whenever an air raid warning was given. This government 'announcement' gave the travelling public a degree of hope, but it is a long way between the making of such a bold statement by a politician and completion of the work. By early November the SR had fitted improved lighting in many of its main line carriages. Its complete scheme involved the darkening of every compartment window by the application of broad borders of a special paint and the fitting of lamp shades designed to direct the light down onto the passenger's book or newspaper and to restrict any escaping light through an open door when the train stopped at a station. The reading lights were fitted with white bulbs, but these were supplemented with the usual ceiling lights still fitted with the unpopular blue bulbs which would not shine out onto the station platforms. A new grade of railwayman was created, that of 'train lighting attendant', who could be identified by the passengers by his armlet inscribed with the word 'lighting'. It was his duty to patrol the train fifteen minutes before blackout time and close any of the windows that had been left open and then draw down all of the blinds. In the event of an air raid warning, the train lighting attendant was tasked with switching off all of the train lights.

The first trains to receive these modifications on the SR were those in use on the Southern Electric 'Portsmouth direct' route between Waterloo and Portsmouth Harbour. The SR publicity department published photographs showing relaxed travellers reading in what appears to be one of the open third–class motor coaches of the type used on the Portsmouth services. It was reported in the national press that the new lighting arrangements used on the SR were the same as that being used on the LMSR's Euston to Heysham boat trains. Other early recipients of new lighting arrangement were a few of the SR's steam hauled trains which ran between Ramsgate and Cannon Street and two other trains on services departing from Waterloo, one to the West of England and the other to Bournemouth West. Early in the war before the German invasion of France, the SR continued to run boat trains for cross-channel services mainly for the use of military personnel, and it was one of these services in each direction on the Victoria to Folkestone Harbour route that was also provided with the improved lighting. The SR hoped that by Christmas all of their main line stock would be equipped with the modified reading lights. The company also announced that the next trains to be fitted were to be the London to Brighton electric expresses – much to the delight of the large number of season ticket holders on that line.

But these much vaunted 'improvements' were only to be applied to the long-distance express services, improvements to lighting on the slower short-distance passenger trains was infuriatingly slow. One correspondent to *The Times* in November 1939 made the claim that there was not any lighting at all in three quarters of the carriages on the LTPB Metropolitan Line services from Baker Street to Watford. As late as July 1940 there remained 70 of the SR's older carriages being used on the suburban services that were still without any lighting whatsoever – perhaps it was not possible to fit the 'modern' blue bulbs? The SR general manager, aware of the public's distaste for darkened trains, ordered that these carriages should be withdrawn from service forthwith.

Following the limited restoration of sleeping car services during the first few weeks of the war, the LNER had a procedure to reinstate the white bulbs in the sleeping cars to enable passengers to read. The railway's solution for providing an acceptable level of lighting in these carriages was for the replacement of the blue bulbs for white but maintaining the blackout with all of the compartment windows fitted with shutters which were closed at night and padlocked shut. On the corridor side of the sleeping car the windows were completely blacked out. Should any passenger not wish to have his sleeping compartment windows shuttered, they were requested to speak to the attendant who would unlock and open the shutters and replace the sleeping compartment's white bulb with a blue bulb. The Pullman Car Company (who continued to operate some Pullman services on

SR electric trains) claimed to have solved the problem of providing passengers in its coaches with adequate light without infringing the blackout when they too fitted wooden shields to the windows. Each shield had a small, narrow shutter to be opened during daylight hours.

One writer to *The Times*, who was a regular traveller on the LMSR between South Hampstead and Broad Street, complained that the blue-bulb blackout lighting was also being used throughout the day on his journey which involved the train having to run through numerous bridges and deep cuttings. In peacetime the standard white lights had been left on all day in the carriages but in the restricted daylight when the only lighting came from the blue bulbs it was proving impossible for the passengers to read their books or newspapers. He compared the LMSR unfavourably with the LPTB Metropolitan line on which he claimed that passengers during the day on the above ground sections of the route enjoyed the 'normal' lighting.

In the early days of the war the German propaganda machine was insisting that Britons could not obtain any food on the trains or at the stations. Untrue, of course, as station refreshment facilities had never been withdrawn, although these refreshment rooms had arguably been inadequately staffed during the period of exceptional demand from 11 September until when October when there was a restoration of many restaurant car services. After the initial withdrawal of on-train catering, the LNER and LMS introduced the use of snack boxes sold at the stations for consumption on the journey. Refreshment rooms were retained at important stations, and, despite wartime restrictions, the opening hours were set to meet the needs of the travelling public. At the GWR's Paddington station the withdrawal of the restaurant cars had resulted in a huge increase in sales at the catering trollies provided on the station platforms and this had unfortunately resulted in crush and overcrowding. The German propaganda asserting that there had been the elimination of all catering facilities on-board the trains had been true for only one week before the SR restored the Pullman operated buffet, pantry and restaurant car services on its electric trains and later, on 5 October 1939, the REC announced what was welcome news to many travellers, the restoration of a limited number of restaurant facilities on the longer distance services.

The new REC edict permitted the GWR to reinstate catering vehicles on twenty-nine express trains on their routes from Paddington to the West of England, Cheltenham, West Wales, Worcester and Birkenhead, but initially from 22 October only ten trains with restaurant cars were scheduled by the railway. This restoration of the restaurant cars was concentrated on trains that ran between the important centres and were used by many business and public service passengers. Special blinds had been fitted to the windows of the restaurant cars enabling the passengers to dine during the blackout periods in what the railway hoped would create the comfortable and well-lit environment that was expected and appreciated by its regular customers in peacetime. The GWR were proud to be able to serve their ever popular *a la carte* breakfast and also provided a *table d'hôte* menu priced at 2/6 for those who wanted an alternative. A charge of 3/- was charged for the on-board mid-day and evening lunches which offered a soup, fish, roast meat, vegetables and potatoes to be followed by sweets and cheese. The GWR wine list had to be shortened but the company claimed that they could still offer a variety of wines. In the light of a reduced service being provided, the GWR requested that diners vacate their seats as soon as possible so that others could be accommodated. The LNER's new timetable might have been what they described as 'less Spartan' but their on-board menus could not match the offering from the GWR, for so as to be able to serve the maximum number of meals in the minimum amount of time, a new wartime menu offered what was described as 'simple meals' costing 2/6 being served. On the LMS restaurant cars were soon to be provided on fifty trains every day, and it too provided simplified menus and introduced a standard charge of 2/6 for all meals whether breakfast, lunch or dinner except its 'standard tea' which cost travellers 1/-. Sandwiches could also be purchased for the same price. The LMSR claimed that due to the wartime conditions it had reduced the cost of the meals to 2/6 in order to simplify meal provision and to take due account for the much-reduced variety of ingredients being offered. The LMSR also added a service charge to the menu as passengers were no longer expected to tip the waiters – but all of the new service charge income was to be passed on to the staff.

Despite the original intention to withdraw all catering vehicles, on 26 May 1940 the Ministry of Transport wrote to the REC asking for information about the provision of on-train catering, the tone of which suggested that the railways were providing a poor service. The ministry at this stage of the war, having had complaints from members of the public, seemed more concerned about restaurant car meal prices and service levels than about the appropriateness of providing restaurant cars on express trains during wartime. The REC responded by stating that meals and refreshments were provided for the convenience of the travelling public. The railways aimed to provide a service which as far was possible satisfied the demands of the majority of passengers but due to the reduced train services available it was not possible to increase the facilities except at the expense of reducing seating on the train. As for what was perceived to be the high price of the meals, the REC explained that the cost of preparing and serving a meal was 'considerably in excess' of the cost of providing the same in a hotel or restaurant. In response to a plea for lighter, cheaper meals, the REC explained that the restaurant cars were primarily equipped to provide full meals and not equipped for a buffet service. The restaurant cars could be used for a buffet service during the 'hours when recognised meals were not being served' but this, it was explained, would require more staff and these were not available due to the shortage of labour.

Not every member of the travelling public agreed with restoration of the restaurant cars. A passenger who travelled with his wife from South Wales to Paddington held the opinion – which he claimed was shared with many 'humble and patriotic people' – that all the luncheon and dining facilities should be withdrawn since such luxury was inappropriate in wartime Britain. In his letter to the REC, he claimed that a third of the third-class passengers on the train, who he described as 'miserably poor', were forced to stand with their luggage in the corridors along the length of the train due to the lack of seating. He noted that many of these were women and children who were forced to stand for over two hours during the journey. Meanwhile, what he described as the 'South Wales plutocrats' also travelling on the train, after vacating their comfortable first-class seats would force their way through the crowded carriages so as to reach the dining car. The writer noted that this situation was an example of what he described as the 'inequalities of wartime sacrifice'. Rather than indulge in a meal on the train he opined that all 'decent' people should take with them on a long journey sandwiches which they had prepared at home before setting off in the morning. If this was a common point of view, and the lack of more letters does not necessarily preclude the possibility that the population as a whole would have also noted the inequality but chose not to make any formal complaint, it does suggest that the REC and the government were out of touch with much of the general public. Arguably they were guilty of looking inward, away from the working-class traveller, and seeing only the needs of those they could identify with – the middle and upper classes, including those that wrote to the Ministry of Transport complaining about the paucity of meals available on the trains during wartime.

Was the other main complaint about overcrowding on the GWR's South Wales services justified? Although some time later in March 1941, a census carried out to count passengers on these trains and record the available seats gives some indication as to the overcrowding or otherwise on the route. The survey was conducted on 13 March and showed that the 8.55am Paddington to Pembroke Dock train had at Reading General station 46 first class passengers spread across 78 first class seats and 437 third class passengers using the available 674 seats, this train might be described as 'busy' but not overcrowded. Another train, the 11.55am from Paddington to Neyland in Pembrokeshire, had its passengers counted as it departed from the London terminus. The train had a total of seventy-eight first class seats occupied by seventy-two passengers and 600 third class passengers finding what seats they could amongst the 524 third class seats. A later train to Neyland leaving Paddington at 1.55pm had when it departed from Swindon seventy-two first class ticket holders spread around 108 seats while the 743 third class passengers had only 624 third-class seats available to them. Another later train, the 5.55pm to Cardiff, upon departure from Paddington had 30 of the 'South Wales plutocrats' in the train who were probably returning home after a day's business in the capital and would find 60 seats at their disposal. Meanwhile, 431 of the 'miserably poor' with their third-class tickets could spread themselves across 600 seats. All of the trains had adequate first-class accommodation, half could be described as being almost full in the third-class compartments, and the other half crowded as the third-class passengers spilled out into the corridors. Those who travel on the 'new' GWR and have had, at certain very busy times, have had to stand in the vestibules outside the toilets might come to the conclusion that on occasions travel in 2022 is not so much different from travel in 1940 in respect to crowded trains.

Patriotic or not, by the spring of 1940, many restaurant and buffet car services had been restored. It was reported that the LMSR were in May daily operating eighty-four restaurant car and ten buffet services, while the LNER were running fifty-seven restaurant car, and forty-two buffet car services. Meanwhile the GWR ran forty restaurant car and twelve buffet car services every day. The SR, which had Pullman vehicles within its electric multiple unit sets, was operating fifty-four trains with restaurant cars and six buffet car trains – many with Pullman service as that company had a contract to provide the railway's catering facility. This might today seem a lot of express trains with full catering, but on any pre-war weekday the SR had run 391 such trains every weekday. The other railways had also severely reduced the number of restaurant car expresses, the GWR had operated 103 on weekdays before the war, the LMSR daily total had been 252 and the LNER had run 274 in all. The reduction in the number of express trains providing their passengers with meals while in transit was therefore quite considerable.

In March 1940 there were questions in parliament concerning the overcrowding on trains between Newcastle and London. Less concerned about the general public who might be making 'unnecessary' journeys, parliament was concerned that because the trains were so full, many soldiers were unable to find seats and were having to stand in the corridors. The reason given for this was because the LNER had been forced to make reductions they described as 'extensive' to services on its east coast main line route to Scotland. These had been announced in February 1940. The minister of transport explained that extra coal trains from Durham and Northumberland had been the reason for these reductions in services and the passenger trains had been extended to the maximum locomotive capacity. The LMSR and LNER both cited 'coal traffic requirements' as the reason why they had been forced to reduce services to the North and Scotland. The REC, mindful that the railways took pride in their public service, did what they were very good at which was to produce a poster for display at stations and for publication in magazines and newspapers. The text of this new poster which hoped to appeal to the passengers' patriotism was not exactly snappy but to the point, it read OHMS (On His Majesty's Service), 'Food-munitions-troops. British Railways are anxious to provide complete services for the public. National duties may prevent them from running all trains which you, and they, might wish, but please be indulgent, remember National Needs Come First'. In an attempt to reduce overcrowding on the daytime trains the LMS – who had not been running sleeping car trains to Edinburgh – in March 1940 introduced a limited number of first- and third-class sleeping accommodation on the Euston to Edinburgh route.

Early in 1940 many of those in authority believed that the apparent peaceful situation was not going to last for much longer and even before the fall of Belgium and the Netherlands there was concern about the locations to which children had been evacuated. Early in May the Ministry of Health decreed that children who had been evacuated to areas in the south of England which were not now deemed to be completely safe must be moved to safer locations. It was agreed to extend the reception areas further west and inland. For the first time Wales was included in the area to which London children were to be evacuated. Once again, the railways took part in the movement of children, on 19 May London children were evacuated from coastal areas of Essex, Kent and Suffolk to Glamorgan and Monmouthshire. On 2 June children were transferred from the coastal areas of Kent, Suffolk and Norfolk to new reception areas in the Midlands and Wales. On 23 June children who had been at first evacuated to the Eastbourne and Hastings localities in Sussex were moved further away from the hostilities to Brecon, Carmarthen, Radnor and Pembroke. On 23 June other children billeted in the Brighton and Hove localities were moved a shorter distance to locations in rural Surrey, and on 21 July those evacuated to Worthing were transported to Hertfordshire. Accounts of the first evacuation of school children by the railways indicate a smooth and relatively uncrowded travel experience for the children on trains neatly fitted in between regular services. There is, of course, the continuing assumption that travel by train during the war was a crowded and unpleasant experience and any journey likely to be subject to massive delays. As already recorded mistakes were made during the first evacuation but it is probable that it is the later, smaller evacuations such as these which became intwined in the disorder created by the later additional and untimetabled occurrences on the railway system which did give rise to the many accounts about unpleasant evacuation journeys being endured by very young children. Or perhaps, as any parent might suspect, there might have been many children exhibiting the 'are we there yet?' syndrome. The Ministry of Health meanwhile continued to put pressure on the local authorities to press for more children to be registered for evacuation, and on 10 May there was a public appeal for volunteers to assist with what was to be the second evacuation of children.

On 30 May the LCC registration efforts were helped when the new minister of health, Malcolm Macdonald, the Labour MP for Ross and Cromarty, broadcast to a nation which was becoming increasing uneasy and concerned about the deteriorating military situation on the other side of the English Channel. Macdonald, not wishing to induce panic, merely hinted that a new mass evacuation was imminent, and that the government would not wait until any air raids began before acting on this plan. The minister insisted that all children would be medically examined before leaving for the reception areas, and furthermore he expected the children who had been evacuated would be regularly checked for disease and cleanliness. To expedite this (it was of course before the introduction of the National Health Service) the ministry announced that it would pay the medical fees for these examinations. When a child had been medically examined this was to be recorded with a mark placed upon their 'label'. To speed up the process a temporary clinic was to be established at Waterloo station.

As in 1939, by May 1940 detailed plans were prepared to transport evacuees away from the cities to the 'safe' reception areas. The LCC Evacuation Branch proposed to evacuate 266,900 children from the greater metropolitan area which included 160,000 from the County of London. On Monday, 10 June at 10.45am the instruction 'evacuation to commence Thursday' was given. Curiously, this new plan for a second evacuation of children from London was announced in a radio broadcast prior to any warning being given to the railways. The radio announcement stated that evacuation of children from London would commence on Thursday, 13 June, and the plan was to spread the operation over six days. Individual rail travel tickets were to be issued and the scheme was to be ready for implementation at a day's notice. Despite what should have been a worrying outlook for parents, there was still a shortfall in the number of registrations. Only 105,000 London children were to be transported to safety between the 13 and

18 June in the summer of 1940. The original LCC evacuation plan had been to use all four of the main line railway companies – the LMSR, LNER, GWR and SR – but on 2 June the minister of health decreed that the LMSR and LNER should not be used for the London evacuation and that only the GWR and the south-western lines of the SR were to be used. Fortunately, despite the very short notice the GWR and SR rose to the occasion. As well as the evacuation of children from London, children living in North Kent joined the LCC children and were evacuated westwards.

In this second evacuation of children, 84 per cent of them who had been registered by their parents, a total of 103,000, left London by train in the charge of 5,625 teachers together with over 1,000 other adults. The LCC were to claim that the young Londoners were greeted by the staff of the local authorities in the reception areas with what they described as a genuine warmth. James, who had originally been evacuated to Luton but subsequently returned home to central London, was now without his sister to be escorted, to Wales, travelling on the GWR from Paddington to Bedwas which is two miles north-east of Caerphilly in what was in 1940 the county of Glamorgan. At the time, Bedwas was a mining village. The evacuees arrived at the GWR Bedwas station which was once part of the Brecon and Merthyr Tydfil Railway, and then escorted by bus to a local assembly point where what was in effect a 'beauty contest' was carried out. Those volunteering to billet London children were asked to select which of the children they wished to take home. All of the girls were picked first – they would provide 'free' domestic help for the households. The boys, unless they looked particularly strong and might be useful for labouring on the local farms, were less favoured. James was chosen second to last, but despite this he was welcomed into the Williams household and remained with them for three years. He recalls that he was fully accepted into the family and when they visited their relatives, he would always go with them as part of the family group. He had no complaints about any harsh treatment while he was an evacuee.

A combination of distance from home and the expense of even the reduced railway ticket, meant that James, billeted with the Williams family at Bedwas, was to receive only one visit by his father during his three-year stay. James' father was a London tram driver and while he was of the same social class as the Williams family and their neighbours in Bedwas – they were miners and agricultural workers – when alighting from the train the visitor from London stood out from the crowd when he arrived wearing his 'Sunday best'. Much to the amusement of the Welshmen, James' father stepped off the train wearing not a cloth cap, but a black felt Homburg hat, a type which was later to be popularised by the politician Anthony Eden.

Any suggestion of extra holiday trains in 1940 was quickly abandoned with the darkening military situation. On 15 May the Whitsun bank holiday was cancelled by royal proclamation on the day following the Dutch surrender to the German onslaught. On 17 May, the SR, which now in 1940 was effectively on the 'front line' in the war, announced that its summer timetable, due to be introduced on 1 July, would not be proceeded with in view of the 'existing circumstances'. In anticipation of an invasion stations were stripped of any posters showing maps. The chief inspector of railways, Colonel Mount, issued the instruction that all signal box and platform name boards which were of sufficient size or so located that they would be visible to a low flying enemy aeroplane, must be obliterated or hooded so as not to be visible from the air. He also suggested that signposts in country districts indicating the direction of railway stations or goods yards should be removed or obliterated.

On 28 May Belgium surrendered, and the German army spilled into northern France and the catastrophic events that are now given the shorthand title 'Dunkirk' played out as the BEF became surrounded by the advancing German army which resulted in thousands of British and French soldiers being trapped in and around the port of Dunkirk. The Nazi army officers would soon be able to look across the Channel to view the white cliffs of Dover through their field glasses. What looked like becoming a humiliating defeat was turned into a triumph as most of the British army, in addition to hundreds of French troops, were rescued from the beleaguered port and sailed to England. From the Channel ports the railways took up the baton to transport the weary soldiers to military bases across the country.

Today the term 'Dunkirk' – as invoked by J.B. Priestley's famous contemporary radio broadcast – usually evokes the folklore image of thousands of 'small boats' gallantly collecting soldiers from the French beaches and safely returning them to home. The truth is more complex. Many small civilian boats did bravely venture across the Straits of Dover, but they were mainly put to use ferrying men from the beach to the larger transports out to sea. The Royal Navy also managed to obtain many Dutch fishing vessels despite the capitulation of the Netherlands. The bulk carriage of retreating troops was either by Royal Navy destroyers – who mainly collected soldiers off the beach – or by the larger civilian ships that had been requisitioned by the Royal Navy and these had the more dangerous task of collecting troops from within Dunkirk harbour. Amongst these larger ships now flying the white ensign were many that were railway owned with others from the Isle of Man Steam Packet Company. Most of these ships were crewed by their regular officers and seamen although many of these would have been Royal Navy Reservists. The ships had neither armour plating nor any weaponry – except, rarely, a single anti-aircraft gun – to defend themselves and many were sunk, including the SR's *Normania* and *Lorina*, while *Canterbury*, *Maid of Orleans* and *Biarritz* suffered considerable damage. The stress on the crews, most of whom had earlier worked for the railway companies, can only be imagined since after returning from the hell which was Dunkirk the ships were quickly turned around to collect even more troops. The Royal Navy did however provide what they condescendingly described as 'stiffeners', that is Royal Navy ratings who supplemented the exhausted and shocked civilian crews. With the code name 'Operation Dynamo', the evacuation exercise officially commenced on 28 May and was deemed complete on 3 June.

Earlier in the war, in September 1939, the railways had risen to the challenge of transporting the BEF to France, but now a second major challenge arose when the tired and shocked servicemen came back from France and after their arrival at the English ports it became the railways' task to move them on to military sites across the country. Long-serving railway staff who had been employed by the South Eastern and Chatham Railway in 1914 would have had a sense of déjà vu in 1940. For the second time in their working lives, they witnessed an evacuation across the English Channel, but this time it was not hundreds of Belgian civilians and their crown jewels that had to be collected from the Channel ports and transported by the railway across England, but the retreating British Army accompanied by very little of their fighting equipment. The enormity of the task confronting the SR can best be illustrated by the operation of the troop trains through Redhill. Between Monday, 27 May and Tuesday, 4 June 1940, a total of 560 special trains passed through the station. The majority of these trains – numbering 324 in total – started their journeys from Dover Marine station, but Folkestone dispatched 64 trains, Ramsgate 82, Margate 75, with 15 from Sheerness. The whole operation was carried out on an *ad hoc* basis – no official 'working notices' setting out timetables were prepared and distributed to staff. Trains would depart from the Channel ports with their ultimate destination yet to be determined as this would be agreed when the train reached a key junction such as Redhill. The *Railway Magazine* complemented the SR for the 'brightness and cleanliness' of the locomotives that it provided for most of the trains as they gave forth 'a little cheer' to the scene. To minimise disruption to timetabled services the evacuation trains avoided the London area and cross-country routes were used wherever possible. Such was the upheaval that it would not have been possible to provide all of the special trains without the severe curtailment of many regular passenger services. All passenger trains in the Redhill locality were cancelled. Impromptu chalked notices appeared at stations informing passengers that no trains would run between Redhill and Tonbridge and between Redhill and Reading. The SR organised bus replacement services to stations along this cross-country route which became a vital link from the ports to the West Country and the Midlands.

It had been a tremendous effort by the railways and on 7 June the REC received a rather understated message on behalf of the Army Council from Anthony Eden – the Conservative politician who had recently been appointed Secretary of State for War – merely asking that the Railway Executive Committee 'pass on thanks to all companies concerned'. Given the disproportionate effort by the SR, the general manager, Eustace Missenden, must have thought his company had been undervalued by the government, but he had already written a letter on 4 June to all of the SR staff thanking them for their efforts expressing his '… unbounded admiration …' for their part in what had been a very successful operation and he also issued a glowing press release congratulating his staff on their efforts.

During this period of huge upheaval, it is unsurprising that a casualty of the heightened war situation was the arrangements for parents to visit their evacuated children. On Wednesday, 19 June the Ministry of Transport decreed that any such travel arrangements would be cancelled. It was duly announced that London parents would not be able to visit their children on 30 June or for the whole of July. It was alleged by some critics at the time that this withdrawal of facilities caused so much anxiety within the families that it led to even more children being brought home. But it was only the railways in the south which were being severely stressed by the troop evacuation, so some leeway was possible in the north of England as five special trains from Liverpool and Manchester did run as planned. When it was noted by the government that the lack of cheap travel for parents during June and July had caused distress to many families, the latest minister of transport Sir John Reith (more famous for his leadership of the BBC than for his very short tenure as minister of transport) told parliament that he hoped 'it may be

Right: Poster displayed at all stations giving details of passenger services during the evacuation period. (Railway Executive Committee)

Below: A post-war view of Epsom Downs station showing the white hoops painted on the stanchions which hopefully helped people to avoid bumping into them during wartime blackouts. This is a most unusual sight of a steam train at this station, as usually only electric trains visited the branch. For the record, the occasion was a day excursion on 20 June 1954 to Margate which had been organised by the supporters of the Carshalton Athletic football club. The assigned locomotive is Nine Elms allocated Maunsell 'N' class 2-6-0 No. 31409. (Mike Morant collection)

RAILWAY PASSENGER
SERVICES
DURING EVACUATION

The Main Line Railways announce that during Evacuation, alterations in the existing Passenger Services will be necessary, and the public are requested to limit their train travel to essential journeys.

The following information will be of guidance :—

LONDON SUBURBAN SERVICES.

Before 8.0 a.m. and after 5.30 p.m. services will be as near as possible normal.

Between 8.0 a.m. and 5.30 p.m. skeleton services only will operate.

PROVINCIAL SUBURBAN SERVICES.

During the hours of evacuation, skeleton services only will operate.

MAIN LINE SERVICES.

The Railways expect to maintain Main Line services, but no guarantee can be given as extensive alterations to existing time tables may have to be made without notice.

The Railways will make every endeavour to provide the best possible services, and are confident that they may rely upon the co-operation of the public in their efforts.

Above: A photograph taken just before the war showing an LNER express hauled by one of Sir Nigel Gresley's A4 locomotives. No. 4469 *Gadwall* is shown here on the east coast main line near Barnby Moor. This locomotive was later renamed *Sir Ralph Wedgwood* in March 1939. It was written off after it was badly damaged by a German bomber during the raid at York in April 1942. (Rail-online/David P. Williams archive)

Below: Another photograph taken just before the war, this time on the GWR at Paddington. GWR Castle class 4-6-0 No. 5013 *Abergavenny Castle* has arrived with a night-time express in 1937. (Rail-online/C.R.L. Coles/Rail Archive Stephenson)

Above: A typical coal train of the period comprised of four wheeled un-braked wagons. This train, photographed before the war in September 1937, is heading south on the LMSR west coast main line near Tring. The locomotive is a former London and North Western Railway 0-8-0 No 9143. (James Herbert Venn (1921-2014); © D P Williams Archive / Rail-Online)

Below: A long LMSR express train hauled by Stanier Princess Royal Pacific No. 6201 *Princess Elizabeth* at Brinklow on 31 August 1940. This locomotive has been preserved in working order and took part in the Queen Elizabeth II Diamond Jubilee celebrations. (Mike Morant collection)

The rapid and efficient DISTRIBUTION of the NATION'S ESSENTIAL SUPPLIES depends upon the smooth running of 1,250,000 FREIGHT VEHICLES worked by BRITISH RAILWAYS

BRITISH RAILWAYS ARE CARRYING ON

Above: GWR Hawksworth 'Modified Hall' no. 6965 Thirelestaine Hall in wartime black livery approaching Oxford from the north in 1945. The picture was taken from Aristotle Lane footbridge (a little to the north of the Walton Well Road bridge) with Port Meadow on the left and the Oxford suburb of Summertown seen distantly on the right beyond the Oxford Canal. The tracks on the right are those of the LMS line from Bicester. 6965 was less than a year old when this was taken and was probably allocated to Swindon motive power depot. It would seem that there is a plate over the cab window when the locomotive was built to reduce glare in blackout conditions. (Mike Morant collection)

Left: Typical of the early publicity distributed by the REC in late 1939 – early 1940. (Railway Executive Committee)

Right: Example of poster based on Mass Observation's report. The locomotive, of LNER origin, probably never pulled trains to Blackpool. Note 'BR' on buffer beam, not LNER number. (Railway Executive Committee)

Below: The Metropolitan line extended out into 'Metroland' and beyond Rickmansworth the electric locomotives were replaced by steam. This train is shown near Chalfont St Latimer on the Metropolitan/LNER joint line heading for Aylesbury. *The Times* correspondent claimed that 'normal' lighting remained 'on' during daylight hours enabling passengers to read when the train ran through gloomy cuttings, etc. It is believed that this photograph was taken in October 1942. The locomotive is an ex-Metropolitan Railway 2-6-4T but by 1942 LNER No. 6417. (Mike Morant collection)

THIS BRITISH ENGINE USED TO PULL
HOLIDAY TRAINS TO BLACKPOOL

LIKE HUNDREDS OF OTHERS IT IS NOW
PULLING TROOP TRAINS OR AMMUNITION
HERE OR TO THE FRONT

THIS IS AN EXAMPLE OF HOW THE
RAILWAYS ARE HELPING TO WIN THE WAR

MORE ENGINES ON THIS WORK MEAN
FEWER PASSENGER TRAINS BUT
SOLDIERS' LIVES AND YOUR SAFETY
DEPEND ON USING EVERY TRAIN
TO THE GREATEST POSSIBLE EXTENT

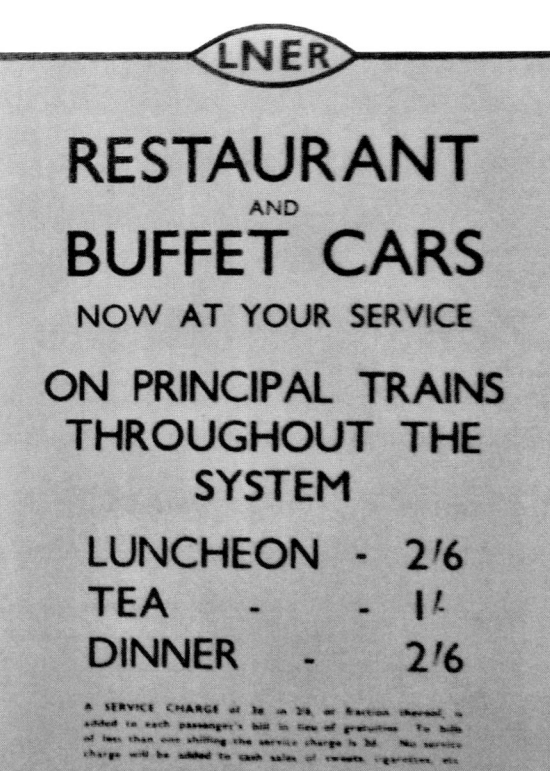

LNER

RESTAURANT
AND
BUFFET CARS
NOW AT YOUR SERVICE

ON PRINCIPAL TRAINS THROUGHOUT THE SYSTEM

LUNCHEON	-	2/6
TEA	-	1/-
DINNER	-	2/6

A SERVICE CHARGE at 3s in 2/6, or fraction thereof, is added to each passenger's bill in lieu of gratuities. To bills of less than one shilling the service charge is 3d. No service charge will be added to cash sales of sweets, cigarettes, etc.

DETAILS OF TRAIN SERVICES AT LNER STATIONS AND OFFICES

Left: LNER poster advertising restaurant car services in 1940. (London and North Eastern Railway)

Below: The *Railway Magazine* applauded the SR for the cleanliness of the locomotives it provided for the Dunkirk evacuation trains. It is unlikely that this Lord Nelson 4-6-0 would have been used in the exercise but if the locomotives that were used were as well kept as No. 859 *Lord Hood*, shown here in 1940 about to leave Waterloo with a West of England train, the magazine was justified in its praise – not that the cheerfulness of the locomotives would have been of huge interest to the relieved evacuated soldiers on arrival at Dover. (Mike Morant collection)

Above: Devastation at Middlesbrough station after the air raid in 1942. The fireman and driver of the locomotive both suffered severe injuries and the fireman later died in hospital. The LNER was able to restore services within hours of the raid. (wwwgazettelive.uk)

Below: LNER class J24 No. 1892 and J27 No. 2339 with a train of petrol tanks leaving Harrogate on 18 April 1942. The tanks probably contain aviation fuel, therefore this was certainly a photograph the censors would have not wished to be published at the time! (Rail-online/ M.N. Clay/Rail Archive Stephenson)

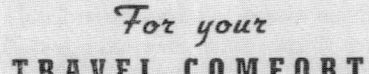

For your
TRAVEL COMFORT

HAVE YOUR TICKET READY—The fumbler is a
travelling highwayman—he holds up fellow travellers
and robs them and the Railway of time.

*

GET YOUR WEEKLY "SEASON" ON SATURDAY
EVENING OR SUNDAY MORNING and cut out
the Monday Morning queue.

*

CLOSE THE CARRIAGE DOOR—this will help the
depleted platform staff to get the train away quickly.

*

KEEP SEATS FREE OF LUGGAGE and give yourself
and other passengers more room

and
Travel only when you must

BRITISH RAILWAYS
GWR   LMS   LNER   SR

Above: One of the S160s sent to Europe during the war. No. 6046 was built by the Baldwin Locomotive Company in Philadelphia, Pennsylvania, USA. This locomotive was not used in Britain as it was exported straight to France in 1945. Later 6046 was used by the Hungarian State Railways and has been restored and preserved on the Churnet Valley Railway. It is shown during a visit to the West Somerset Railway in March 2018 hauling a demonstration freight train. (David Lindsell)

Left: A more subtle and 'public service' message from the REC. Using gentle humour, tips are given to avoid overcrowding, followed by the 'travel only when you must' message at the end. (Railway Executive Committee)

One of the Southern Railway's 'mixed traffic' Merchant Navy class locomotives in its original condition. 21C9 *Shaw Savill* at Waterloo station on 6 May 1943. The locomotive is in wartime black livery. (SR Official)

W.H. Whitworth/Rail Archive Stephenson

Above: The war is over and in 1946 LMSR Coronation Pacific No. 6225 looks worse for wear when it was photographed at Crewe. The original crimson lake with yellow 'speed' stripes has been replaced with plain black for the duration of the war. The locomotive is not only filthy but it has also had its 'streamlined' tender replaced with a substitute tender built to the standard non-streamlined design. (Rail Online/W.H. Whitworth/Rail Archive Stephenson)

Right: The updated 'Is your Journey Really Necessary?' poster. (The National Archives AN 2/11.16)

IS YOUR JOURNEY REALLY NECESSARY?

TICKETS

RAILWAY EXECUTIVE COMMITTEE

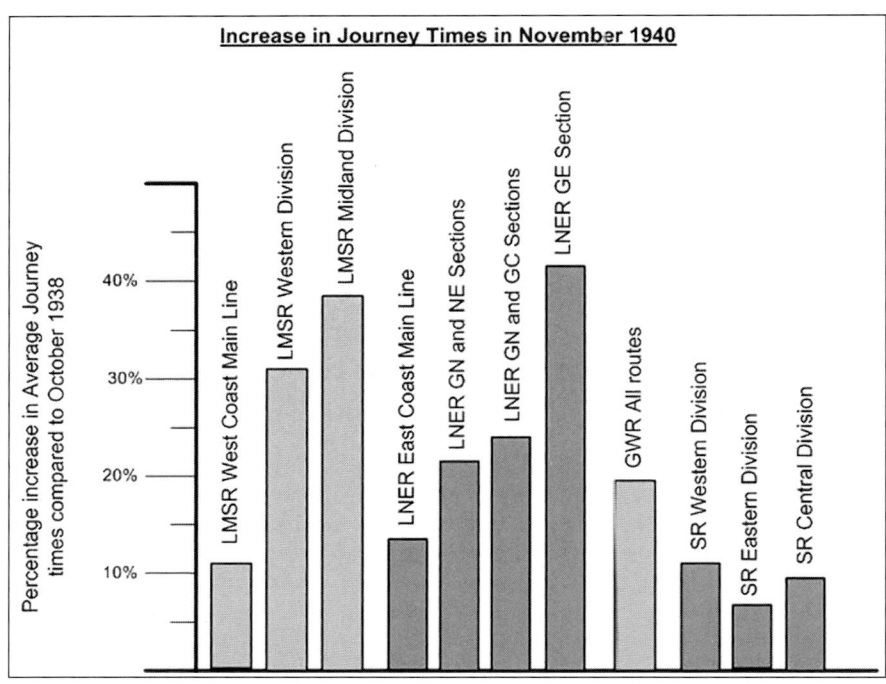

Source: Railway Magazine February 1941

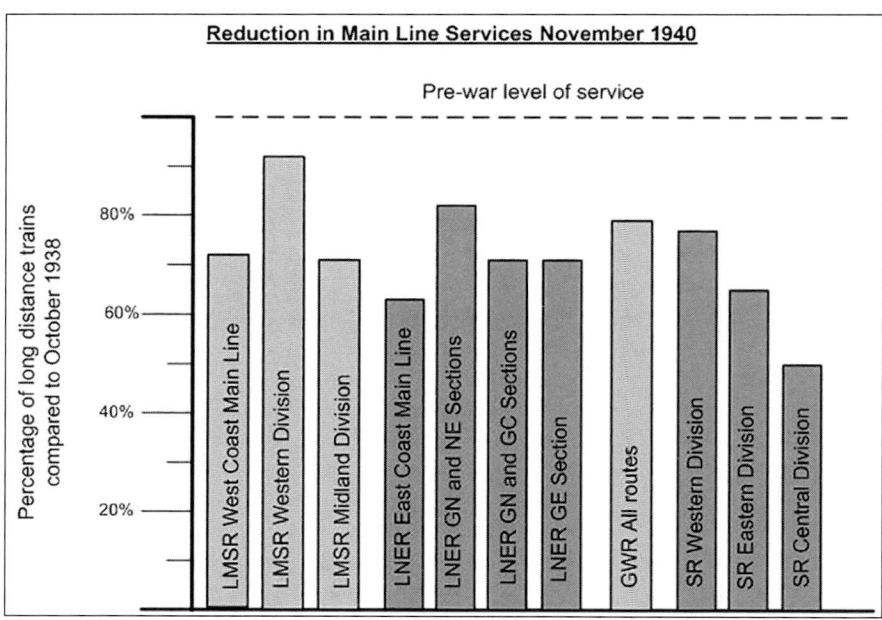

Source: Railway Magazine February 1941

Adaptation of 'Is your Journey Really Necessary Poster' to encourage the populate to take 'holidays at home'. (Railway Executive Committee)

(Railway Executive Committee)

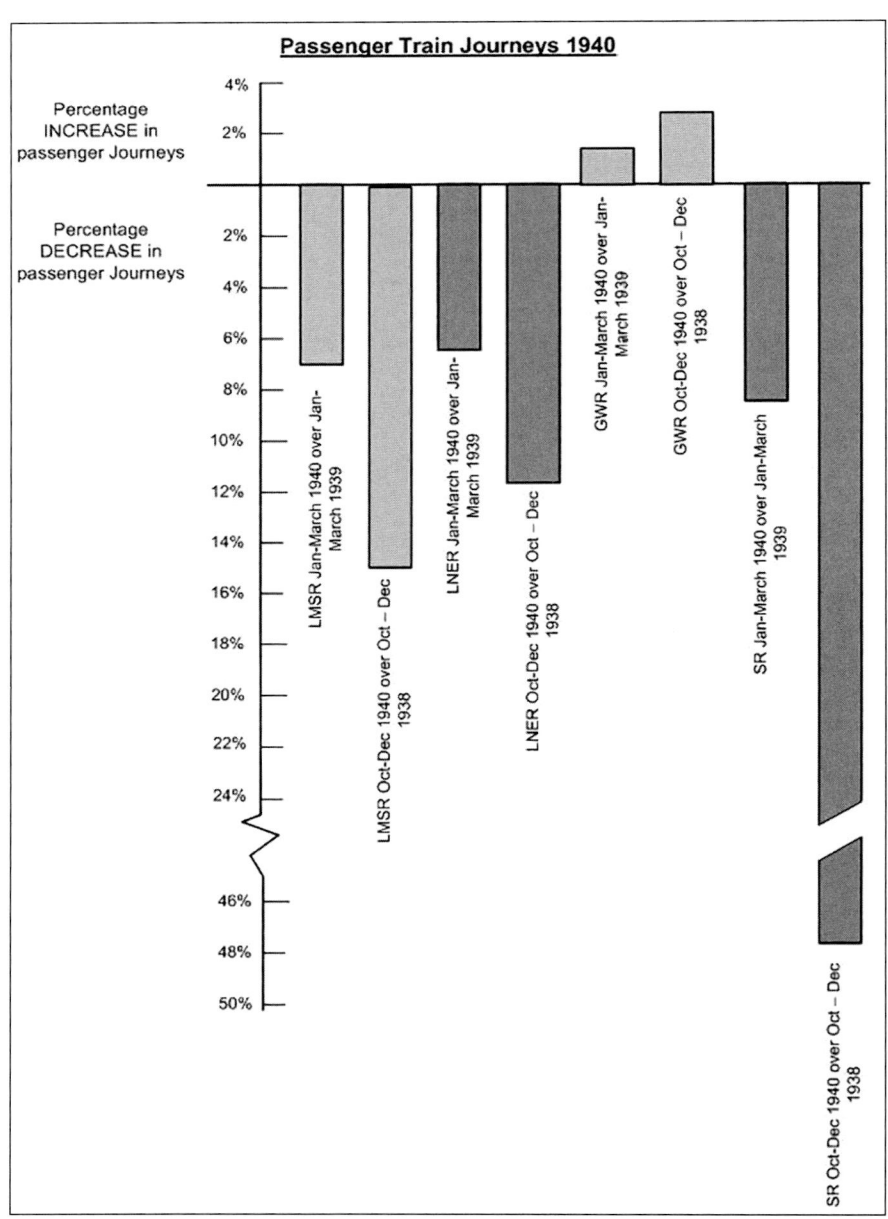

Above and opposite: Reduction in Passenger Travel, etc. These graphs indicate the extent of the fall in traffic prior to the dramatic increase later in the war. Source: The National Archives AN 2/820

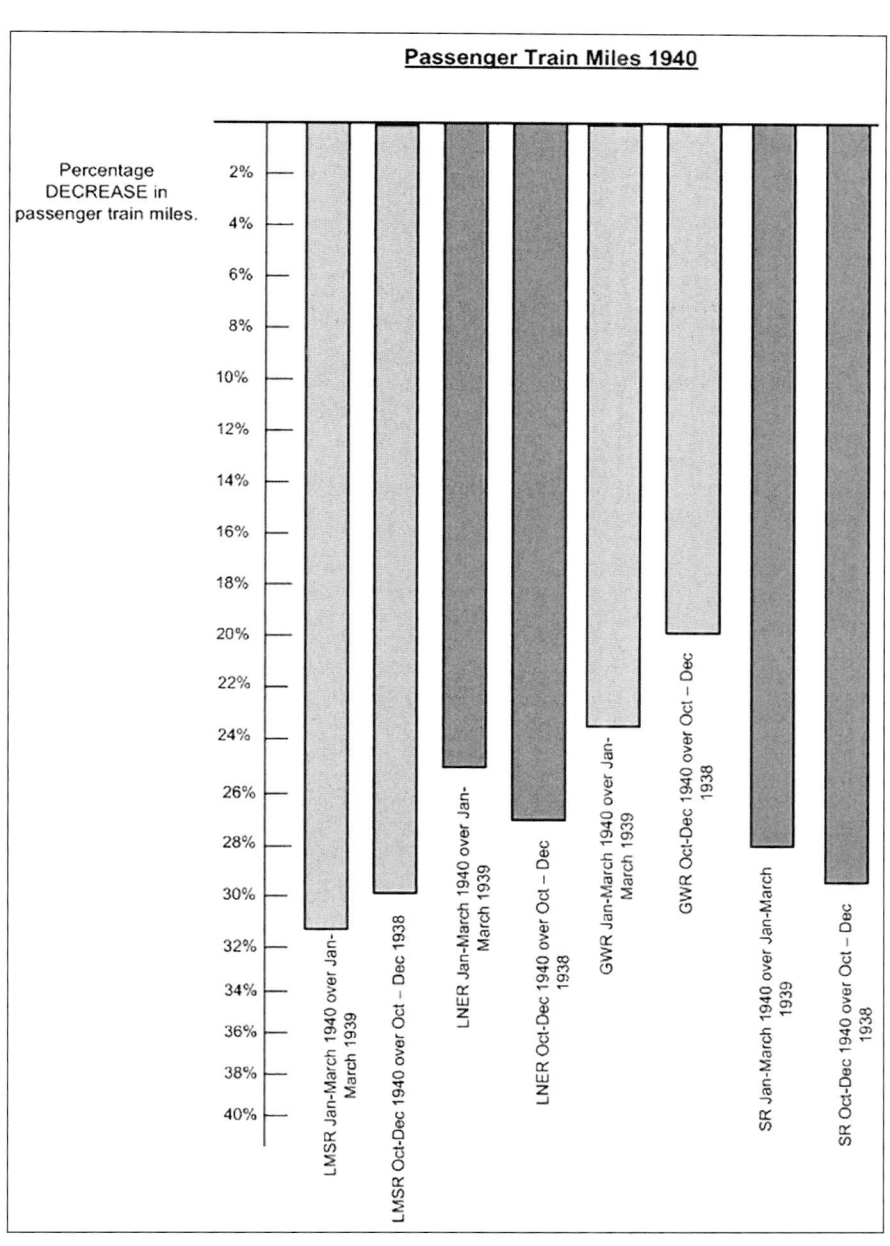

Passenger Train Miles 1940

Percentage DECREASE in passenger train miles.

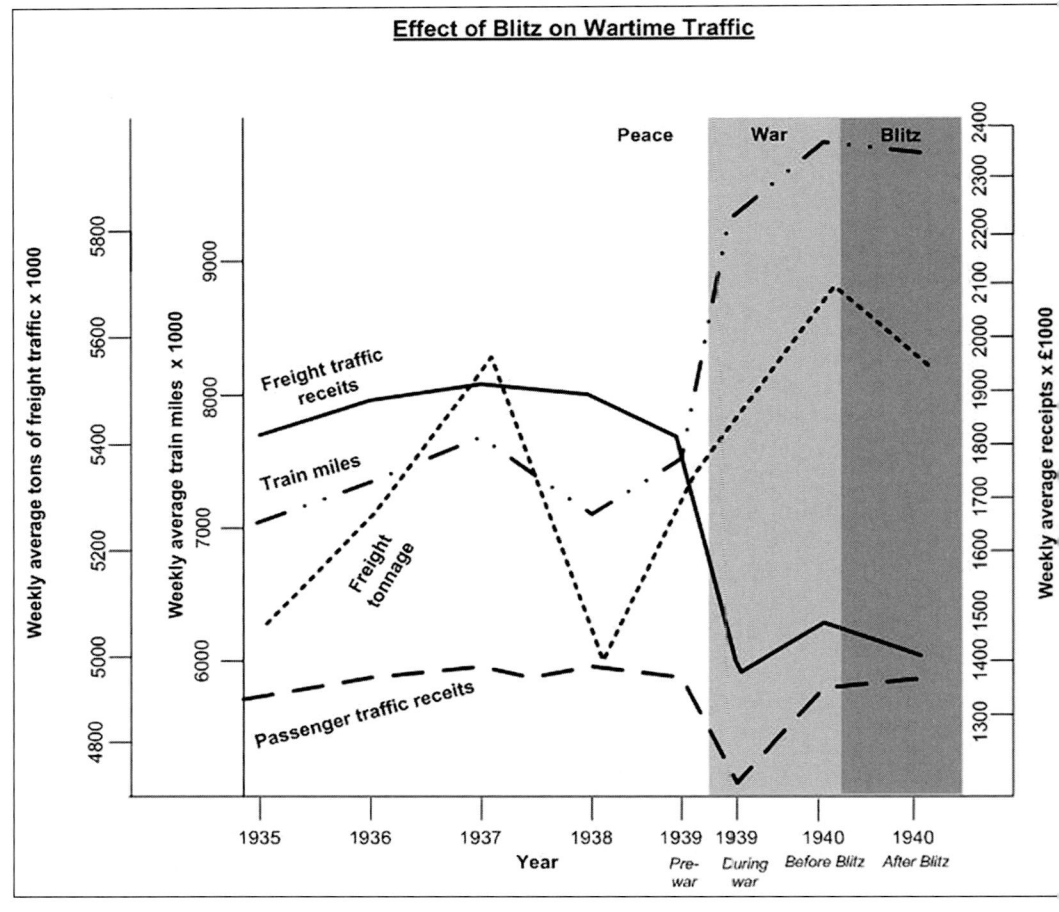

Source: The National Archives Cabinet Papers CAB 123/69

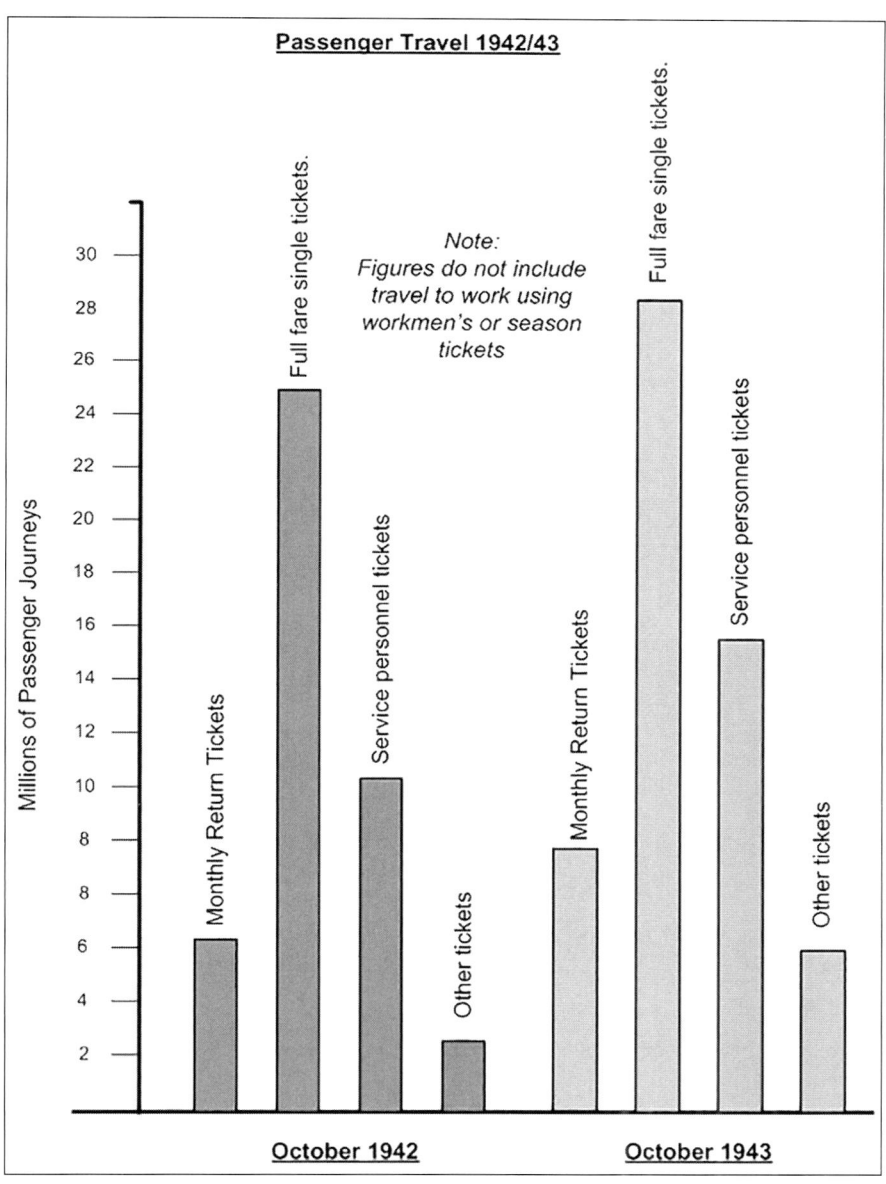

Source: The National Archives Railway Executive Passenger Sub-Committee
AN 3/18

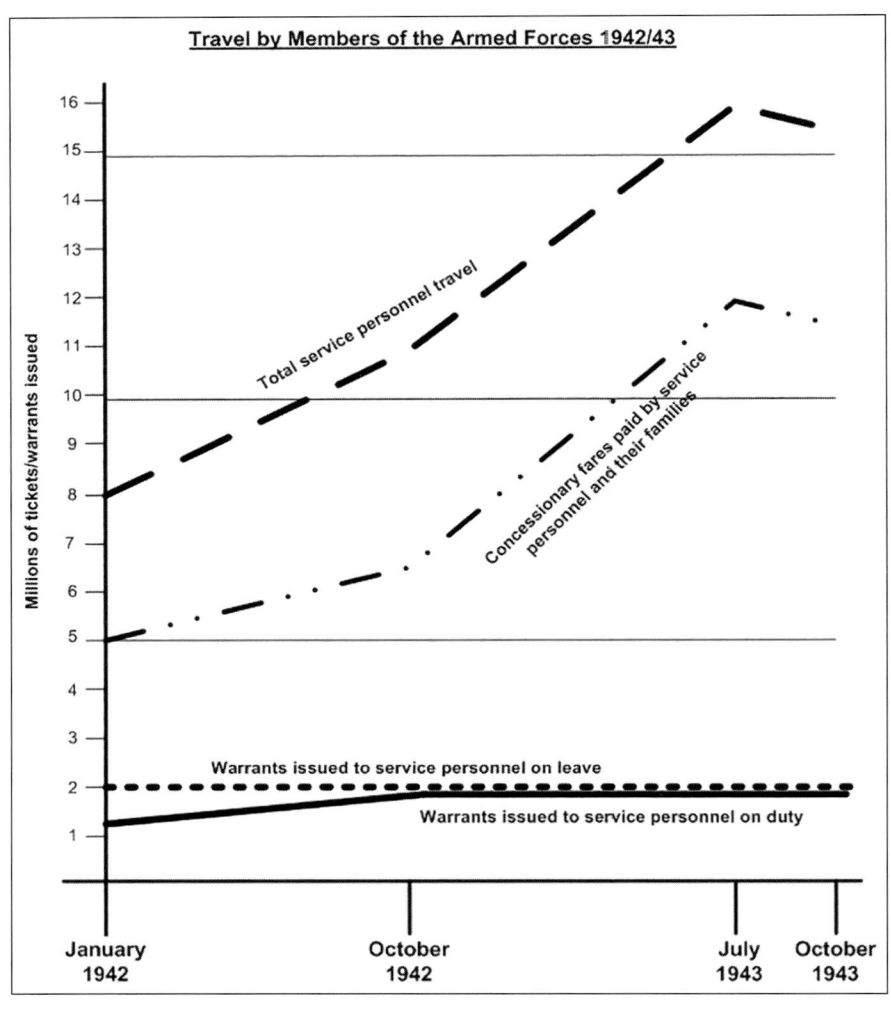

Source: The National Archives Railway Executive Passenger Sub-Committee
AN 3/18

possible to provide cheap facilities – but this had to depend on the military situation'.

After this hiatus matters did improve for any parents wishing to visit their evacuated children. It was decided that vouchers were to be issued for any day of the week, and the validity of the tickets purchased was to cover two days (or three days if there was no Sunday service when tickets were issued on a Saturday as they would be valid for the return journey the following Monday). This meant that the parents would travel on 'ordinary' trains. If an overnight stay was necessary due to distance and the railway timetable, the voucher would not be issued without proof of the recipient having booked accommodation – parents were not allowed to 'take a chance' on finding a bed for the night. Also, once again, parents had to undertake not to return home with their child. The new ticketing arrangement was a major improvement since with the experience from the previous November it had become clear that the one-day tickets were causing real hardship for parents making the longer distance journeys. The Ministry of Transport civil servant dealing with evacuation issues, Alfred Rake, acknowledged that all of those concerned with the organisation of these visits would be subject to bitter criticism if parents travelling to distant destinations had to take extra early trains and arrive home extra late thereby enduring two nights 'sleep' sitting upright in a third–class carriage. Another reason given for the extra flexibility was that with the increase in wartime traffic, Sundays were increasingly becoming a 'normal' day, and furthermore many parents who wished to visit their children were now working on essential war work on Sundays.

The new revised arrangements required that every parent had to register with their local authority giving their name and address, the name or names of their children and their location in the reception area. Every parent would then be allowed to apply for up to two vouchers each month for each child and were to be given a card upon which would be recorded the issue of each voucher. The new scheme would permit parents to buy day or two-day return tickets to visit their children without any restriction on distance to be travelled, date of travel, or train service to be used. Vouchers had to be obtained three days before the date of travel and on presentation at the ticket office the bearer would be entitled to the cheaper tickets. Many local authorities continued to have misgivings about the scheme. There was the ever-present risk that homesick children would be brought home or that the 'routines' that had been established by the host families would be disrupted. The LCC cautioned that it would be inadvisable to travel by an overnight train and thus arrive very early at a child's billet at an hour or so before the household was awake. Therefore, those travelling overnight were advised to have a 'picnic' breakfast in the station waiting room so as to delay their arrival at the billet until after the family had their routine breakfast. By the same reasoning, parents were told that they should not overstay their welcome at a billet beyond the child's normal bedtime but instead return to the railway station to await their return train.

The SR, despite its gallant efforts in moving the troops during the Dunkirk crisis, was the overall loser in terms of passenger traffic. A large proportion of the railway's income was from commuter traffic, which while this did not fall away completely, the reduction in the numbers of civil servants travelling up to town each day did have an impact. Potentially worse than any loss of trade due to businesses and government departments evacuating from London was the closing off to the public of a huge chunk of the territory served by the SR. With the nation now under threat of imminent invasion after the Dunkirk retreat, the Minister of Home Security, Sir John Anderson, issued an official order creating what was described as a 'defence area' along the coast from the Wash to Rye in Sussex extending twenty miles inland. Only residents were permitted to travel to the area unless there was a genuine business need, and police were expected to enforce this Order which specifically barred anybody making a journey for holiday or pleasure purposes. Later, in July, this defence area was extended as far as west as Portsmouth and also included the whole of the Isle of

Wight. These restrictions were to continue throughout most of the war period but were modified from time to time.

Rather than produce a map (perhaps it was reasoned that this would be of assistance to the enemy), the extent of the defence area was conveyed to the public by a list of railway stations that they could not buy tickets to without having a very good reason for visiting the area. This may have placed a degree of responsibility upon the railway clerks behind the ticket office window. No doubt they would have advised any potential traveller that they could not travel to say, Hastings or Canterbury or Swanley but it is questionable about how much authority they had to actually refuse the ticket. The police however would stop travellers at the railway stations and decide if the ticket holder had a *bona fide* reason for entering the defence area. A business or military reason for travelling into the defence area would be accepted, such as for example, the member of the Home Guard having to travel to Portsmouth to collect a critical gun spare part had to obtain a written letter from his commanding officer giving the reasons for the visit. An octogenarian, who as a boy lived in Kent, told me that his family did not often travel away from home by train during the war as 'there was nowhere to go' – an unfortunate situation for a youngster effectively barred from all the relatively local seaside resorts in Kent and East Sussex. He did however also voice the opinion that, as far as he can recall, when they did travel by train, it did not seem to be any more crowded or slower than either before or after the war. There was a concession given by the minister of home security that parents visiting their children billeted in defence areas would be allowed access. This concession was not likely to make much of an impact, the restricted zone along the south-eastern coast was an area from which most children had by 1940 been evacuated away from, not into.

The other three companies also had to concede early in 1941 that they too had suffered a considerable loss in main line traffic. The exact details of this loss of traffic were however something of an unknown since as a wartime economy measure the reduction in clerical staff had led to the 'suspension of the majority of information'. This resulted in the REC not being able to properly analyse the traffic data to make a reasoned comparison with the pre-war traffic statistics. Other industries were also suffering due to staff being called up for military service. The British Federation of Master Printers informed the REC that it was becoming increasingly more difficult to print railway timetables as many experienced printers were being 'called-up'. The reluctance to make significant timetable changes was one answer – but given the constantly changing disturbance to regular passenger traffic not the only answer – to a letter received by the REC late in January 1941 from Gilbert Szlumper who had now moved on from his duties for the War Office based at Southampton to be the railway control officer at the Ministry of Transport. The former SR general manager presented his views in what otherwise might have been seen as a personal letter, but as he was now a senior civil servant overseeing the railways the full committee had to take notice of his comments and formulate an answer. Szlumper wrote that recently he had heard from several sources on several occasions that there seemed to be only a tenuous link between the published railway timetables and the actual running times of the trains. In his view, the general public had a very good appreciation of the causes of late running, and he had received only a small number of complaints due to this. His concern was that many trains were running habitually late – very often by more or less the same amount each day and it was therefore misleading for the printed timetable to state that a train would arrive at say, 10.43am, when it never got there before 11.57am. According to Szlumper this incongruity had not only been observed in government circles but among his own travelling friends. He proposed that the railway companies' timetables should be reviewed and related to the actual traffic activities.

Meanwhile, for those regretting the loss of many of the dining cars offered by the railways, at many stations the station refreshment rooms were augmented by platform trolleys which the railway companies endeavoured to increase in number but difficulties due to platform congestion and the blackout restricted the use of this facility. In January 1941 due to the high demand for station railway food, which was available to the public 'off-the-ration', there was a shortage of food supplies to the railway station buffets. The REC wrote to the Ministry of Transport requesting a clear statement of policy in respect of food supplies for railway passengers. They did not receive a helpful reply, so the REC decided to place advertisements around the stations which proclaimed to the hungry public that the inadequate supply of foodstuffs was entirely due to the railway's inability to obtain sufficient food to meet the demand of members of HM forces and members of the public.

On 18 February 1941, the first meeting of a new REC subcommittee was convened. This was the catering committee which consisted of a member from each of the four main line railways. It was chaired by the LMSR representative, Arthur Towle. The committee secretary was Mr E.W. March who had catering experience working for the LNER. As well as the shortage of food supplies, an early issue was the replacement of crockery at the railway canteens which was being 'lost' due to theft and breakage. The government had recently made the proposal to grant fifty per cent of the cost to replace the shortfall, but this, the committee argued, would be insufficient to maintain the running of the refreshment facilities without making direct arrangements with the voluntary organisations staffing the canteens.

The shortage of available food meant that all of the companies were having difficulty in obtaining supplies for Army, Navy and Air Force personnel who were travelling by train. The committee argued that there could be no hardship to other caterers in giving priority in the supply of certain foods to the railway companies since services provided to troops and other travellers in no way conflicted with those of other caterers. Furthermore, the committee argued that since the provision of meals for troops was in the national interest and for the most part unremunerative, priority should be given to the railway companies and their suppliers so as to perform the important work of catering for the troops, a task that had been given 'so much attention in parliament and the press'. The Ministry of Food had offered to give assistance towards catering for service personnel travelling to and from their depots – that is 'official' military transport – but refused to contribute towards the serving of food to troops or naval ratings making 'leave' journeys or to the general public. The committee noted that the public were continuing to demand food when travelling particularly when trains were regularly delayed due to important freight movements or enemy action.

The railways' catering efforts were to be further handicapped due to the introduction of the registration of female labour in March 1941. The REC approached the Ministry of Labour requesting that their female workers at station refreshment rooms and on the few remaining restaurant cars should be considered as doing 'national work' and therefore exempt from other employment. Women were not keen to be employed in refreshment rooms or kiosks until they had the assurance that they were officially performing 'war work'. The REC catering committee put forward a strong case that the women were carrying out war work during a time of extreme national emergency. It was argued that due to the frequent and inevitable delays to train services, food and drink had to be provided to the large numbers of troops, soldiers on leave and refugees from bombed areas who often had long waits at stations awaiting connecting trains. Furthermore, if all men of military age other than those who were physically incapable of serving were removed from railway service, the companies believed that most of the restaurant and buffet car services could be retained staffed by men who were over military age and by women. In September 1941 the Ministry of Labour and National Service decreed that dining car and refreshment staff men of non-military age and women would not be taken for other work of national importance, but railway hotel staff were expressly excluded from this agreement. Many of the railway owned hotels had been taken over by the government for military and other purposes, with only those at the principal termini in the major cities and some remote locations such as Kyle of Lochalsh remaining available for passengers' use.

The subcommittee stressed that it was important that the few remaining dining car services should be maintained. It cited the negative experience of the early days of the war when it had been hoped that the dining cars could be safely withdrawn and meals supplied to passengers from the refreshment rooms, lunch boxes and snack boxes. In 1941, due to the strict rationing of food, the supply of food in boxes for passengers to take onto the trains had proved to be problematic. It was asserted it was not possible to replace the thousands of meals that were served each day on the restaurant cars by alternate means. Dining cars were providing meals more economically and with less waste than simple snacks from refreshment rooms, trolleys or kiosks. Furthermore, due to the shortages there was insufficient meat or other suitable foods to provide packed meals of any kind. The subcommittee asserted that immediate action was necessary to prevent a serious breakdown in services. On 24 March 1941 it finally decided that the luncheon basket scheme was to be discontinued due to the lack of suitable food and equipment. In July the provision of breakfast and tea baskets was reduced and only available to passengers at a few locations where it was practical to have this facility, and any reference to the supply of these baskets withdrawn from all railway publicity.

A later decision by the catering subcommittee in October 1941 was that due to the lack of staff and supplies, many of the services offered to passengers would have to be withdrawn or reduced. These included tobacco kiosks at stations, individual refreshment rooms and platform trolleys. The full Railway Executive Committee insisted that this bad news should be not published by them, but that the railway companies should announce the withdrawals themselves.

Despite the early fanfare of publicity for a few selected trains, overall, the standard of lighting on the trains continued to remain poor and any improvements was going to take time to fully implement. The

SR, despite being joint pioneers with the LMSR, conceded that the improved lighting on the suburban trains was a more difficult problem to solve. They cited the need for most trains to make frequent stops at stations and the consequential opening of the many doors along the length of the train would cast a stream of visible illumination along the whole platform length. Despite the early progress on certain main line rolling stock, such practical difficulties were to result in very little being done to solve the difficult problem of providing better lighting in all trains. Three years had to elapse before the Ministry of Home Security, a government department with responsibilities far removed from the practicalities of operating a railway, suddenly pronounced that improved lighting would be provided to allow all passengers to read in 'reasonable comfort' on the trains.

Those who regularly had to travel by train would have known that after the initial flourish of activity in 1939, it would be fair to say that as far they could observe, overall, very little had been done to provide adequate lighting in the carriages during the blackout and thus the minister's announcement was met with scepticism and disbelief. The initial public outrage of not being able to travel in lit carriages during the blackout had largely dissipated after the phoney war. Passengers had come to terms with the fact that they were now engaged in a 'real' war with life threatening dangers following Dunkirk, the Battle of Britain and the start of bombing. To enable the essential freight operations to be carried out at night however much work had been done to improve the level of lighting in the marshalling yards. In February 1941 experiments were carried out in the vicinity of Balleymoney in Northern Ireland to determine what was likely to be visible to an enemy bomber flying overhead and to thereby determine what level of lighting could be used by the railways. A spotter aircraft was used to fly above test lighting rigs situated in a non-industrial area on six moonless nights when conditions were judged to be average or below average for winter.

The results from these experiments led to an REC subcommittee instigating a code of practice for railway lighting. This covered lighting at goods and passenger stations and included the shielding of signals and the cabs of steam locomotives. In brief, the code permitted two levels of lighting for use at all of the railway premises. What was defined as 'category B' lighting was either blue, amber or white, which was so screened that no light was thrown above the horizontal and the level of illumination did not exceed 0.002 ft. candles at ground level or on any surface visible from the air. (A foot candle was the unit used in pre-SI days and was equal to 10.76 Lux.) This type of lighting was installed at many passenger stations as it was a very low level of illumination and could remain switched on during the air raids and this innovation was welcomed by passengers. Category C lighting was white lighting which was so screened that no light was thrown above the horizontal and did not exceed 0.2 ft. candles at ground level or on any surface visible from the air. This level of lighting was used in the marshalling yards, motive power depots and goods yards. Category C lighting was defined as 'exempted lighting' and spotters were posted to ensure that it was extinguished when an alarm was given, or hostile aircraft were spotted. The railway staff used as spotters had to be positioned such that they got a clear indication of any immediate danger, which did not necessarily have to be high up on a rooftop. The railway had to ensure that its spotters were provided with some reliable form of communication to enable them to give warning of the imminent raid. The lighting was extinguished immediately following an alarm from the Royal Observer Corps or the railway's own spotter. This arrangement seems to have worked well, but the police often intervened when they judged that the railway company had infringed the code of practice that had been agreed with the Ministry of Home Security. Notwithstanding the need to create blackout conditions, all of the signal lamps (screened if possible), lamps at level crossings and other safety lamps were retained during air raids. The improvements to lighting in the marshalling yards proved to be successful allowing 'normal' operation during the nights that were not subject to air raids.

Even with 'improved' category B lighting at the stations, they remained dangerous places for passengers. A writer to *The Times* in 1942 commented on what he described as 'platform dangers' claiming to have witnessed five accidents occurring when passengers alighted from trains at blacked-out stations. The unlucky passengers had not realised that the train had not yet come to a complete standstill. On one occasion a mother had been carrying her baby, she instinctively pushed the baby clear of danger but then partly slipped between train and platform. The writer blamed the railway for these unfortunate incidents stating that the trains on that line were coming 'to a stop in a much more dilatory way than usual', and he suggested that this was intentional in an attempt to save brake wear. The Railway Inspectorate reported that in 1940 – before the agreement to install category B lighting – there had been twenty-eight fatalities due to attempts to enter or leave a train; thirty-one died falling from trains and twelve more falling off platforms. In the 'slam-door' era when passengers had control of the opening and closing of the train doors, many accidents were caused by careless and impatient individuals. The Railway Inspectorate however concluded that the station blackout conditions had been a contributory factor in twenty-five of these incidents. And, of course, for every fatality there must have been more 'near misses' that did not become part of the fatality statistics.

What was described by the government as a standard to ensure reading in 'reasonable comfort' was a huge task. Before the date of the announcement there had not been any substantive progress made on fitting improved lighting and to carry out the ministry's promise would have required work on 250,000 compartments and this would often have meant modifications to lighting circuits and painting white the black internal surface of lampshades. It was questioned if such an effort in time and labour was appropriate during the war particularly as the blackout rules were regularly being broken by passengers who would refuse to lower the blinds at night and, worse, blinds would be damaged and lighting fittings tampered with. Furthermore, no doubt as a result of the wartime rationing in place, many less honest members of the public saw the trains as a ready source of difficult to obtain items. Despite the public's craving for better lighting, a prime target for these thieves were the easily removed light bulbs in the railway carriages. The SR issued a poster with the bold title 'THEY STEAL YOUR LIGHT'. The smaller text below the title claimed that thousands of bulbs and – the very necessary in blackout maintenance – shades had been stolen and that the railway had successfully prosecuted twenty-six individuals who had been duly fined up to £5 plus costs. The SR requested that its passengers assisted with keeping the train lights on by reporting to a member of the railway staff anybody stealing bulbs and other fittings.

It was not just a lack of lighting that was the result of criminal activity; other commodities began to disappear from the train toilet compartments and the public lavatories at the stations. Solid soap was being rationed and this quickly disappeared, resulting in the provision of this type of soap being discontinued on 23 February 1942. If liquid or powdered soap could be obtained this would be provided on the trains. There was a similar issue with the disappearance of toilet paper, but the railways did continue to provide this essential item. Given that it was generally the better-off in society who dined on the trains, it is perhaps surprising that the freshy laundered linen napkins were also disappearing from restaurant cars and consequently the railways soon had a shortage of the napkins, and these had to be withdrawn. In the months before the inevitable decision to withdraw the linen items was reluctantly made, the railways' staff had resorted to reducing the size of and carrying out darning repairs on the table clothes and napkins.

Compared to the pre-war delivered levels of service, by the end of 1940 the railways' timetables showed a significant reduction in the number of main line train services being provided and an increase in overall journey times. Passengers were making less use of the railways and there was a further significant reduction in passenger journeys after the fall of Dunkirk. The LMSR and LNER passenger journeys decreased significantly in 1940. The SR's passenger numbers fell even more dramatically due to the establishment of the 'defence zone' in south-east England, the reduction in commuter traffic into London and a disproportionate amount of disruption due to enemy action. Only the GWR seemed to be taking an early advantage of the inevitable increase in passenger mileage. Later in the war there was to be an increasing need to travel due to the demands of war, therefore the end of 1940 may be seen as the low point in passenger traffic numbers.

Chapter 7

Surviving the Blitz

Throughout the period of heavy German air raids on this country, the arteries of the nation, the railways, with their extensive dock undertakings, were subjected to intensive attacks. Yet the grim determination, unwavering courage and constant resourcefulness of the railwaymen of all ranks has enabled the results of the damage to be overcome very speedily and communications restored without delay.

Winston Churchill, 1944

Any residual hopes that the railways would be able to operate a wartime service that was as near as possible to the peacetime 'business as usual' soon evaporated after the Dunkirk evacuation in 1940. The enemy was now only a short distance away across the English Channel and threatening invasion and the Battle of Britain began in July and lasted until October. Thwarted by the RAF's Fighter Command the enemy held back from a full invasion and began to do what had been feared and predicted; that was the bombing of the civilian population. In August there were bombs dropped on London, but this was only the prelude to what became known as the 'Blitz' during which 40,000 civilians were killed. The Blitz continued until May 1941 with most of the bombing raids occurring during the hours of darkness. London had half of the national total number of casualties, suffering more than any other city across Britain. Ports on the west coast where the essential supplies were being imported were the target for many Luftwaffe raids. Principal among these was Liverpool which suffered bombing damage that was second only to London. Other ports in the west that the Luftwaffe bombed included Belfast, Bristol and Cardiff, while on the south coast the cities with the Royal Navy establishments, Plymouth and Portsmouth, were also attacked. Hull on the English east coast was doubly unfortunate, because the bomber squadrons flew directly over the city every night on their way to and from other targets and should for any reason the attack was abandoned due to say, poor weather conditions, it was convenient to make the town the secondary, alternative target. Inland cities such as Coventry, Manchester and Sheffield were also bombed. It will be noted that the towns where the government departments had been relocated to in 1939 such as Bath, Harrogate and Colwyn Bay were untouched during the main Blitz period, Bath was only later to be a target during the Baedeker raids. During the Blitz period the Luftwaffe caused extensive damage to the railways' track, stations and rolling stock. Railway services were often also disrupted due to bomb damage to adjacent non-railway locations, when there were fires at lineside locations or when debris was strewn across the tracks. Unexploded bombs lying on the rails or on railway embankments also stopped traffic until they were made safe. The German air force concentrated its attacks on ports and factories, but several important railway stations were bombed, often with much loss of life to the passengers and staff. Not surprisingly, the Blitz was also a reason for a reduction in passenger rail travel. In May 1941, Gilbert Szlumper requested that the REC issue a notice requesting that passengers refrain from travelling to the heavily bombed city of Liverpool except on urgent business.

The commuter services running across the extensive suburban network around London also suffered severe disruption. For the SR, one of the worse nights was on 7 September 1940. Commuters intending to travel home that evening took refuge in the public shelters at Waterloo station but found that when they emerged in the morning all traffic from Waterloo had ceased and they had to find alternate routes home by bus, tram or taxi. A direct hit on the line between Waterloo and Vauxhall had opened a fifty-foot-wide crater spanning six of the eight running lines and leaving the other two severely damaged. This was probably the worst disruption to passenger services as this, one of the busiest of the London termini, was closed until 19 September, almost two weeks later. At other locations down the line from Waterloo there was more war damage, also at Vauxhall a bomb severely damaged the bridge at Juxon Street; at Clapham Junction bombs struck the carriage sidings, derailing and damaging rolling stock; at Wimbledon a bomb was dropped on the north side of the station damaging an LTPB train standing at the platform and many other incidents at stations on the south-western network from Waterloo at Norbiton, Tolworth, Wandsworth and Putney. Following any air raid, the SR's regular commuters had to be made aware of where enemy action had caused disruption, so the railway established travel information posts in kiosks at its most important stations. To further assist the travelling public, the SR also made arrangements for the latest travelling information to be available at a number of local shops. By providing up-to-date travel information it was hoped that regular passengers would be able to avoid fruitless journeys to their usual station on a day when it was often possible to travel by any of the alternative services that the railway had been able to offer nearer to their homes. The information posts and posters in shops provided the intending passengers with news of the alternative routes or the emergency bus services. The addresses of the shops where the emergency travel information posters were to be found was displayed at the local stations.

On 13 October 1940 the GWR's London terminus was bombed. The main line station suffered indirect damage, but the railway's hotel and offices were severely damaged. Worse, the Praed Street underground station took a direct hit where there was a crowd of passengers waiting on the platform. Six of these were killed and others received life-changing injuries such as the loss of limbs. The previous night, which might be described as a 'typical' night during the Blitz, other GWR locations in west London were bombed but without fatalities, these being on the Brentford branch, on the West London Railway between

Clapham and Willesden junctions that was part owned by the GWR and at its principal locomotive depot at Old Oak Common.

Despite all the obvious dangers and difficulties, during the months of the Blitz the railways resolutely continued to operate as best they could. Operating a railway system through what had become a war zone was challenging, but the evidence shows that the railway staff did not shy away from maintaining the service as far as was possible in the circumstances and often exhibited great heroism, ingenuity and presence of mind. The mobility of the civilian population who were required to travel long distances was seriously disrupted as trains were frequently delayed and forced to divert away from damage locations. Travel during the latter months of 1940 was a starkly different experience to travel in the same months in 1939 when initially, apart from a reduction in speeds, very little had changed. A *Manchester Guardian* journalist offered an intriguing account of a journey that he had made from London to the Midlands. Setting off from his home in north London he was aware of the recent destruction, noticing the damage to the Victorian buildings, with their windows often boarded up and the neat continuity of the rows of houses broken as large sections of brickwork had been blasted away. Adding to the usual mix of people to be seen on the streets were firemen and air raid wardens busy attending to the human and physical damage in the aftermath of the recent air raids. London had been the target for three raids already that day so a fourth was anticipated. On arrival at the unnamed London railway terminus – but surely it was St Pancras – his first impression was the lack of passengers waiting. He described the station as being 'not full'. Most of the passengers waiting at the station or boarding the train, the journalist observed, were wearing military uniform of some description. The train did quickly fill up with passengers and left the station at just after 7.30pm, ominously travelling north under a clear blue sky punctuated by barrage balloons. Any chance to enjoy the beautiful full moon – a 'bomber's moon' – illuminating the camouflaged lineside buildings was restricted as when it grew dark the guard came through the train making sure that all of the window blinds had been properly pulled down. The train pulled into a small country station and came to a halt. The train's dim lighting was switched off and overhead could be heard the familiar drone of the enemy bombers. Two very familiar low thuds were heard indicating the detonation of bombs that had been dropped not very far away from the stationary train. The sound brought the realisation that at that moment they were all in mortal danger. A party of previously very boisterous sailors further down the train immediately stopped singing and a communal feeling of great trepidation spread throughout the train as they all waited to see if any more bombs would be dropped. After about ten minutes the sky lit up with anti-aircraft fire and if you peeped behind the window blinds, a solitary aircraft could be seen in the moonlight sky which one of the more knowledgeable passengers assured the others in the compartment that it was 'ours'. After being stationary for about ten minutes, much to everybody's relief the train moved off and continued on its journey. On arrival at his destination the journalist was told by the ticket collector that the last day or two had been without incident.

During the Blitz, the railway staff regularly exhibited bravery and devotion to duty in their efforts to keep services running. In September 1940, an attack on the LNER's Channelsea carriage sidings at Stratford set many carriages on fire, the shunters on site managed to couple up locomotives to pull carriages out of the yard before they were all consumed by fire. Only eighteen carriages – all spare stock – were badly damaged by the fire. The SR's extensive electrified railway network suffered difficulties due to a Luftwaffe attack on its Durnsford Road generating station at the height of the Blitz on 14 October 1940. This power station provided about half of all the electricity used by the Southern Electric services. A German bomb struck one of the station's chimneys and caused serious damage to the boilers below, thereby severely reducing the station's output. Fortunately, there was no damage to either the generators or the switchgear, but there was disruption to the station's water supply. Within a few days the water supply was not fully restored, but 10,000kW – only about one third of the station's maximum output – was available, but a fortnight later the situation did improve when it was reported that 21,000kW was now available. Due to the wartime timetable fewer trains were being run, but during the electricity supply emergency those that were running had to travel at a reduced speed. This was because the reduced electrical capacity available resulted in a much lower voltage on the conductor rails at many locations thereby slowing the trains. The passengers on the electric trains suffered double because to further save the precious electricity the train heating fuses had been removed. As usual little was publicly divulged at the time and Bernard Darwin was to assert later in his *War on the Line* – the Southern Railway's 'official' history of the war – that the passengers were not made aware of any specific problem as such foibles as slow running trains were what they had come to expect in wartime. A very glib statement for it was winter, and the passengers must have been suspicious that the very cold trains indicated that something was amiss. The emergency situation lasted until the remedial work was completed on 3 February 1941, this included a new chimney which for expediency and speed of erection was made not from the usual masonry but from what was in wartime a very precious commodity – steel.

Adding to the frustrations due to the compounding effect of reduced train services, the reduction in overall speed of the trains and the need to hold trains to allow the passage of troop trains, because of the need for wartime secrecy the railways were forbidden to offer any explanation for the delays to their passengers. During the Blitz in 1940 there would be sudden and quite random attacks by the Luftwaffe which effectively closed down sections of the line which would halt passenger trains at inaccessible locations or force these trains to have to take laborious unplanned diversions. The wartime passenger may have understood the problems ('Don't you know there's a war on?'), but the railways were soon to become something of an 'Aunt Sally' to some who were frustrated by the reduced timetables and delays, and by December 1940, many regular railway travellers were developing an attitude of resignation. A weariness was setting in, too much time was being spent standing and waiting at railway stations. Many Londoners whose workplace was in London, and before the war had lived in the city, moved away from the centre to the relative safety of the outer suburbs for what became known as 'dormitory purposes'. This resulted in extra daily travel to reach their offices. While those making infrequent long journeys to the provinces might tolerate a few delays, interruptions to an extended daily commute soon became a morale sapper.

It was to be a bleak Christmas in 1940, but nonetheless the railways provided extra trains which many people used to temporarily unite families. Many of those who had made their own evacuation arrangements and left the cities for what they hoped would be 'safer' locations, began to have second thoughts when the bombing became nationwide. The thought of a Christmas at home was often the final incentive to return. The returnees included Mrs. Grady, a young mother who had evacuated with her two sons to live with friends in Bolton. The final decision to return was made after hearing the German bombers flying above them every night on their way to bomb Liverpool. They feared that Bolton was now as dangerous a place to live as it was back in the London suburbs. The family made the brave decision to return to Bexley and re-join the father who had remained at home to carry out his essential war work at Woolwich Arsenal. This small family group found that all the trains bound for London appeared to be full, with many passengers travelling in the corridor perched on their luggage. After standing for a while the guard escorted the three of them to a compartment with spare seats. It is most likely that the 'full' compartments did have the odd single unoccupied seat, but the compartments might have appeared full because the passengers were spreading themselves and placing small items of luggage on an empty seat. The assertive guard, noting the young mother standing in the corridor, organised the seating rearrangement which probably provided them with two seats – the smaller boy sitting on his mother's lap. Perhaps one of the occupants with a spare seat beside them was asked to move into an adjacent compartment which also had a spare seat. It was the same guard who later kindly walked through the train with the mother and her little boys to the restaurant car where it had been arranged for those with children to be served first. The LMSR's 'simple menu' of three courses on that day was tomato soup, stew and jam roll.

The journey south was long and slow, and frustratingly the train was brought to a halt by signals at Crewe for over two hours. Exactly why the train was so slow was not known to those on board, but the guard did walk the length of the train doing his best to offer reassurance and to keep all the passengers informed as best as he could. Delays to trains were not necessarily due to enemy action on the route ahead. The effect of even relatively minor damage to the railway could cause the tail-back of trains onto lines that otherwise were undamaged and safe to use. And direct damage to railway infrastructure was not the only reason to halt trains. Delays were also due to the presence of unexploded bombs that had been found either on railway land but clear of the running lines or on land which was just the other side of the boundary fence. Another hindrance to the passage of trains were buildings next to the railway which had been bombed, these might have been judged to be in imminent danger of collapse or were on fire. It is hardly surprising then that the train that Mrs Grady and her two boys were travelling on made frequent stops, since these could have been due to a number of causes, perhaps a hundred miles from where the train was brought to a halt. During December 1940 the main line into Euston suffered relatively little direct damage except for one very serious incident at Queen's Park station, four miles north of Euston, on Tuesday, 3 December. At 10.07pm a bomb fell on the electric lines, killing two of the railway staff and five passengers. Debris covered all six of the running lines through the station. Despite the upsetting circumstances staff promptly cleared all of the lines, and the fast line was back in service as early as 10.58pm.

Mrs. Grady and her two small charges had to endure the onset of darkness sitting in a stationary train illuminated only by the unhelpful blue bulbs. The passengers could only imagine what terrors were occurring outside the train, horrors that were unseen due to the drawing down of the blinds, dreading the drone of enemy aircraft overhead or the sounds from nearby bombs exploding on impact and the staccato of anti-aircraft fire as tracer bullets were sent high into the night sky.

Progress to Euston continued to be slow, but eventually the blacked-out train arrived at Euston. Luckily the family were spared the terror of being trapped in the train during a raid for as the train entered the station the air raid sirens sounded. The exact date of his childhood journey from Bolton to Bexley was not recorded by Derrek Grady in his testimony to the BBC's 'People's War' survey, but during December 1940 the LMSR lines north of London were repeatedly under attack. Throughout the late afternoon and the night of Sunday, 8 December there was a particularly heavy raid on London when there was severe damage to many important public buildings such as the House of Commons, Westminster Abbey, the Royal Mint, the National Gallery and the Royal Naval College at Greenwich as well as seven hospitals in and around London.

The only significant damages that occurred during this raid likely to indirectly affect the Euston main line were in the north of London away from the LMSR main line. At Caledonian Road and Barnsbury station at 7.20pm a bomb fell directly onto an electric train on its way from Broad Street to Watford, killing four of the passengers and a further seven receiving injuries. An LMSR staff member was also killed, and the train guard was injured. The station was closed to all traffic until 3.30pm the following afternoon. A bomb fell on the railway at Woodgrange Park station on the line that had once been part of the original London, Tilbury and Southend Railway. The only track damage was to two sidings but there was damage to signalling equipment. Another bomb fell on the track on the North London line near Dalston Junction, blocking the line south towards Poplar, westbound trains had to be terminated at Victoria Park in Hackney and the passengers transferred to a bus to take them on to Dalston Junction.

Having arrived at Euston, Mrs Grady and her sons then had to cross London to reach London Bridge station so as to travel on by an SR train to Bexley Heath. This proved to be a frightening experience, for having used the Underground to reach Bank station they were advised that they should walk from there to London Bridge because no trains were running during the air raid either over or under the Thames. Being outdoors in the middle of an air raid was a scary experience, but they pressed on as they were anxious to get home. On reaching the SR station the small party was greeted by porters who scooped up their luggage and briskly led them to their waiting train. The family was reunited at Bexley Heath at the end of a gruelling eighteen-hour journey from Bolton. Derek Grady's account highlights the dedication of the railway staff, the LMSR guard who went further than he needed to so as to look after the welfare of his younger passengers and the SR porters at London Bridge station for whom it would have been perfectly acceptable for them to have taken cover in a shelter during the air raid.

There was public recognition of the work by railway staff to keep the railways operational during the Blitz period. Press articles described in detail how what were euphemistically described as 'incidents' were dealt with in a professional and often heroic manner. Shielded by censorship the press was able to describe incidents such as a bomb that was dropped just before daybreak one morning onto the arches carrying a section of SR main line into London. Despite extensive damage to track and signalling, the SR's engineering department had partially repaired the signalling apparatus by midday, the track partially repaired later in the day at 5.30pm allowing three of the four running lines to be back in service. This feat, so it was claimed in a newspaper account, was made all the more praiseworthy as there were some delayed action bombs in the vicinity so the repairs were carried out by volunteer gangs. Presumably a bomb disposal team had made these bombs safe before trains were run through the repaired section. Other newspaper reports applauded how railway staff would have to stumble across the railway tracks in blackout conditions to ascertain damage, a task that would be dangerous enough in the dark but made more so as it was onto a railway on which trains were still running, and all the time fearful of the bombs falling all around. One example of extreme courage was that of a railwayman who pushed a wagon loaded with munitions clear of another wagon which was on fire. Such tales of cheery heroism might be dismissed as part of the wartime mythology generated by propaganda and over enthusiastic patriotism. Certainly, for every brave volunteer there may have been a more cautious railwayman hunkered down in the air raid shelter. But the evidence shows that all the bomb damage was repaired with incredible speed and the most extreme dangers would not necessarily have come from the initial bomb damage but from the subsequent dangers relating to work on unstable structures and possibly in close proximity to traffic on lines which had been partially restored to service.

Despite the dangerous travel conditions due to the Blitz, over the 1941 holiday period (counted as the day before Christmas Eve until the day after Boxing Day) the GWR ran 59 additional long-distance trains, the LNER 71, the LMSR 148 and the SR 18; an impressive total meeting the nation's desire for families to get together in wartime. In 1940 all four companies ran services on both Christmas Day and Boxing Day which is in stark contrast to the meagre service provided by the train operators today when it is usual for no trains to run on Christmas Day and Boxing Day, either 'normal' or 'extra'. The number of extra trains run, and it can be assumed that these were 'relief' trains to the scheduled trains that appeared in the public timetables, were however less than was required on a 'normal' weekday, and none of the railways needed to run any additional non-relief trains on Christmas Day. The GWR averaged 26 relief trains on a normal weekday, but an average of only six extra trains over the Christmas period. The corresponding count for the other railways was for the LNER 24 extra trains compared to an average of 12 over the Christmas period, for the LMSR 50 extra trains compared to 26 at Christmas and for the SR 10 on a normal weekday compared to only four at Christmas. On one day, Boxing Day, the SR did not run any extra trains.

Important railway locations continued to attract the Luftwaffe even after the intense period of aerial bombardment that constituted the Blitz. One of the important stations bombed was at York. Ninety-four people died in the attack during the early hours of 29 April 1942. This attack has been grouped with the so-called Baedeker raids, but those who witnessed the raid were in no doubt that the principal aim of the assault was to cause maximum damage to the railway station, sidings and locomotive depot and not to the historic York Minster. The iconic overall roof above the station and a train standing in one of the platforms below were set ablaze. The train was an overnight express from King's Cross to Edinburgh. It was reported that this train was composed of twenty coaches, and while some of these 'coaches' may have been parcels vans, it was not uncommon for such very long trains to be run in wartime. It was prompt action by both passengers and railway staff that saved much of the station and rolling stock. One lady passenger kicked incendiaries safely off the platform before moving on to administer urgent first aid to casualties. Shunters and an unnamed soldier uncoupled the carriages which were on fire which enabled the locomotive to pull fourteen of the twenty vehicles safely out of the station. The locomotive shed at York (now part of the National Railway Museum) was also bombed. The shed was set on fire, but LNER staff managed to recover over twenty locomotives and only three were damaged beyond repair. Sadly, for railway enthusiasts, one of the locomotives destroyed that night was one of Sir Nigel Gresley's magnificent A4 class pacifics, No. 4469 *Sir Ralph Wedgwood*. Not to be defeated by the enemy, station staff dragged desks out of the damaged buildings and had soon set up a temporary booking office which they had in use within a few hours of the raid. All of the through running lines were cleared of debris and were back in use only two days later. As was usual for security reasons, the public had to wait three months before the story was released to the press.

Another station bombed was the LNER's Middlesbrough station on August Bank Holiday Monday 1942. The German propaganda machine was to claim that it had destroyed 'military targets' and 'port installations' in the area on that day. Aided by the obscuring low cloud, what has been reported as a single German Dornier Do 217 aircraft – a twin engine heavy bomber – dropped two bombs through the station's glass and steel overall roof. In 2012 James Henwood gave the local newspaper his account of the bombing. He recalls that he was with his mother and older brother at the station seeing off his aunt when they heard the shrill wail of the air raid siren. This was a regular occurrence and, as usual, none of them took any notice. The two brothers with their mother watched from the station barrier as their aunt got into the Newcastle bound train which fortunately was the only train in the station at the time. They had just waved goodbye when the first bomb struck. James described the effect as a 'deep whoomph' rather than a bang and vividly recalls the ensuing chaos; he could not see anything, and he had knocked over his mother and brother as the whole roof structure collapsed onto the platforms and the Newcastle train below. The initial terror subsided, and thoughts turned to the injured. The boy's aunt was unhurt, and she was able to scramble out of the wrecked train but was, not unsurprisingly, in a state of deep shock. The first bomb had fallen through the roof and exploded immediately in front of the locomotive while the second bomb landed on part of the station buildings. The explosion had created a fourteen-metre gap in the roof and a steel beam had crashed down across one of the carriages. The driver and fireman on the locomotive were both injured, the driver survived but the fireman died of his injuries in hospital nine days later. Another fatality was the train guard. Many people were rescued from the wrecked carriages, and these included an LNER ticket inspector.

A total of eight railway employees and passengers were killed. It was not until 3 November that, due to censorship, details of the station bombing were to be revealed to civilians in the northeast.

Such an event caused severe disruption, but as a priority the LNER immediately organised alternative routes for the local freight traffic. For its passengers the railway enlisted the help of the local bus operator, United Automobile Service Ltd, who provided a fleet of buses for the emergency replacement road service. It was claimed that specialist railway staff had cleared the track sufficiently that within two and a half hours goods trains could pass through the station. The passenger services were restored only one and a half days after the raid.

The bombing raids were soon contributing to the rise in civilians travelling by train. Due to the destruction of housing and a wish to reside well away from locations that were the targets for enemy action, by the end of the recognised Blitz period, the SR was transporting 20,000 passengers daily into Portsmouth, Southampton and Plymouth. This necessitated the provision of special trains for this new class of 'commuter'. At Southampton many of the local workers whose homes had been destroyed were issued with extra 'workmen's' tickets for use on the special trains provided for the unfortunate displaced men and women so that they could travel into the blitzed city to reach their place of employment early in the morning and at the end of the day travel back to what they hoped would only be temporary accommodation. Southampton based workers travelled into the city from locations as far away as Bournemouth and Andover. Similar arrangements were made by the GWR in Bristol and the LMSR in Liverpool.

Due to damage as a result of enemy action, the railways often had to pay local bus companies to provide a bus replacement service. These amounts paid out do not seem huge when viewed from the twenty-first century. During the second half of 1943 the total paid out by all of the railways was £2,095, this was the bus companies' income from the special buses ordered by the railways and no statistics were collected to assess the extra revenue generated by bus travel due to the general disruption of railway services during the blitz. Due to shortages of clerical staff after 1943 the REC did not continue to collect the wartime bus replacement statistics.

The figure of £2,095 was mainly due to a single incident at Brighton. The SR paid £2,039 of it because of the damage to the London Road viaduct at Brighton which on 25 May 1943 was attacked by a Focke-Wulf fighter-bomber. One bomb demolished two arches, leaving the tracks suspended in mid-air. Within 24 hours the SR had completed temporary repairs and instigated a limited resumption of traffic; the full service was operating within a month. It is not recorded, but it is probable that train services between Brighton and Eastbourne were diverted via Wivelsfield on the main London to Brighton line, and the buses provided a local service on part of the Lewes to Brighton line.

Not unexpectedly it was perceived that the Blitz had a detrimental effect on the amount of traffic carried by the railways. One civil servant however did an analysis of the traffic performance during the war and claimed that, against expectations, any detrimental effect was relatively lower than might be expected. He analysed the railways' performance using industry standard measures of performance. These were freight tonnage carried, train miles, and passenger and freight traffic receipts. These were compared with results from the pre-war years, the early days of the war and the Blitz period. All four metrics show a modest rise during the 1930s following the Great Depression, then the 'bad year' of 1938 when receipts fell but paradoxically train miles and freight tonnage increased, clearly showing why the 'Square Deal' campaign was so important to the railway companies. Receipts continued to decline in 1939 but started to rise at the outbreak of war as extra traffic boosted income. The figures did dip at the start of the Blitz but remained higher than at the beginning of the war. Given the extreme pressures that were placed upon the railways during the Blitz the results were, in the circumstances, surprisingly good.

Chapter 8

The Government's Dilemma as Passenger Numbers Rise

The slogan 'Is your journey really necessary?' was originally introduced by the railway companies, to whom is due much of the credit for the considerable success which it has had.

Noel–Baker, Parliamentary Secretary to the
Minister of War Transport, Hansard, 2 March 1943

There was a huge population shift during the Second World War when a staggering total of sixty million changes of address were recorded as workers and their families relocated to take employment at new wartime manufacturing or research establishments; evacuated themselves from danger areas due to fear of being bombed; or they were forced to move some distance from their place of employment after their homes had been destroyed. Overall, this disruption of extended families created new and diverse mobility needs which often resulted in additional travel by train. Every individual would have had his or her own specific mobility requirements and the government would have expected them all to consider whether or not any of the journeys that they made were strictly 'necessary'.

But all of these completely understandable and valid needs of the passengers had to be balanced against the increasing demands on the railways in respect of goods traffic. With Britain defeated on the land in Europe, it was left to the RAF to fight off the enemy in the sky and consequently the threat of invasion diminished in March 1941 when Hitler, thwarted in his attempt to conquer Great Britain, turned his troops eastwards for another campaign – this time attacking Greece and Yugoslavia and later to invade the USSR. Meanwhile the Royal and merchant navies continued the war in the inhospitable Atlantic Ocean. The maritime operation to supply military equipment, raw materials, food and fuel for the nation has since been given the name the 'Battle of the Atlantic'. As part of this tremendous endeavour the imported goods from the United States and elsewhere had to be moved by the railways from ports situated on the west coast of England, such as Liverpool, to inland destinations which were spread around the country.

As well as coping with the increasing demands to carry the imported traffic, the railways had to cope with another coal shortage crisis during the winter of 1940/41 which necessitated the REC having to contemplate the withdrawal of some passenger trains so as to clear the lines for the additional coal trains. One estimate in an REC internal memo stated that three passenger trains would need to be withdrawn to accommodate a single slow-moving coal train comprised of the small, unbraked coal trucks. Such a massive passenger service reduction was not deemed to be possible, but it was decided that some of the less important passenger trains could be suspended to free up the track and as a bonus release the locomotives and crews for use on the extra coal trains. The LNER had already made passenger service reductions in the north-east of England to permit additional coal trains but further reductions were deemed necessary in the south. The REC was keen to ensure that as far as possible any services that were likely to be used by industrial workers employed in war production were safeguarded. Given the nature of the underground network in London it was unsurprising the LPTB did not need to cut any of its services, but one bottleneck was situated on one of its lines. This was the former Metropolitan Railway's 'widened lines' route which carried coal (and other goods traffic) from the LNER and LMSR across London from King's Cross and St Pancras to the yards in the south of London. The line runs below ground through Farringdon and emerges at what was then Snow Hill Junction, next to the SR's

Holborn Viaduct station. The line then crosses over the River Thames at Blackfriars. It was decided that from Monday, 6 January 1941 additional coal trains to the SR would be routed through London using the widened lines. The LNER had running powers over the LPTB track from King's Cross as far as Farringdon before its trains branched off to Moorgate. To be able to accommodate the upsurge in coal traffic the LNER was instructed to terminate its Finsbury Park to Moorgate service at King's Cross. The LPTB claimed that they had sufficient capacity on its Metropolitan and Circle lines to accommodate the former LNER passengers beyond King's Cross who it described as 'black-coated' workers, that is office clerical workers. The SR, whose electric trains joined this route at Snow Hill junction before crossing the Thames, removed from the timetable thirty trains a day which been previously operated between Holborn Viaduct and Crystal Palace (High Level) station. To compensate for the loss of these trains the SR operated a shuttle service along the branch from Crystal Palace (High Level) to Nunhead – a station where passengers were able to travel onwards to London by changing to other trains. This branch was later to be an early casualty of railway closure, for despite it being a relatively recently electrified railway, it was to be closed to all passengers in 1954. The destruction of the Crystal Palace building by fire on 30 November 1936 was a contributory cause for the line's demise, since previously the line carried crowds to the events held at the venue.

Also, from Monday, 6 January 1941 the LMSR was forced to make alterations to its services in the Birmingham locality due to the coal situation. Many services had to be suspended on each working day including three trains in each direction between Birmingham and King's Norton via Camp Hill, a Saltby to Whitacre train and a Whitacre to Birmingham train. Another train suspended was a Birmingham to Leicester service which did carry important war workers, but in this case a bus replacement was provided. Other trains were diverted to run by different routes such as a Derby to Birmingham train which was diverted through Whitacre. Some trains did not run for the usual full distance, for example one Birmingham to Ashchurch train in each direction daily started or terminated at Barnett Hill.

A REC subcommittee also began to investigate ways of persuading the public not to take unnecessary journeys and met the editors of *John Bull* and *The People*, urging them to impress upon their readers the necessity for avoiding needless travel. For purely commercial reasons a proposal that propaganda posters be displayed in railway carriage compartments was rejected by one committee member, John Elliot, the assistant general manager of the SR and a publicity mastermind for that railway company. He advised caution – these precious spaces brought in advertising revenue for the railway companies; and posters in the carriages would only be seen by those already on the train, possibly already partaking in an 'unnecessary' journey. The railways continued to believe that they could not refuse the reasonable 'traffic that presents itself' and looked to 'manage' the situation by producing less aggressive, more people-centred posters advising the public as to how to travel in comfort; these used humour to seek the cooperation from passengers making their 'necessary' journeys. The need to reduce passenger demand with the decreased number of train services and the perceived increase in congestion and overcrowding on the trains provoked the *People* newspaper in early 1942 to invite suggestions from its readers. In a spirit of public service the REC reviewed all of these amateur proposals which had been sent to the newspaper. Subcommittee members Elliot and Grand reviewed all the suggestions and produced a report. Several proposals involved service personnel's travel arrangements such as stationing soldiers closer to home or modifications to the length of home leave, bizarrely attaching essential freight traffic to passenger trains but all were deemed to be impractical or were outside of the REC's authority.

Parliament published its 'Tenth Report from the Select Committee on National Expenditure Session 1940 – 1941' which commented on the increasing congestion at the ports. It was noted that as the war progressed the type of import had 'in some important respects' changed. It was argued that as the fabricated material that was then being delivered was of 'greater length and heavier weight' than before the war and therefore the railways needed to build special wagons to accommodate this new class of traffic. For the railways however the most important comment came towards the end of the report which was the strong recommendation that the Ministry of Transport should immediately give urgent consideration to issuing an instruction to the REC to implement drastic reductions to the railways' passenger services but opined that these reductions should only be made on specified days. Early in 1941 a report entitled 'Land Transportation in Great Britain' was prepared for Sir John Anderson, who was by then the Lord President, in which recommendations were made for steps to be taken to regulate passenger traffic. The main recommendations included the proposal for a standard charge based on journey mileage. Given the current costs, the rate of one old penny per mile was suggested and this amount would also be charged for the return journey, thereby removing the passenger's saving when buying a 'monthly return' ticket. This, it was hoped, would discourage any unnecessary return journeys. To further discourage unnecessary journeys, it was recommended that many of the valuable concessions that were given to assist both government and public travel should be withdrawn, and all passenger rail travel would be charged at the proposed standard mileage rate. While this would undoubtedly have reduced passenger travel, politically this was not going to be popular with a war-weary public, and like many suggestions emanating from Whitehall, once subjected to the scrutiny of the railway companies it was quietly dismissed.

In April 1941, after the British government had signed the 'lease lend' agreement with the United States, it was anticipated that in the following months the railways would be called upon to handle many more imported goods – including munitions. This would increase the volume of freight traffic to a level considerably exceeding what was so far being transported. Consequently, the REC was put under extreme pressure to make arrangements to prioritise the conveyance of this increase in imported goods which was soon to arrive from America – but with the caveat that the movement of the imported materials must not interfere with the important coal traffic. This was a huge challenge but nonetheless, Sir James Milne, the REC member from the GWR, was able to inform the government that his railway could accept an additional 300 to 400 wagons a day from the South Wales ports without interfering with coal or passenger traffic and this was despite the perceived issue of the Severn Tunnel 'bottleneck'. Sir James also promised that a further 300 wagons could be transported but this would unfortunately only be possible by temporarily suspending a 'limited number of passenger trains'. In such a difficult situation the losers were only ever likely to be any of the travelling public who wished to make train journeys, and the REC subcommittee responsible for operations considered that a thirty per cent reduction in passenger services would be required to accommodate the anticipated additional freight traffic along the main lines and heavily loaded secondary routes. Such a reduction would require that any remaining passenger trains would be loaded up to, but not beyond, the practical maximum for punctual and operational convenience. This reduced passenger traffic would, it was estimated, permit an increase in freight train mileage of between ten and fifteen per cent. The REC accepted that such draconian cuts might be needed in due course and as an indication of a lack of trust between the ministry and the railways, it made it clear to the government that it expected them to make it clear to the public, probably by a radio broadcast, that the reductions to passenger services were being made at the government's request and not that of the railways.

The REC was requested to find more ways to increase track capacity for the freight trains. The need for this task was not only to provide the paths for these extra freight trains but also release locomotives and crews from other duties to operate these extra trains.

The subcommittee's brief was to assess any means of reducing traffic when the expected rise in freight traffic volume peaked as the war progressed. It was not expected however that any immediate action needed to be taken but the necessary planning and preparations had to be made. The subcommittee argued that the Ministry of Transport's suggestion that goods trains be given priority through known 'bottlenecks' on the network should be discarded as previous experience had shown that any holding back of passenger trains to make way for freight trains only added to the congestion on the lines and resulted in the unintended consequence of the holding up and further delaying the important goods traffic. The government were reminded that the slowing down of passenger trains at 'bottlenecks' had been tried earlier in the war but failed and was soon abandoned.

Another government suggestion that was given little respect by the subcommittee was to introduce a 'one-way' traffic arrangement. This would involve what the REC described as non-standard operating practices to be used if both of the lines on a double-track railway were used for trains travelling in the same direction. It was pointed out that this method of operation could only have been used for passenger trains operating to and from stations at which there were adequate facilities for holding empty trains. The normal practice was to use the carriages from an arriving train for an outgoing departing service as soon as possible. It was not the usual practice to move an empty train out from the platform to make way for the next incoming service, and then retain the carriages at the station, but this would have to be done if one-way working was employed. It was asserted that there was not sufficient space at the termini to hold empty stock ready for the time when the direction of travel was reversed. This was an important and crucial practical difficulty, but the REC's main concern was that any system of one-way working would require complex alterations to the signals and structural alterations to the terminal facilities for both the passengers and the railway staff. Such extra expenditure, the REC insisted, would involve a heavy cost and would take a considerable time to complete.

Suggestions had been made to introduce 'non-travel' days. Again, the REC opposed this suggestion, declaring that there would be much less inconvenience to the public if there was to be a level decrease across the week rather than to apply any extreme severe reductions only on certain days. The REC insisted that the government should give consideration to taxing long distance rail travel. This suggestion, which was promptly rejected by the ministry, was that a one hundred per cent tax should be imposed on tickets for any journey over thirty miles. The REC saw taxation as a very attractive solution as any tax would be levied by the government, not the railways, so it would be the government that would incur all of the 'blame' for the cost increase and not the railway companies. The response from the Ministry of Transport came in a robust letter signed by Gilbert Szlumper, clearly stating that taxation was not an option and opining that such an arrangement would not affect the 'idle rich' but would restrict travel to many who had good, valid reasons to travel.

Before the REC could formulate its considered response to the government's appeal for a curtailment of passenger services, a restructuring within Whitehall established the new Ministry of War Transport on 1 May 1941. This new ministry led by Frederick, the first Viscount Leathers, effectively combined the ministries of shipping and transport and with great vigour proceeded with its primary aim of coordinating the nation's transport, in particular the process of coordinating the offloading and forward distribution of the vital imported war materials arriving from across the Atlantic at the west coast ports.

Lord Leathers, upon taking up his new duties, was unimpressed by the wartime railway organisation and was quick to make it known that the titular head of the REC, the chairman, Sir Ralph Wedgewood, should be removed and new management structure put in place. He was not convinced that Sir Ralph was securing the necessary coordination between the railway companies which he concluded were not working fully together to ensure that the railways made the maximum effort to provide what the nation required, and he had the full support of the wartime cabinet in his efforts to take a tighter control on railway operations. The new minister of war transport wanted to sack Sir Ralph Wedgewood and install a deputy chairman. This was not precisely stated by Leathers, but one can presume that the 'deputy' would be answerable directly to the minister who would assume the duty of 'chairman'. This would have allowed Lord Leathers to have much tighter control of the railways but leave the routine work to his appointee deputy. The matter appears to be resolved when Sir Ralph retired in 1941 – in fact he had already 'retired' from the LNER in 1939 but had stayed on to lead the REC.

Leathers was also unhappy about the original agreement that had been made with the railways at the start of the war in 1939. In the first half of 1941 the railways' net profit was already £22.5million and were therefore on course for exceeding the anticipated £40million. He had some allies along the corridors of Whitehall as some senior government figures were also unhappy with the original agreement with the railways which in 1939 had established the REC as the body to 'take control' of the railways on behalf of the government. When the details of the proposed Defence Regulations were being discussed prior to the war, some civil servants scratched their heads and tried to understand precisely what the minister of transport meant by his phrase 'take possession of the railways'. Despite this phrase, these civil servants had the clear impression that the minister had always intended that the directors of the railway companies would continue to be responsible for the day-to-day administration of railways, not any government body. There were those, such as the Lord Privy Seal, the Labour politician and future prime minister Clement Attlee, who in 1941 were unable to understand how the 'big four' railway companies who were separate profit-making entities could not only be expected to work harmoniously together with each other but also work in unison with other transport providers – a clear case was being made here for full public ownership of the railways.

After much deliberation and behind-the-scenes discussion, Leathers relented, and the REC was allowed to continue much as before but with more intense surveillance from Whitehall and a new financial agreement was imposed upon the railway companies. After long and delicate negotiations, the new agreement capped the railways' income at £43million and they were forced to accept lesser compensation under the government's war damage scheme. This revised war damage arrangement brought them into line with other public utility organisations and was estimated to cost the railways £2.5million every year.

This restructured ministry continued to take an aggressive stance by insisting on a significant reduction in passenger numbers. The ministry did rule out the one simple and easily achieved option for managing passenger numbers which was to introduce a fare structure that would be effectively 'rationing by price'. Such a simple measure had been strictly forbidden by the government at the outset of the war, when it had insisted that the railways must not increase fares beyond what could be fairly justified by the rapidly rising costs. Sir John Anderson's proposal for a standard charge based on journey mileage which would eliminate the cheaper return tickets fell into this category. The government's policy not to increase fares other than as a result of increases in the railways' operating costs had resulted in the railways making a claim from the government of £11.8million due to the 'lag' between increase in costs and the government's approval to increase fares. Nonetheless, despite their lack of any practical solutions the reformed government ministry insisted that in the national interest the REC must find ways to reduce the number of passengers carried and to instigate cuts in passenger services to allow the much-desired freer movement of freight. The reluctant REC countered with the usual argument that the railways were legally obliged to carry 'the traffic that presents itself' maintaining that any further reduction in services would not reduce the number of passengers travelling but would result in even more over-crowding on the trains with the consequential outcome of further delays. One option that was available and promoted by the REC was for the War Office to assist by cutting out any unnecessary military personnel travel on ordinary passenger trains.

With continuing pressure from the revitalised ministry, the REC promptly produced a paper entitled 'Means to be Adopted for Limitation of Passenger Travel' which surveyed the sources of passenger traffic and highlighted what was directly attributed to the wartime situation, and thus could be deemed to be priority or essential traffic. The REC insisted that it had been made clear to the public that it was their duty not to travel (for example over the recent Easter holiday) but unfortunately, the appeal had not been sufficient to impact on the number of passengers who travelled over the holiday period.

In its report to the ministry, the REC outlined what it described as its new, wartime, traffic problem which was the steady increase in the number of passenger journeys. This was due to the large concentration of HM forces in various parts of the country; the widespread evacuation of many civilians, government departments and private companies and the upsurge in the number of munition factories across the country which required the railways to operate many additional workers' trains.

There was according to the REC, two main categories of passenger travel. The first of these was the shorter distance journeys which were made on local or suburban trains. Many of these shorter services were used by workmen while others were predominantly used by passengers with season tickets or cheap day return tickets. Much of this traffic was carried over short branch or minor lines, neither of which would ever be likely to be used for the additional wartime freight trains. The second main category was travel on longer distance trains, and these did generally run over the important freight arteries. The railways had reported that during the early war years there remained a considerable amount of first- and third-class travel by traders and businessmen using the long-distance trains so any reduction in passenger services would cause hardship both to the individual passengers and the businesses and organisations they represented.

The REC directly confronted the new ministry by pointing out that what they classified as 'government' traffic had become the major component of wartime railway travel. It was this additional travel that was often resulting in the overcrowding on the long-distance trains when many extra passengers were travelling either at the government's expense or with a government subsidy. Service personnel were regularly travelling at the government's expense on ordinary service trains and only very rarely on special 'troop' trains. Servicemen and women in uniform were conveyed at half ordinary fares, either in large parties, smaller drafts or individuals. If a serviceman was on leave, he also travelled at a reduced rate but had to pay for the ticket himself. Tickets for passengers who were government department personnel were charged at the 'public' individual or bulk fare, and for those who had been evacuated to the provinces and were travelling either home or back to their workplace in the provinces on leave, belatedly, arrangements had been made for subsidised travel. Conscription had been introduced and for those called up for national service the government funded travel from home to a base for their medical check-up, and then on to their first posting. The ministry of labour had arranged special rates with the railways so that trainees could travel to and from the training centres. There was of course the scheme for the relatives of the vulnerable children who had been evacuated by their local authority with railway tickets available at a special rate. Unfortunately, the number of parents who had made their own arrangements to evacuate their children was not known and they were not able to take advantage of the reduced rate tickets through the voucher system but nonetheless their travel need was just as compelling. The Government were also assisting the civilian population in making additional war related journeys by providing concessions for agricultural workers toiling to combat the food shortages and these included women in the 'land army' and young people taking 'holidays' to assist in the fields.

The REC also claimed in their report that there was also considerable extra passenger traffic due to the many larger companies who had evacuated themselves to the provinces. Those travelling 'home' from the provinces paid the ordinary fares as did scholars travelling to and from the many private schools which had been relocated from urban areas deep into the countryside.

The elimination of 'non-essential' travel was seen by many outside the railway industry as an easily achieved and acceptable solution to the reduction of passenger services and also to reduce overcrowding on the trains. The REC, taking the opposite view, attempted to persuade the ministry that any non-essential traffic was only ever likely to be a very small part of the whole. Unfortunately, the REC was unable to make any statistical argument and was adamant that it had no information in numerical terms as to what was 'essential' and what was 'non-essential' travel as it did not have any data as to the 'mix' of each. Unless the question was directly asked of every passenger, just how would the railway company know why any individual was making a journey? The REC also refused to offer any opinion as to how 'essential' could be defined but did concede that this definition might include journeys on account of illness, voluntary evacuation, or the removals of workers to new, remote locations – all of which was regularly taking place.

The report did offer a few possible solutions. One option which had first been proposed by the ministry was the introduction of 'limited' trains. This, the REC believed, was difficult to implement, and then would only be possible on a restricted number of trains. It argued that a system which controlled the number of tickets issued on a 'first come, first served' basis would be both unpopular and unfair. A full seat reservation system was discounted for similar reasons – and passengers would have difficulty in locating their seat when their train arrived at a blacked-out station. Another possibility for reducing passengers on long-distance journeys was for a 'permit-to-travel' system, but the response by both the government and the REC was lukewarm. A decision to implement such a proposal required the difficult appraisal of the likely effect on passenger numbers relative to the numbers of precious railway staff required to manage the scheme. Price control by abolishing discounted fares such as the withdrawal of cheap day return tickets was discussed, but the railway professionals on the REC maintained their commercial instincts, opining that this would be detrimental to business travel. The only other option was to continue to allow passengers to 'go as you please' and make the further reductions to services with the consequential overcrowding. It was hoped that the public would accept that the trains would be crowded trains and that those with 'unnecessary' journeys would stay away. This was to be effectively the 'solution', but the REC, despite being dismissive of all other options, saw this as an admission of defeat. With this policy it is unsurprising that overcrowding proved to be commonplace throughout the war as passenger traffic increased, the GWR was to provide 60 million passenger journeys in 1944 – 64 per cent more than in 1938, with a passenger train mileage of only 10 million miles – 23 per cent less than in 1938. That is, more people were travelling on fewer trains. The REC did however also question the emphasis that was being placed by the government on the reduction in passenger traffic. It argued that providing fewer passenger trains would have no effect whatsoever on what it described as the 'next' problem which was that there was inadequate marshalling yard and terminal capacity to be able to cope with the anticipated increase in freight traffic.

Despite the REC's robust response with its rather negative conclusion, the government continued to insist that the railways find a solution to the problem themselves. The LPTB representative on the REC, Lord Ashfield, was delegated the task of preparing a formal report outlining the difficulties and the options for practical solutions. Given that the LPTB was a step away from the other railways in the operational sense due to the unique nature of its traffic, Lord Ashfield, while being a full member of the REC, could be seen as somebody who could potentially provide an unbiased 'outsider's' view. Lord Ashfield returned to his office at 55 Broadway SW1 to write his long memorandum which he titled 'Restriction of Passenger Travel' and dated it 22 August 1941.

Lord Ashfield was aware that as the war dragged on, the strains on the railways would increase as the demands for war related traffic increased at the same time as the railways' resources came under greater pressure. He did not believe that it was necessary to make any sudden draconian changes. He did however concede that it might soon become necessary to consider doing so when the railways had to accommodate further additional wartime traffic. It was not stated, but here was the strong hint that any substantial additional wartime traffic would most likely arise should the British with its allies return to mainland Europe. Nonetheless it was the time to look towards solutions to alleviate stress on the railway network. Due to backlogs of maintenance, fuel shortages – particularly locomotive coal – and reduced staff numbers due to many experienced staff entering military service, any policy on passenger volume would have to ensure that the railways would employ no more rolling stock, fuel or staff than was absolutely necessary. He assumed that to achieve the maximum operating advantage, any measures to reduce passenger travel would only be applicable to longer distance travel in excess of 50 miles.

He outlined three suggested methods to reduce passenger travel; these had been proposed in outline in the REC's recent report to the ministry of war transport, but detailed study of these proposals was required. The first of these options was the simplest to implement which was to increase the cost of the tickets. Second, a system of 'limited trains' be imposed to restrict the number of passengers using any service. The third suggestion was that a system requiring passengers to obtain a 'permit to travel' should be developed.

Increasing ticket costs had the merit of being easy to implement but would limit travel by ability to pay, not by necessity to travel or for travel which he saw as 'nationally desirable'. Furthermore, past experience had shown that any increase in ticket price did not reduce passenger traffic – unless the increase was so drastic as to a wholly unreasonable burden on those who had little choice but to travel. Furthermore, the rising of ticket prices was disliked by the government and of course it went against its 'stabilisation of prices' policy.

Nonetheless there were those who advocated another version of rationing which was not by price, but as an addition to the national ration system by using a variation on the coupon arrangement. An editorial in the *Railway Gazette* promoted a rationing system refuting the statements from government and the railways that any rationing of travel would be both costly and difficult to administer. The editorial opined that a simple solution was available using the spare page in universally issued ration books. The seat reservations system had been withdrawn at the outbreak of war but could be reintroduced only for passengers with seat tickets – either 'rationed' or on first-come-first-served basis. Despite the 'official' line of the journal delivered in the 7 August 1942 edition, the idea was gently lampooned in the cartoon which depicted typically long war era queues at a 'Seat Reservations' desk behind which was a list of trains, all of which were indicated as 'fully booked'.

The second option offered by Lord Ashfield was a proposal to operate a system of only running 'limited trains' on the long-distance routes. This would create a system whereby tickets would only be issued up to a predetermined number for a particular train. This he criticised because only those able to plan their journeys would be able to travel. Many passengers – and Lord Ashfield cited the needs of service personnel – had urgent needs to travel with immediate notice. If space were left for any late arrivals who had urgent national business this would only result in many trains running with empty seats. In an age long before any national computerised booking system, he stressed the practicalities of issuing all seats at the station booking offices. The limited train arrangement would be easy enough at the 'starting station' but along the route many passengers would detrain at intermediate stations, making the number of tickets available for issue at these stations difficult or impossible to quantify.

The third possibility was to operate a permit system, and this was favoured by Lord Ashfield, who took a contrary opinion to the government and the REC as a whole. He proposed that any intending passengers would first obtain authority to travel from 'a specially organised establishment' set up by the government but administered by the railways. Permits would be valid for a limited period but would not restrict the passenger to any particular train. The issue of the permit would follow scrutiny as to the reasons and need for the journey. The time limited permits would not stipulate the number of journeys to be taken. The advantage of the system was that the railways' sacred duty to 'carry the traffic presented' was maintained as the issue of the permit was only one step removed from the individual buying a ticket at the station booking office. Lord Ashfield opined that the permit system he proposed was the only way of eliminating journeys which were not essential or 'nationally desirable'. If civilian journeys were restricted by the permit system, it would make it politically more acceptable to restrict the level of service leave travel which at the time was considerable. Lord Ashfield stated that in his opinion the only objection to a permit system was that it involved the establishment of what he described as a 'substantial administration staff' who would need to be suitably qualified to make judgements as to what was 'necessary' travel and if any journey was 'nationally desirable'. He also commented upon the proliferation of existing concessional fares which had been introduced which, he claimed, were encouraging non-essential travel. The introduction of a permit scheme would present the opportunity to consider if the time had come for such schemes to be withdrawn. Lord Ashfield's LPTB were shortly to abolish first class travel on its trains, but if the main line railways were to retain it, he suggested that railway staff should be allowed to use their discretion and allow third class passengers with a permit to travel to move into first class when the train was crowded.

At the time that the main committee received Lord Ashfield's report, it noted with interest a report in the *Railway Gazette* dated 22 August 1941 that in parts of Germany a system of permit to travel was being introduced. The *Railway Gazette* has to be complimented on how it was able to provide detailed information about foreign railway operations during the war. This was particularly impressive when it was able to publish detailed accounts of the enemy's railway activities.

In October 1941, the REC Publicity Control Committee again discussed ways of persuading the public not to take unnecessary journeys. They reviewed the current National Savings Campaign which had produced advertising encouraging the saving of resources, such as locomotive coal, by avoiding unnecessary travel. The committee's opinion was that the slogan 'Leave the Trains to the Tanks' was a better slogan than a simple 'Don't travel by Train'. They also met the editors of *John Bull* and the *People* urging them to impress upon their readers the necessity for avoiding needless travel. They also requested the pressmen for suggestions as to how to put this message across to the public. The proposal that government posters such as 'Safety in the Blackout' and 'Avoidance of Rush Hours' should be displayed within railway carriage compartments was again treated with disdain by John Elliot, who saw these precious spaces bringing in advertising revenue for the railway companies. To ensure the American public that Britain was not taking undue advantage of the recent 'lease-lend' deal, the committee proposed an American press release to describe how the railways were doing their utmost to meet war needs, citing curtailment of passenger services, overloading of trains, numerous troop trains, abnormal coal traffic and difficulties due to the blackout.

Despite much research, discussion by the publicity subcommittee and further report writing, none of the more radical solutions was ever to come to fruition. By this time the United States had entered the war following the attack on Pearl Harbor in December 1941 not only was the volume of war related imports being accelerated, but also in January 1942 the first American troops began to arrive in Britain. This was the beginning of the massive military build-up given the code name 'Operation Bolero' which was ultimately to lead on to the Normandy landings on D-Day in June 1944. The Ministry of War Transport continued to apply pressure upon the railways and issued a statement in February 1942 that insisted that the railways tighten up their arrangements for the regulation of passengers at stations. At busy times objection was taken to the practice of advertising any extra trains, which internally the railways described as 'relief' trains, as being either 'extra' or 'special' services. With the Easter holiday approaching, 'all necessary steps' must be taken to persuade the public not to make long-distance journeys. The ministry demanded that appeals were made both by the BBC, notices in the national and local press and posters displayed at stations. The ministry also prepared themselves to be able to answer any questions posed by questions in parliament from errant MPs or Lords. In this context the well-remembered 'Is your Journey Really Necessary' campaign was introduced in March 1942, which was to lead the way in the attempt to reduce passenger numbers.

The attractive artwork for the campaign for the 'is your journey really necessary' campaign was provided by the respected artist Bert Thomas. A later version of the poster showed a menacing soldier 'guarding' the front of the booking office window, but the version originally used (and remembered) depicted a well-dressed, middle-aged couple with a small dog looking as if they were going up to town to do a bit of shopping. Therefore, quite intentionally, the potential passengers illustrated were not soldiers, young civil servants or working-class parents visiting children evacuated to 'safe' areas away from London. They were drawn to appear as two well-off people perhaps anticipating a leisure trip, perhaps they intended going to the theatre or possibly merely proposing to take their small dog for a walk at a beauty spot somewhere in the country. Quite obviously the poster was aimed at those making an optional, not an essential journey by train.

The posters were prominently displayed next to the booking office window at every station. Consideration was given to also displaying the poster at travel agent's shops such as in the Thomas Cook shops, which from 1942 were to be railway owned. No immediate decision was made but it was confirmed that Thomas Cook had withdrawn all posters advertising holiday resorts.

Typical of the target audience who might relate to the couple and dog, was the lady who lived in Cranleigh, Surrey who had complained that she was unable to conveniently travel up to London due to time of day restrictions. Cranleigh would have had few shops, but would it have been 'necessary' for her to travel to London when advantage could have been taken of the bustling shops in Guildford where she had to change trains?

The advice given by the MO organisation to the REC in 1939 had advised that the viewer of any poster had to feel that the message applied to them, thus the use of the personal pronoun '*your*' within the text. The new poster was adaptable – a small line drawing version also appeared in newspapers, often with an additional text message such as 'Don't help Hitler by travelling this summer'. As the campaign entered the public consciousness the slogan became transferrable, a road vehicle servicing and repair company in Sussex, Caffyns, often used the phrase when advertising in the press and reminding the motoring public that they were still in business for those with 'necessary journeys'.

Despite a bullish opinion given to the House of Commons later in March 1943 by the Parliamentary Secretary to the Ministry of War Transport Mr Noel-Baker that the campaign had been a 'considerable success', the REC had their reservations and in October 1943 the publicity control committee reviewed the campaign and agreed that it should be played down for a while. The posters should remain on display adjacent to the booking offices, although the committee were not satisfied that the slogan had in fact made enough impact as 'unnecessary' travel had continued. Cynically they believed that the slogan's real value had been that the public now accepted the overcrowding of trains knowing it was due to their own fault, selfishly insisting on making a train journey and therefore no blame could be placed on the railways or the government. The belief that the railways were overcrowded and uncomfortable suited the government's purpose and is one factor creating the persisting impression of uncomfortable wartime railway travel. When the publicity control committee's recommendation that the campaign be suspended was placed before the full committee, Sir William Wood – the President of the LMSR – declared that he was not satisfied that the slogan had produced positive results claiming that there had, as always, been considerable unnecessary travel. Mr Richmond Temple, the REC's public relations and propaganda expert who was attending the meeting, disagreed. He reasoned that the slogan had caught the public's imagination and it was not possible to assess the poster's retardation effect in respect to unnecessary travel. Concurring with the views expressed at the publicity control committee's meeting, he added that in his opinion the campaign had been successful and agreed that the posters had fended off criticism from the general public, the press and from parliament about the overcrowded trains by implying that it was the selfish passengers who were making unnecessary journeys and crowding onto the trains. The poster campaign, he maintained, had induced a sense of guilt in those who were travelling without justification.

Without any contemporary data about the public's reaction to the campaign, despite Richmond Temple's professional opinion, it is only possible to speculate as to the success or otherwise of the posters. The MO report may have stipulated that posters should be easily visible to the public thus they were placed adjacent to the booking office windows. Visible yes, but any uncertain traveller arriving at the station would probably by then have committed to travelling and unlikely to have a late change of mind. The survey had noted that the highest group of railway travellers were middle-class men, but most individuals would not relate to the wealthy couple in the picture and were likely to convince themselves that relatively speaking *my* journey was much more necessary than *theirs*. Anybody approaching the booking office did however have to face a booking clerk who might well give an intending passenger a stern gaze. It is uncertain if the booking clerks were ever formally or informally instructed to ask any questions about the ticket purchaser's reason for travelling, but the fear of having to provide a 'good answer' would have deterred the shy and nervous souls from attempting to travel, but the more robust individuals could brashly declare that it was 'none of your business.' Unlike the travel restriction denying any access to the coastal defence areas, there was no legal prohibition on travel to any other destination. Many intending travellers would have taken the view that if they wanted to travel, had paid for their ticket and were prepared to endure any overcrowding, why should they not travel since the train would run whether or not they were a passenger aboard? Another failing of the campaign was that the definition of 'necessary' was never quantified, thereby diluting the clarity of the intended message. But there is another possibility to be considered which is that the posters did have more impact than was believed at the time but any resulting reduction in traffic was swamped by the increase in other – perhaps much more 'necessary' – wartime passenger numbers.

Given all the concern about too many passengers travelling, how crowded were the trains? On Friday, 24 October 1941 a survey was carried out on the passenger numbers on eleven SR trains running from Waterloo to Bournemouth. The total number of passengers carried in first-class over the day was 531 who had 870 seats available for their use. The corresponding numbers for third-class was 3,343 sharing 5,016 seats. The closest the trains came to being significantly short on seating capacity was the 1.40pm departure when 403 third-class passengers had 456 seats available for use. In the same train 78 first class ticket holders spread themselves over 104 seats. This might indicate that there was more than adequate seating provision but four of the trains, the 11.20am, the 1.20pm, the 3.20pm and the 5.34pm, were all classified by the SR as 'relief', that is extra trains provided by the railway due to the anticipated high number of potential passengers. The total number of passengers who made use of these extra trains was 166 first class and 1,205 third class. One of these 'relief' trains, the 1.20pm, had only 39 first class passengers but with relatively few – 42 – seats available and the 261 third class passengers had the choice of 456 seats.

The GWR also surveyed the number of passengers on seven trains on the South Wales to Paddington route on Monday, 13 October 1941. On these trains a total of 263 passengers with first-class tickets spread themselves across 492 seats and 2,906 third-class ticket holders had to find seating from a total of 3,206 seats. The survey did not show which of these trains had restaurant cars, but where applicable the seats in them were not counted. This GWR survey also included what were effectively 'relief' trains as two of the services from Nyland to Paddington were run in two parts and were counted as separate trains.

A similar survey on the LNER covered eight trains run on Friday, 6 February 1942. The train services on which passengers were counted were, unlike the SR and GWR surveys, spread across different services using the east coast main line – to and from King's Cross to Edinburgh either stopping at York and Darlington or York and Newcastle and to and from King's Cross to Newcastle only. Across these trains the 669 first-class passengers had 942 seats available to them but the 6,219 third class passengers had to find themselves seats in compartments with only a total of 6,020 seats. There was a mix of crowding in the third-class carriages, the 491 third-class passengers on the 8.05am Newcastle to King's Cross train had the luxury of 812 seats at their disposal but please spare a thought for the 1,084 third-class passengers on the 9.50 King's Cross to Edinburgh train who had a mere 872 seats for their use.

These three surveys, with others, were undertaken as part of an investigation into the possible introduction of what was described as a possible 'limited train permit', that is a variation on the permit-to-travel concept, and as such might be seen as 'worst case' scenarios. This data would also have been of use in order to deduce what the effect of withdrawing any 'relief' trains or running trains as a single unit, not as two parts. The overall conclusion of these surveys might be that all of the trains were 'very busy' but occasionally they could be classified as being overcrowded. A well-filled train that does not become overcrowded represents good transport economics. Another conclusion which can be drawn is that the railways were adept at matching provision with demand – hence the number of reliefs and second separate trains and consequently the non-running of extra trains or reduction in timetabled trains would have resulted in gross overcrowding in the third-class carriages.

On 7 March 1942 an official at the Ministry of War Transport let it be known that the minister was to insist that all restaurant cars must be withdrawn from service. The rationale for this was that smaller or lighter locomotives could be used which would result in a reduction in the consumption of the precious locomotive coal. The withdrawal of the cars would also release staff for other duties. The REC conceded that if there was to be a ministerial edict, they would have to implement the withdrawal of these services but requested that factors such as the needs of the passengers who had to travel over long distances such as from London to Liverpool and the Scottish destinations should be taken into account. The REC also requested clarification as to whether or not the restaurant cars on the SR electric trains which had catering vehicles as an integral part of electric multiple units should also be withdrawn from service. It was for these trains, of course, that the arguments about the continued use of these trains at the very beginning of the war had effectively prised open the original complete embargo on catering vehicles, and this in turn lead to a phased reintroduction of many restaurant cars on routes across the railway network.

On 27 March the REC received the official memorandum from the Ministry of War Transport confirming that the minister had decided that it was now necessary to cease the running of all restaurant cars. Lord Leathers had concluded that the time had come to tell the public that when travelling they should take their own food with them. He dismissed representations that he had received from the railways that restaurant cars should be retained on boat trains and business trains between important centres. He believed that the retention of catering services for important business travel would cause more dissatisfaction than benefit and could not accept the logic about catering on boat trains as meals would be available when the passengers boarded the ships. He did show some sympathy for travellers on the very long-distance trains to Scotland. Further representations were made, and the minister did eventually relent when the railways presented a short list of services for which they considered the retention of catering facilities was justified. The result was that the railways were, reluctantly, permitted to run some restaurant car services.

The GWR continued to run express trains with restaurant cars to the West Country from Paddington with services to Penzance, Kingswear and Plymouth. Further restaurant services from Paddington were permitted to run to Bristol, Cardiff, Swansea, Wolverhampton and Birkenhead. The Bristol trains would have been of use to Admiralty staff outstationed at Bath. The GWR claimed that the reason for retaining these services was that these trains were used by passengers engaged in 'important business and government' activities.

The LMSR list of retained services included the Euston to Holyhead boat trains connecting with sailings to Ireland. Notwithstanding the minister's comments on meals being available on the ferries, the railway was able to argue that these trains were also used by businessmen travelling to and from Manchester and they enabled business passengers to make an out and home visit in a single day. This seems a strange justification because the day-return businessman would have had to change trains at Crewe. The route to Holyhead was along the North Wales coast, making these boat trains a convenient service for the Ministry of Food staff who were based at Colwyn Bay. The same reasoning was given for continuing to provide catering on other express trains serving Manchester. Other LMSR services which carried those engaged in 'important business and government' services included trains from Euston to Liverpool and Blackpool. The LMSR did however manage to persuade the ministry that a restaurant car service should be retained on some boat trains such as Euston to Heysham and Euston to Stranraer – but the restaurant car was detached at Crewe. From St Pancras restaurant cars continued to be provided on trains to Derby. Some non-London LMSR trains retained restaurant cars on services within Scotland. These were services between Aberdeen and Glasgow, Inverness and Helmsdale and Aviemore and Perth. The small village of Helmsdale on the east coast of Sutherland might seem an odd destination but this choice of train was made for wider operational reasons rather than any local passenger need although the RAF had built two radar stations in the locality. The LMSR argued that the Inverness to Helmsdale service provided connections to northern destinations such as Thurso and Wick for passengers travelling on the sleeping car trains from Euston, a service that was used by many service personnel. The return Helmsdale to Inverness working was the return 'balance' working for the restaurant car. Similarly, the 6.40am train from Perth to Aviemore also made connection with the overnight sleeper service from Euston. The 12.30pm return from Aviemore was to return the car to Inverness.

The LNER continued to run several restaurant car express trains between King's Cross and Leeds. These too were justified on the grounds that they carried important business and government traffic and would have been used by the RAF, Ministry of Aircraft Production and GPO staff who were based at Harrogate. Restaurant cars were retained on a few Aberdeen to Edinburgh and King's Cross trains. The 6.35 Aberdeen to King's Cross train had the restaurant car attached but only as far as Edinburgh and this provided a breakfast for those who had travelled south to Aberdeen overnight. The 9.55am Edinburgh to Aberdeen was a train which connected with trains from London

King's Cross and London St Pancras. The 5.50am train from Glasgow to Fort William provided breakfast in the restaurant car for travellers on their way to the Western Islands who had arrived in Glasgow overnight off the 7.15pm train from King's Cross to Aberdeen. There was the corresponding 2.50pm return working from Fort William to Glasgow to provide afternoon tea or an early dinner.

The SR was only permitted to run six restaurant car services. These were three trains each way on weekdays between Waterloo and Exeter. These trains, it was claimed, also regularly carried passengers engaged in important military and civil business. The wartime SR restaurant car express trains were now all steam hauled trains to the West Country and all of the Southern Electric catering vehicles had been withdrawn and sent to storage.

All of the railways' restaurant cars were withdrawn during the Whitsun holiday in late May 1942, and thereafter only the 62 services that had been agreed with the ministry were to be run each day. These were spread across all four of the railways. The LMSR provided 28 of these, the GWR 16, the LNER 12, and on the SR their six. This was a drastic cut in service provision; the maximum service previously during the war had been 90 trains on the LMSR, 147 trains with buffet or restaurant cars running on the LNER, 52 trains with buffet or restaurant cars running on the GWR, and 141 trains with restaurant, buffet or Pullman catering on the SR.

These restaurant car services, despite government disapproval, continued to do good business and were popular with the passengers. During the month of October 1942, the 8.30am Euston to Holyhead train which was used by passengers to North Wales and Ireland served 5,706 breakfasts, 5,635 luncheons and 9,353 teas and morning coffees. Another LMSR service linking Euston with Heysham departed at 3pm from Euston and returned south leaving Heysham at 8.30am the following day, and served a total of 4,970 breakfasts, 3,703 luncheons, 11,648 teas and morning coffees and 5,644 dinners in the same month.

With the on-train catering doing such good business and with an obvious public demand for this service, why was such a draconian measure as drastic withdrawal of most restaurant cars deemed necessary? It was not likely to have been due to the kind of resentment displayed earlier in the war by the letter writer who urged that all 'decent' people should provide their own food when travelling – even if this had been originally implied by Lord Leathers as part of his original proposal. Compared to travel times today, the railway journeys were long – especially during wartime when there were delays – so even the less affluent third-class passengers would wish to partake in an 'off the ration' meal in the third-class dining saloon. Sitting at a table with a 'knife and fork' meal was the norm in the 1940s, decades before the current 'grazing' culture emerged with the popularity for consuming take-away food. It will be recalled that the young mother with her two small sons who travelled south towards Euston during the Blitz had a three-course 'standard' meal in the LMSR restaurant car. Possibly due to the lack of any progress in getting passenger numbers down, the new minister thought he 'had to do something' and pounced upon a blanket ban on train catering. To suspect this would do Lord Leathers a disservice, the railways were struggling with their task of conveying the additional wartime freight which was made all the more difficult due to a shortage of labour and locomotive coal. The term 'restaurant car' suggests a single vehicle but typically there would be two coupled together, a kitchen and first-class dining car and a separate open saloon for third-class diners. These vehicles were heavy and did not contribute to the count of available seats. If a train could be reduced by these two carriages, the replacement vehicles could carry about 120 extra third-class passengers. Alternatively, the lighter train could be pulled by a smaller engine. Another major problem that the railways had was the shortage of labour. In September 1942 it was reported that 95,000 railway staff members had been released to serve in the armed forces. This drastic reduction in on-train catering would enable the railways to redeploy the staff who had been working on the restaurant and buffet cars.

The flexibility afforded by being able to use smaller locomotives on restaurant car free trains was attractive to those running the operating departments. The acute shortage of locomotives was regularly recorded in the minutes of the REC mechanical and electrical engineer's subcommittee when tables were produced enumerating the number of locomotives awaiting heavy overhaul or repair which could not be attended to due to a lack of skilled fitters and that the railway workshops were fully engaged in non-railway war production. The locomotive departments were hard at work maintaining an aging fleet of locomotives for use on the additional freight trains and the crews were working them harder than they had been designed for often thirty years before. The main line passenger trains were much heavier, for example on the express trains on the LNER's east coast main line trains northwards from King's Cross by 1942, the weight behind the steam locomotives had risen from around 500 tons to 650 tons. The war had not reduced the demand on the LNER's suburban services. Locomotives and coal had to be found for the 194 trains – mostly short distance suburban workings – that entered or left Liverpool Street station between 4.00pm and 6.30pm, a rate of one train every forty-six seconds. This activity was much the same in the morning peak time between 7.30am and 9.30am. There is little evidence that the war had significantly reduced the passenger numbers on trains into the City of London.

How much of a reduction in passenger numbers was achieved by the REC and government's campaign? The simple answer might be 'none', but what is uncertain is the degree by which any falling away of passenger demand due to a patriotic reluctance to make any unnecessary journeys was swamped by the numbers of new passengers who had not previously had any need to travel by train. At the end of 1942 when the railways published the winter timetables, critical observers would note that despite all the pressure to reduce railway travel, the latest schedules were little different to those that had been in force during the relatively calm phoney war period at the beginning of 1940. Despite the expectations in 1941 that passenger services would have to be reduced, very few services had been withdrawn and the point-to-point timings had not perceptively changed indicating that there had not been any deceleration of trains, but, due to the many extra stops being made, the overall journey times had often increased.

The following year proved to be just as depressing for the government officials who wanted to see a reduction in passenger traffic. 1943 was the busiest ever recorded on British railways. Between them the 'big four' carried a total of 1.268 million passengers with a total mileage of 32,210 million miles. It was estimated that there had been a 10 per cent increase in the total number of passenger journeys with a 60 per cent increase in journey length. This was achieved with a 30 per cent decrease in passenger train miles compared to 1938. Consequently, the average load carried by the passenger trains was 125 per cent above pre-war levels. This massive increase in traffic was largely due to additional – often 'unnecessary' – travel by service personnel.

Chapter 9

Travel by Service Personnel

Soldiers, sailors and airmen [creating] crowded railways necessitating holidaying families having to squeeze into the trains.
James Marsh, *A 1940s Childhood* 2014

Throughout the war, service personnel regularly travelled on the
public trains using either 'leave' or 'duty' warrants which were
issued by the military, or at their own expense by purchasing railway
tickets at a concessionary rate. Fare concessions were also granted on
29 September 1941 to Home Guard and Civil Defence staff for return
travel between their home and normal place of work at the cost of a
single ticket. Free travel warrants were provided for relatives visiting
'dangerously ill' servicemen in hospital and also at reduced rate for less
seriously injured patients. And it was not only the service personnel
themselves that were to be granted cheaper travel – it was soon to
be also available to their wives and families. From 1942, American
servicemen were stationed in Britain and these too were eligible for
the same personal travel concessions. In addition to service travel on
timetabled trains during the war period, the railways ran 70,000 special
troop and equipment trains. During the first two years of the war the
LMSR alone carried more than 4 million servicemen on special troop
trains with 104,694 tons of baggage, 350,000 wagon loads of stores,
equipment and ammunition carried on 10,328 special freight trains.

Some confusion arose during 1940 as to what travel concessions the
wartime service personnel were entitled to receive. To clarify the issue,
in August the War Office issued a statement explaining that service
personnel were entitled to two seven-day periods of leave every year.

For these leave periods travel warrants were issued to the serviceman or servicewoman for free travel from their base to home and for the return journey at the end of their leave period. As an exceptional case for those who had so recently taken part in combat, any soldier who had returned with the BEF from France or who had taken part in the Norway campaign were also entitled to an extra free warrant to return home. Should anyone in military service be granted any additional leave they could journey home and back at the standard concessionary rate which was a return journey at the cost of a single fare.

As described in Chapter 1, one of the most significant changes that was observed by railway passengers at the beginning of the war was the sudden appearance of many service personnel on the trains and at the main stations. The War Office were not able to provide any amenities in the form of refreshment facilities or accommodation for those waiting overnight for connecting trains, but the railways obliged by keeping refreshment rooms open later than usual and often permitting soldiers to sleep in carriages at the stations. The railways' help was welcomed but proved to be insufficient to meet the demand. The War Office made a request to the railways to allow 'private' organisations such as the YMCA to operate catering facilities at railway stations. Accordingly, the Archbishop of York formally opened a services hostel which was to be operated by the Salvation Army at York station. Bunks for up to 57 men were provided at York for servicemen who were waiting overnight for connecting trains. Also provided at York was a reception room and washing facilities. Other organisations such as the Church Army, the WVS and the YMCA began to operate canteens for the refreshment of travelling servicemen at important junctions such as at Birmingham (New Street and Snow Hill), Reading, Crewe, Perth and Inverness.

Early in 1940 there was to be further progress in the provision of facilities for servicemen provided by a variety of organisations in association with the Council of Voluntary War Work (CVWW). This association included a mix of philanthropic and religious organisations such as YMCA, Salvation Army, Catholic Women's league, Church of Scotland, Methodist Church and Toc H (the international Christian movement). The Salvation Army, for example, established a hut for servicemen on the forecourt of St Pancras station. Toc H did not concern itself with providing canteens within the railway stations – leaveng this work to the Salvation Army and the YMCA – but outside Crewe and Peterborough stations they opened a club and canteen.

The YMCA also arranged dormitories in locations such as libraries. At Bristol, 60 beds were provided in a concert hall. At Reading, 70 beds were provided, distributed across a lecture hall, the library and what was described at the time as a 'parlour'. YMCA also provided a 'get you home' service – probably lifts by private cars – from the railway station to the serviceman's home.

In the months before the German invasion of France a 'new normal' evolved with minimal military activity occurring and there were many service personnel who were serving with the BEF in France. In December 1939 many of these servicemen stationed on the other side of the English Channel were granted home leave for the Christmas period. Additionally, many of those serving 'at home' throughout the land were also granted Christmas leave. Between 21 December and 30 December 1939, the GWR operated 143 special trains transporting an estimated 62,000 servicemen on Christmas leave journeys. The SR also operated 114 leave trains plus 77 special trains for the benefit of what they described as 'naval and military authorities'. Complex travel arrangements had to be made for the BEF soldiers stationed in northern France who were granted their most welcome home leave. All the BEF officers and men coming home on leave were provided with a printed 8-page booklet. These booklets provided the soldier with the authority for leave embarkation, sea and rail travel, when necessary Underground travel across London, and, if required, any overnight accommodation in the capital while awaiting a train to a remote location anywhere within the country. For those stationed at 'home', representatives of the railways visited the various camps to assist the inexperienced younger travellers with the issue of tickets, timetables and travel advice for the journey home for Christmas leave. Nationally, the REC estimated that over the extended 15 days of the Christmas period special trains covered an aggregate half a million miles, transporting 900,000 men from the 'fighting services', auxiliary services and civil servants who had been outposted to 'safe' locations. These special trains transporting personnel to and from leave were in number 299 and 305 respectively. All these non-public trains were given priority over the timetabled public trains and the REC admitted that despite the best efforts of the railways this did unfortunately cause delays to the ordinary services but, due to wartime secrecy, the reasons for any delays could not be explained to the public.

None of the leave trains from France – in the relatively peaceful days before the German onslaught in the spring of 1940 – could follow a fixed timetable but nonetheless the running of the special leave trains was well organised by the railways. Troops arriving at Dover would not have been aware that one of the two usual routes to London – through Shakespeare tunnel between Dover and Folkestone – was blocked due to a cliff slippage. Servicemen arriving at Dover passed into the customs shed to be greeted by SR staff with the words: 'have your part III ready'. The 'part III' was a combined leave pass and railway tickets booklet giving full details of each soldier's journey. Part I would have been left with the soldier's unit, part II would be collected at the port of embarkation. The Part III counterfoil surrendered at Dover was not a railway pass, but it helped transport arrangements at the London end. On one typical occasion, 350 men were duly loaded into the train, six men to a compartment. The destination of each man was collected and the LPTB informed to be prepared for troops travelling onwards via other London termini such as Paddington or Euston. During the journey, an 'RTO assistant' would walk through the train advising each man as to his way to his ultimate destination. Part IV of the 'green booklet' was collected by SR ticket inspectors from those whose journeys would finish at Victoria. When the non-stop train arrived at Victoria, a fleet of LPTB buses would be waiting to facilitate the cross-London transfers.

Following the repatriation of any injured British soldier, the railways played their part in conveying distressed relatives to visit them in military hospitals. In mid-June 1940, the War Office announced that any relatives of seriously wounded soldiers who had received an official telegram from the hospital notifying them that the soldier was dangerously ill and who could not afford the cost of a railway ticket could travel at public expense to visit them in hospital. For those relatives who could afford to buy a ticket, they were requested to obtain a travel warrant from the nearest police station. Relatives of less seriously injured soldiers who had not received a telegram were still able to visit wounded relatives at a reduced rate using concessionary vouchers which they could obtain from the military unit to which the soldier belonged. The procedure for relatives to visit the wounded in hospital became much easier in July 1940 when the railway companies agreed to supply the British Red Cross with vouchers for it to issue for travel for hospital visits.

In 1941, further concessions were given to service personnel who needed to travel by train. Commanding officers were given the authority to issue free warrants to any soldier or officer below field rank who had been granted compassionate leave to visit their homes which had been severely damaged due to enemy action. This concession also applied to military personnel who wished to visit relatives who had been seriously injured in the bombing raids. It was confirmed that these warrants for free rail travel were in addition to the regular two leave travel warrants issued each year. The military authorities authorising these first- and third-class warrants were charged by the railways on the same basis as the usual 'service' tickets. On 29 September 1941 another fare concession scheme was introduced, this time for return travel at the cost of a single ticket for Home Guards and civil defence workers who were travelling by train between their home and normal place of work. This brought them into line with the servicemen's concession. Those eligible for this concession were able to buy tickets on presentation of a certificate from their employer or civil defence authority. Simplification of the bureaucracy in issuing concessionary tickets was achieved in late 1942 when a new scheme for issuing travel warrants in a form valid as a ticket was introduced. The new form deemed to be the equivalent to a conventional railway ticket, and this relieved the railway staff at the station ticket office of the task of having to check the documentation. There appears to have been little consistency in government policy on the subject of concessionary travel for service personnel, for in June of the same year the minister of war transport wrote to Sir Kingsley Wood MP, the chancellor of the exchequer, acknowledging that the number of railway passengers had increased by fifty per cent with a decrease in passenger train miles run, he had several suggestions to alleviate the overcrowding problem, one of which was to restrict service leave. He also let it be known that he was to withdraw the 'cheap day return' ticket facility as he adjudged that many of these were being used by the public to make 'unnecessary' journeys.

Despite the best efforts that had been put in by the YMCA and others, questions continued to be asked in parliament concerning the lack of facilities for soldiers in transit. Euston and King's Cross were cited as two of the London termini where facilities for service personnel were inadequate. Complaints were received that men who had suffered due to the war, such as those who had returned from the recent unsuccessful Norway campaign, were having to sleep on the ground overnight awaiting their trains. As a result of this parliamentary concern, it was announced that canteens, kitchens, rest rooms, cloakrooms, washing accommodation and inquiry bureaux for troops waiting for trains were to be provided at all of the main-line railway termini in London. The War Office gave strict instructions that only troops and members of the Home Guard travelling in uniform were to be served at the special railway canteens and allowed to use the other facilities provided. The REC agreed that the canteens, rest rooms, etc. would be given rent free to the charitable organisations running the facilities such as the YMCA and Salvation Army. It was agreed that the War Office would reimburse the railway companies the rental costs. On 26 August the War Office announced that all washing and left luggage facilities at railway stations in London would be free of charge for service personnel. Despite all the goodwill from above the 'deplorable' conditions of the services canteen at Carlisle – which was run by voluntary workers and catered for 15,000 troops a week – became the subject of a further question in parliament. It was claimed that troops who arrived late at night would find that there were no refreshments available at all. The government would not directly answer the specific charge but responded by stating that recently at fifty main line stations the facilities for service personnel had been improved. In January 1941 as part of the continuing programme to provide more and better amenities for service personnel, the Ministry of Transport insisted that at Perth station the third-class dining room must be given over to the military for use solely by service personnel and the first-class dining room become a general refreshment room for the public.

In 1940 arrangements were made for the provision of meals and refreshments for troops in transit. Lists of stations where refreshments could be provided for service personnel were provided by the railways. There were three categories of stations. List A were stations where the railway could handle demands for refreshments in any reasonable quantity without outside help. Should there be a peak in demand, help was by military or voluntary bodies. This list of stations included Salisbury, to be provided Birmingham New Street, Guildford and Liverpool Central. The second list, list B, were stations where only a limited demand for refreshments could be met, and should they be used frequently permanent voluntary military help was required. The list of B stations included Dover Priory, Newton Abbot, West Croydon and Scarborough. The third list, list C, were stations where refreshments could only be supplied in an emergency and then only with military or voluntary help. List C included Newbury, Ilfracombe, Kew Gardens and Rhyl. In a typical month, June 1941, the GWR, LNER, LMSR, and the SR through their two catering contractors, Fredericks and Bertrams, served 26,393 meals and 45,466 cups of tea to service personnel.

In March 1941, in line with the Food Order 1941 (Restrictions on Meals in Establishments), it was agreed that the meals offered to members of HM forces in dining cars and refreshment rooms would be reduced. The new breakfast, priced at 1/3d, was thereafter not to include the hard-boiled egg to accompany the two sausages, bread and butter (or margarine) and a cup of tea. The previous luncheon menu, which was sandwiches or small meat pie with fruit, was no longer available. A reduced offering for the dinner menu was also offered. For 1/6 the soldier could select from a menu which now contained less meat, but naval ratings retained their right to a one third pint of ale with their meal. Due to the large increase in the cost of beer, in September 1941 any sailor wishing to enjoy his third of a pint of beer – but only during licensing hours – had to pay an additional 2d. Supper was still to be provided at a cost of 8d, where the choice of having both a meat pie and a sandwich was removed, and the serviceman or servicewoman had to choose to either eat a pie or a sandwich. At the forces' canteens at the London termini, it was decided that civilians were not to be admitted, but there were a few exceptions such as sailors from the merchant navy provided they produced their official papers; railwaymen who were both on duty and in uniform at stations where it had been agreed with the railway company; members of the fire brigades in exceptional circumstances at the discretion of the canteen manager and soldiers' families when public facilities were closed. Railway police were counted as railway staff, but civil police were to be excluded entirely.

As well as preferential treatment at the main stations, service personnel also benefited from on-train catering not available to the civilian population. While buffet and restaurant services were removed from most of the regular passenger services, special trains run only for the services were often provided with buffet cars staffed not by the usual railway employees but by staff from the Navy, Army and Air Force Institute, better known as the NAAFI. In early 1940 the LMSR and the NAAFI joined forces and together ran several buffet cars for use on special trains provided for servicemen. These cars were used on the longer journeys and provided both table seating and an over-the-counter service. They proved to be very popular with the troops and the NAAFI claimed to serve as many as 500 soldiers during the longer journeys. Two and a half years later the NAAFI claimed that since its buffet car service had been introduced on many of the long-distance leave trains, nearly four million snack meals had been served to members of the armed forces. One regular special train service which was provided by the LNER, commencing in January 1943, ran every day from King's Cross to the north of England and Scotland for the benefit of troops returning home on leave. The train consisted of ten coaches and two buffet cars which were staffed by personnel provided by the NAAFI. The LNER gave this special leave train a clear road to secure punctual running. To ensure that the troops got home without delay, the company arranged for it to run ahead of the 'Flying Scotsman' so as to enable use to be made of all connections which were held for that famous train. A daily return special train for servicemen returning to their units was also provided by the railway company. The operation of these trains would have the beneficial effect of reducing overcrowding on the east coast main line from King's Cross where complaints had reached parliament about overcrowding, mainly due to servicemen with their bulky kit.

While the 'is your journey really necessary?' campaign was promoting the elimination of unnecessary travel, the provision of special trains for service personnel did not go unnoticed by a frustrated and irritated public who were then suffering from a reduction in services and a decrease in the number of trains provided with restaurant or sleeping cars. On 2 June 1943 the parliamentary secretary for the Ministry of

War Transport, the Labour MP Phillip Noel-Baker, was questioned by another Labour MP, Samuel Viant, about a particular special train being run by the LMSR. Viant claimed that this train, which was not shown in the public timetable, had been booked to run daily in each direction between London, Euston, and Glasgow, St. Enoch, leaving at 8.40pm. It was claimed that the train was composed of 12 vehicles weighing 437 tons empty, with accommodation for 60 first-class sleeping passengers, 56 third-class sleeping passengers and 290 ordinary third-class passengers. Of the total weight of the train, 210 tons was taken up by the 60 first-class passengers. Given that Samuel Viant was able to give such precise details of the train formation, it has to be assumed that it was the railway staff, not members of the general public, who were agitated by the over provision of facilities for the few at a time when their regular passengers were suffering. Viant requested that, as there was not a public sleeping-car train in each direction on this route, would the government take steps to have such 'luxury travelling' withdrawn as its provision was causing resentment amongst railway staff and members of the travelling public? Phillip Noel-Baker replied that these trains were only a temporary measure to cater for the current exceptionally heavy demand for travel by service personnel and 'others.' He did, rather lamely, attempt to pass on part of the blame to the railway company by stating that any spare capacity on the train was 'placed at the disposal' of the LMSR. All that Viant could extract from Noel-Baker was the promise that this 'really essential' traffic would be kept to a minimum.

Given the largesse shown to service personnel travelling on Britain's railways, what was the effect of what was quite obviously a considerable increase in passenger numbers due to service travel and the consequential effect upon any overcrowding on the trains? The traffic surveys carried out by the railway companies in late 1941 and early 1942, as well as recording the number of first and third class passengers to ascertain how full the trains were, they also noted what proportion of those on board were service personnel travelling in uniform and thus either in possession of warrants or tickets purchased at the concession rate. The SR survey showed that on the eleven Waterloo to Bournemouth trains surveyed on Friday, 24 October 1941, of the 531 first-class travellers, 205 – 38.6 per cent of the total – were officers in uniform. In the third-class compartments where 2,020 passengers were counted, 1,323 of these were service personnel in uniform, which was 65.4 per cent of the total. The survey was carried out at Waterloo immediately prior to the trains' departures. The large number of service personnel on these Bournemouth trains does cause some surprise. Had the trains been on the Waterloo to Exeter route a large number of military passengers might have been expected as this line to the West Country passes through Salisbury which is the gateway to the many surrounding military establishments that are associated with the Salisbury Plain military training zone. In 2020 one elderly gentleman remembered travelling with his mother from Waterloo to Overton in Hampshire on the SR main line to Exeter via Salisbury. The reason for him travelling to the large village set in the heart of the Hampshire countryside – whose main claim to fame is that at Overton Mill the Bank of England banknotes are printed – was a very common one. He was taking part in the unofficial 'self-evacuation' process and was being escorted there by his mother so as to stay with a relative to avoid the dangers of living in blitzed London. The train was so full of passengers that he had sit on an uncomfortable suitcase as all of the seats had been taken by the adults. While he could not remember very much about his fellow passengers, he agreed that many of them were in uniform.

On the GWR South Wales services similar results were obtained. The percentage of first-class seats occupied by military personnel when the trains called at Newport ranged between 20.9 per cent and 66.7 per cent. The lower percentage was counted on the second part of the 8.15am service from Nyland to Paddington on Monday, 13 October 1941, and the 66.7 per cent in the first part of the same service on Saturday, 18 October 1941. The percentage of lower ranked service personnel on the same trains revealed by those counting at Newport, ranged between 26.2 per cent and 73.9 per cent. The lower figure – and it does stick out as being well below the average – was on the 7.35am Carmarthen to Paddington train and the higher figure was recorded on the second portion of the 12-noon train from Nyland to Paddington. Typical values for the percentage of third-class service travel however hovered around 60 per cent.

A survey was also carried out on the LMSR Euston to Glasgow service as the trains ran between Crewe and Carlisle on Wednesday, 29 October and Thursday, 30 October. The combined data from both the 'Up' and 'Down' trains showed that a total of 979 passengers found space to sit down in 1,190 seats. A staggering 80.5 per cent of the passengers were service personnel in uniform.

A traffic survey conducted on the east coast main line on Friday, 6 January 1942 was a single day 'snapshot' but surveyed the passengers on eight separate trains with starting times ranging from 8.05am until 3.50pm. Some of these trains ran the full King's Cross to Edinburgh route, others were shorter journeys starting or finishing at either Darlington or Newcastle. The high numbers of service personnel travelling on this route was again confirmed by this survey. The percentage of first-class seating that was occupied by the more senior personnel was on average 56.2 per cent. The lower ranks travelled in the third-class carriages and, on average, were 79 per cent of the total third-class travellers using the trains. The servicemen travelling third-class, many of whom would have been heavily loaded with their kit, together with their civilian fellow travellers, totalled 200 more than there was seating provided on the train. These trains might not necessarily have been overcrowded for the whole journey however, while the highest passenger figures were on trains that ran between King's Cross and Edinburgh, the surveys were actually taken at intermediate locations such as at York or Darlington.

The REC noted that there was a concentration of traffic around the many dispersed military establishments which caused local overcrowding at certain times on certain passenger trains. There is plenty of evidence for this assumption. One of the busiest lines for service traffic was the LNER route to Yorkshire where there were many new military bases. To alleviate any overcrowding on these and other trains, an instruction had been given that servicemen should be permitted to travel in first class compartments when the third–class seating accommodation had been fully taken. A question was asked in parliament in April 1941 querying if this instruction had ever been issued. The origin of this concern was the severe overcrowding on a 5.50pm departure from King's Cross when there were 300 more passengers than there were seats on the train. The reply offered in parliament was that there was no evidence that the instruction had not been given and on the date in question the railway had run a relief train to ease the congestion. Later in the war in a written answer to parliament on 10 February 1943, the parliamentary secretary at the Ministry of War Transport claimed that soldiers, even when travelling on leave, had to travel fully equipped as fighting units and had to take all of their equipment with them; and this often meant the placing of rifles in the luggage racks, but kitbags could be deposited in luggage vans. Despite the minister's assertion that any soldiers on leave carried all their equipment, this would only be so on the leave travel to and from home and base. Soldiers however, when they travelled encumbered by their kit, were not prepared to let their personal or service issued equipment out of their sight and evidence from a former soldier recalls travel on the LNER main line with trains packed with soldiers and with their kit obstructing the corridors and preventing access to the toilets. He also commented however that at his home in Cheam, Surrey, the overcrowding on the SR trains was 'not too bad'. This was confirmed by another correspondent who, while only a young boy at the time, has no recollection of the local trains on which he travelled on in the south of England being overcrowded during the war.

It will be noted that there was a large number of what the surveys deemed to be 'service' travel in the first-class compartments. Serving officers would have expected to receive warrants for first-class travel but the strict definition of the passengers on the train was 'service personnel in uniform'. Many politicians and senior business leaders had commissions in the Territorial Army and given that in wartime there was only a paper-thin distinction between 'civil' and 'military' administrative affairs, many government officials would have deemed it appropriate to put on their uniforms to carry out their official duties. There was a very good practical reason for this, anybody of military age but engaged in any form of 'office' administration would not get labelled 'conscientious objector' by a fellow passenger in the same first-class compartment. With the dispersal of many of the most important state departments across the land to the provinces, these senior officials would have to make many train journeys to Bath, Harrogate or North Wales. Throughout the war the government would reserve whole first-class carriages for the use of these important government and military officials, but not on any of the trains that were surveyed.

The tacit understanding that it was permissible for passengers to use a first-class compartment if the third-class was full resulted in a contributor to the *Railway Gazette* reporting that during his regular travels by train, he noted that many regular long-distance passengers with third-class tickets – both military and civilian – would head immediately towards the first-class compartments assuming that their chance of being ejected was remote. He observed that many passengers seemed to believe that 'it's all the same now'. Nonetheless, the writer opined that many passengers, even if they have seats, would wish to stand in corridors for large parts of their journeys, and this would contribute to the corridor congestion which made any movement through a lengthy train of say, fifteen coaches, a very tiresome business – especially for any servicemen with full equipment. The writer concluded by reporting that the SR used station announcements to inform waiting passengers as to the parts of the trains which have unfilled seats – a 'regular and commendable practice' that the other railways should follow.

In July 1941, the REC was requested to prepare a brief for the Minister of Transport in preparation for a debate in the House of Commons instigated by MPs advocating the removal of first-class accommodation from all trains to reduce overcrowding. The REC's response in its brief to the ministry was that this would not improve the quality of travel for the third-class passenger since the first-class compartments were limited in number and generally well filled. Fearful of antagonising their most influential customers – which during the war included the most senior civil servants and high-ranking military officers – they argued that their peace time obligations to the travelling public still held true and there remained a public demand for first-class tickets. The government concurred, for in a show of blatant self-interest, Colonel Llewellyn on behalf of the Ministry of War Transport insisted that members of parliament, government officials and senior officers needed to occupy the first-class accommodation. This was necessary, Colonel Llewellyn told the House of Commons, not only because these very important people required privacy in which to do their work but also, they had to have the certainty that they would be able to find a seat on the train if they turned up only a few minutes before the train was due to depart. He insisted that the government had no intention of abolishing first-class on long-distance trains. A month later, a Manchester correspondent to the *Railway Gazette* wrote saying that he had witnessed local suburban trains with first class compartments empty while passengers were standing in the third-class compartments. He also noted that tired workers returning home and servicemen travelling long distances on leave were only very rarely offered a first-class seat. Thousands of railway passengers in the north-west of England, he maintained, had no doubts as to whether elimination of class in rail travel would add to their comfort, despite what the writer described as 'the senseless statements of transport officials'.

Given that there was an expectation that service personnel could use unoccupied first-class compartments when all third-class seats were occupied, as late as 1944 the ministry of war transport parliamentary secretary continued to have to face searching questions in the House of Commons after MPs had heard continuing complaints that members of HM forces were continuing to stand in the train corridors on long journeys owing to the absence of third-class accommodation. The implication was that the railway companies were not permitting servicemen to use the first-class compartments.

The effect that service travel had on the wartime increase in passenger numbers was highlighted in February 1944 when the REC's passenger traffic subcommittee discussed passenger numbers. They examined four monthly periods: January 1942, October 1942, July 1943 and October 1943. For service personnel journeys either on duty or leave warrants or on concessionary fares, the figures for October 1943 totalled 15,887,781, which was an increase of only 0.26 per cent above July 1943, but 48 per cent more than in October 1942 and a massive 92 per cent increase since January 1942. The massive rise in 'service' journeys was attributed to the concessionary fares bought by servicemen and their families, not just the travel warrants issued by the military. An explanation for the rise in service personnel travel was attributed to the ever-increasing spread of military establishments necessitating long distance rail journeys. It was confirmed that there was no limitation on the distance travelled on the concessionary tickets that were available not only to HM Forces but also to members of the US Forces that had arrived in the UK. The 15,887,781 journeys recorded in 1943 can be judged as the peak of service travel since it was after the arrival of the American troops in January 1942 but before the invasion of Europe in June 1944. The majority of the service personnel journeys were made after obtaining tickets at the concessionary rate and not after obtaining a warrant for an 'official' or leave journey. It might be inferred, as the REC did, that these 'service' journeys were longer distance journeys on main-line and cross-country services, but many might have been 'nights out' trips from a local station to a nearby town. It was noted that the journeys using concessionary fares exceeded the journeys travelled with a warrant.

This raises the question as to how much of the servicemen's personal travel might be described as being strictly 'necessary'. Even in wartime, the servicemen would get occasional twenty-four-hour leave passes and many contemporary photographs show groups of servicemen without any luggage. Such photographs confirm the service travel statistics that indicate that most 'service' journeys using the public trains were not for any military or leave-taking purposes but for what might loosely be described as 'leisure' outings and as such it is arguable that the 'is your journey really necessary' ethos was not being followed. The author's father claimed that when he had a short 'holding' post near Portsmouth, after the early morning rollcall he was then free to spend the day doing whatsoever he wished, so he would travel to his family home in Guildford every day by train. This was an extreme instance of service personnel wanting to take every opportunity to be with their families before being posted – perhaps never to return. Whole families were able to travel close to a serviceman's base for family reunions, and American servicemen were able to make tourist visits to places in Britain when off-duty.

The REC was completely aware that the service journeys were the tipping point resulting in the overcrowding on the trains. It noted that while at any moment in time leave was given to only a small number of servicemen or women relative to the total complement at any military establishment, the very low percentage nonetheless constituted a large number of travellers as each leave event constituted two separate rail journeys. To add to these journeys to and from any of the remote bases there was often also the requirement to convey personnel away from the base to attend training centres. Consequently, the REC became increasingly concerned that the trains were becoming overcrowded with noisy soldiers, sailors and airmen who were often guilty of clogging up the corridors and luggage racks and monopolising the available seating. The travelling public's view of the servicemen travelling on the railways also began to shift. The original concern for the young servicemen, seemingly out of their depth in strange environments, began to evaporate. Resentment began to grow amongst the civilian population who were being subjected to government propaganda trying to dissuade them from travel or from taking any holidays – but when they did travel, they were faced with having to fight for seats on the trains and have to make way for servicemen who had been granted generous leave time which was more than they had been allowed for holidays from their essential war work in factories or offices.

While many of the travelling public may have been developing a less than tolerant attitude to the masses of soldiers travelling on the railways, the politicians continued to show concern and to remain loyal to the wellbeing of members of the nation's loyal and brave fighting forces. Despite all the noble efforts by the voluntary organisations, as the war progressed questions continued to be asked in parliament about the perceived shortfalls in the welfare and sleeping provision for service personnel who might be stranded overnight at major junctions and termini. The secretary of state for war responded by stating that what he described as 'decent' night-time accommodation had been provided for servicemen at 70 of the stations that were most used by the troops and that a further 45 facilities had been provided for servicewomen which were either at, or very close to, the railway stations. The secretary of state also asserted that in the event of what he described as a 'more or less permanent change in direction of troop traffic' created a new need, an appropriate level of welfare provision would be provided. He conceded that at many other stations where troops were occasionally stranded, the provision of new dedicated dormitories could not be justified due to the shortage of labour and materials. The minister reminded the House of Commons that it was often possible to obtain beds for the night in most of the larger towns. In 1944 the welfare of the troops was still an urgent issue which was duly being recognised by the REC who knew that service personnel were sleeping rough in stations (sometimes in empty carriages) and they too suggested that hostels close to stations was the solution.

There was one government location that was strictly a 'civilian' government institution but had of necessity solid contact with the military and employed many service personnel. This was Bletchley Park and is probably today the most famous outposted government department which during the war had of absolute necessity as its military intelligence gathering work had to be kept top secret and was therefore completely unknown to the public at the time. What had once been a large private estate was to metamorphose into the home for the government's code and cipher school. This organisation, founded after the First World War, was in 1939 part of the nation's secret intelligence service, better known as MI5. The term 'school' should not be misconstrued. This unit was set to work to decode the enemy's secret messages. It has often been claimed that the staff at Bletchley Park shortened the war by two or three years.

Bletchley Park is located in the Aylesbury Vale and has now been consumed within the huge footprint of the 'new town' of Milton Keynes. In 1939 however, it was in a semi-rural location with only a seven-minute walk to the LMSR's station on its west coast main line. Bletchley station is 47 miles from Euston, today the journey takes about 30 minutes by a fast electric train but in wartime Britain the many visitors to Bletchley Park would have had to allow over an hour to travel north by a steam hauled train from London. The station at Bletchley also served another important railway route – the LMSR's 'Varsity Line' which ran between Oxford and Cambridge. This line crossed the LMSR main line at Bletchley and would have been useful for the many academics at Bletchley which included Alan Turing who is renowned for his pioneering work with computers and had been recruited from Cambridge University. Many of the junior staff were to be billeted at Bedford, about eighteen miles to the east on the Varsity Line.

Turing may have been the most well-known mathematician at Bletchley, but he was only one individual in a small group working within a much larger group of codebreakers. In 1939 there were no more than 200 people working at Bletchley Park. Such was the enormity of the task – even after the acquisition of one of the German Enigma encrypting machines – that the number of staff allocated to the code and cipher school at Bletchley Park rose to a maximum of almost 10,000 people by 1944. Just under threequarters of the staff at Bletchley were women. The Royal Navy provided women who had enlisted in the Women's Royal Navy Service (WRNS) and were posted to Bletchley to work on the decoding by operating the 'bombes', which were electromechanical devices that tested possible coding solutions. There was a large staff of indexing clerks, both civil and military, who were all working hard to collate hundreds of thousands of decrypted messages. Office space within the original mansion at the centre of the park soon became inadequate, resulting in the building of many wooden huts and concrete block buildings and some of these have survived and are now part of the museum on the site. Civilian and military personnel worked side-by-side at Bletchley, and it has been argued that as they were unconstrained by military protocol or long-established bureaucratic civilian procedures, they were able to produce practical and workable ways of solving organisational problems. During the war the work progressed from being primarily a codebreaking operation to become a fully integrated intelligence operation encompassing the interception of enemy messages, cryptanalysis, translation, intelligence analysis and intelligence dissemination to the government and to the military. Being centralised on a single site there was a concentration of expert staff enabling co-operation between specialists resulting in many innovations and consequently many technical innovations were developed in the fields of codebreaking techniques, mechanical, electromechanical and electronic devices, and data management methods.

Recruitment for such secret work was problematic, particularly when more civilian staff were required. All recruits had to be British born with British parents. The senior administration officers had to be men, and all had to be able to speak German or Italian – or both – but the spread of their abilities could range between being described as a 'linguist' to having 'knowledge of German'. Junior administration officers usually had to be men, but a few women were recruited to these posts provided they had some knowledge of German. In 1941 there was a requirement for an additional 60 girls for work that was to be described to them only as 'routine but interesting clerical work'. Details of the recruitment process gives an insight into the work and conditions of service. The posts were not conventionally 'advertised' but an appeal to locate what we can assume to be the 'right sort' of young ladies was made to the Conference of Headmistresses which was the association representing the elite private schools. Due to the sensitivity of the work, direct formal application to the schools was not allowed, so much furtive backdoor searching must have been employed by trusted headmistresses. The location of the work was described as being at a country house at the outskirts of a small town. The young ladies aged 17 or 18 would be safely billeted in private houses. The work at the country house was continuous across the 24-hour day such that staff would work on a three-shift system. Normal hours would not exceed 48 hours a week and any hours worked above 44 would be paid as overtime. Third class railway fares were paid for both the travel to attend the initial interview and for the journey to Bletchley on being appointed. If the girl's billet was further than a reasonable walking distance from their workplace at Bletchley Park, transport would be provided for which they would be charged three shillings a week.

Billeting Officers at Bletchley had been appointed to survey the neighbourhood so as to find suitable discreet accommodation for staff. Local geographical areas were located to each Bletchley Park department, as this would hopefully keep the departmental groups socially apart such that each staff member had a very narrow picture of what work was being performed at the top-secret establishment. The rules around billeting had been tightened up after the early mistakes at Bath and other locations at the very beginning of the war. Householders providing the accommodation were told that they were 'bound by law' to provide breakfast, an evening meal, sleeping accommodation and what was described as reasonable facilities for personal cleanliness – but these criteria did not include the duty to provide a bath. The householder was not obliged to provide a fire in their wartime guests' bedroom or to invite them into their living room. Those billeted could not insist that the householder cleaned their room or made their bed, but many householders would do so without extra payment. It is unsurprising then that many of the younger staff craved the comfort of their family home during their all too brief and infrequent leave periods.

The billets being spread across a wide geographic area and the constraints of the 24-hour shift pattern made the use of public transport for Bletchley Park staff difficult. Despite the on-going wartime issues concerning road transport such as petrol rationing and the need to reduce tyre wear due to the shortage of rubber, initially road coaches were provided for staff to travel to and from the establishment. The use of road transport did have the advantage that it allowed staff to join the coach at more convenient locations. The incensed mother of one young lady wrote to Bletchley Park complaining that her daughter had to stand outside a public house to wait for the coach – surely, she could be collected from outside her billet. After consideration it was agreed that if the girl was ready and waiting outside the house in which she was staying at the time the coach passed by, it was not unreasonable that it should stop and let her aboard. This arrangement, however, does not seem to have been adhered to for very long as it soon became obvious that it was only the mother, not the daughter, who was agitated about being seen anywhere near a public house.

Many civilian staff were seconded from the British Machine Tabulating Company to work on the Hollerith data processing machines. This company was based at Letchworth in Hertfordshire. By 1943 this company was dispatching 2 million tabulating cards to Bletchley Park every week. These essential cards were delivered by road in the British Machine Tabulating Company's own van. The company believed that their road delivery task was unnecessary and enquired if the cards could be sent by rail. The Foreign Office (who were the 'owners' of the establishment) were dismissive of the suggestion. A passenger using the railway route from Letchworth, which is situated on the LNER's line from Hitchin to Cambridge, would have had to take the short journey to Hitchin to change onto a main line service to Sandy at which station a further change was required to travel to Bletchley on the LMSR's Varsity Line. Any of the security sensitive and 'unattended' packages taking the same route would have had to be transferred by railway staff between trains and a road vehicle would still have had to be sent from Bletchley Park to collect the cartons of cards from Bletchley goods station. The use of the road vehicle did not chime with the national need to conserve imported fuel for the van's engine and rubber for its tyres, but the official view that was taken was that this use of valuable resources was acceptable for such vital government work.

By June 1942 there were 2,420 staff working at Bletchley Park. The Royal Navy provided thirty officers and seven Sergeants and other ranks. WRNS on the site totalled 289 of which eleven were officers. Also employed were 1,462 civilians – 360 men and 1,102 women. Working on the continuous shift pattern the staff were allowed one day off duty every seven days. For those who had to travel a considerable distance to enjoy their leave at their family home – almost certainly involving a rail journey – two consecutive days leave a fortnight was permitted. In exceptional circumstance three consecutive days leave were grudgingly permitted in a three-week period – but not regularly and was subject to their section head's approval. By 1942 in addition to staff at Bletchley Park the code and cipher school had sprouted several branches across the country. Some coding and cipher personnel were outposted to the City of Oxford, others to Northleach tucked away in the Cotswold Hills, some more to Knockholt in rural Kent and others to Denmark Hill in London. What were described as 'special duty WRNs' were outstationed in nearby Buckinghamshire villages such as Wavendon, Adstock, Gayhurst and Stanmore.

It was over 20 miles between Bedford and Bletchley and on 24 April 1943 a 26-seater coach bound for Bedford with a full load of passengers was in collision with a 12-ton diesel lorry and trailer which resulted in five passengers and the RAF corporal driver requiring hospital treatment. It was however the increasing number of staff, not concerns about road safety and petrol shortages, that prompted the increased use of the railway as transport for the Bletchley Park shift workers. The numbers of potential travellers amounted to between 50 and 60 staff who arrived at Bletchley at 4.00pm and departed at midnight, and between 10 and 15 who arrived at midnight and returned to Bedford at 9.00am. A further 10 to 15 normally departed at 4.00pm. In September 1943 this was manageable using road transport, but by November 1943 it was anticipated that due to extra staff and the requisition of many more billets in Bedford, these numbers would increase to a level that was more than double the previous count. After negotiations between the regional transport commissioner, Sir Henry Piggott, and the REC, the LMSR were forced to agree to the provision of extra trains to be run to and from Bedford and Bletchley. The first of these weekday trains was the 11.10pm train from Bedford to Bletchley. Although the LMSR deemed that 150 passengers were needed to make each of these new services viable, Bletchley Park could only promise that at first only twelve passengers would make use of one of the new services in one direction. The train would return to Bedford at 12.20am with an anticipated 60 passengers. At 9.25am another extra train would run from Bletchley to Bedford, the senior officers at Bletchley Park estimated that about twelve shift workers would regularly use this train. On Sundays only, the LMSR was to provide two extra trains, the 4.25pm from Bedford to Bletchley and the 4.25pm Bletchley to Bedford, both of these with an anticipated thirty-five shift workers on board. It would seem that strings had been pulled by the regional transport commissioner to persuade the LMSR to provide loss-making services – although it was possible for ordinary, non-Bletchley Park staff to travel on the trains.

Later in the war transport to and from Bedford had evolved. The earlier transport difficulties, despite the increase in staff, were in part eased by reassigning shift workers to more convenient billets. In June 1944 the transport arrangement consisted of a mix of rail and road transport. On weekdays a train departed from Bedford at 8.10am, arriving at Bletchley at 9.00am. This train did run on Sundays but left Bedford 10 minutes earlier. A second train left Bedford at 3.11pm and arrived at 4.00pm – this service was replaced by a motor coach on Sundays departing from the LMSR St. Johns station in Bedford slightly earlier at 3.00pm. The midnight arrival at Bletchley was also a motor coach, leaving the garage in Midland Road, Bedford at 10.45pm. Those leaving Bletchley at 9.00am travelled by road and those leaving at 4.00pm travelled by train as did those leaving at 6.00pm. Both of these trains ran slightly later on Sundays. Shift workers returning to Bedford at midnight were provided with road transport. Civilian workers paid 3 shillings a week to use this transport, both road and rail, service personnel had different arrangements with their respective service.

The average age of the Bletchley Park staff was low, as it was made up of many young unmarried women, both civilian and the WRNs, working with many bright young academics who had been recruited straight from the universities. Few were local and had been recruited from far and wide across the country and would have been living in billets close to Bletchley. Despite the strictures not to travel, they would have wished to regularly visit their families at home and so join the ranks of the railway passengers making up the 'extra' passenger journeys created by the war situation. Obviously, the Bletchley Park staff had to do their work in conditions of absolute secrecy, making any discussions around 'what are you doing for the war effort' when they returned home completely out of the question. It is also hard to imagine that the draw of London, which was not a great distance away by train, would have been irresistible to so many young people looking for excitement to break the tedium of their work on their precious days off-duty. Other 'extra' railway passengers were the result of considerable 'business travel' resulting in a steady interchange of senior military staff between Bletchley and Whitehall.

There was no limit on the distance travelled on the service personnel tickets, warrant or concessionary, so when passenger numbers rose and war related freight traffic increased, the REC wished to take control of a situation that was beginning to become uncontrollable; it requested that the government instigate some curtailment of the concessionary travel for service personnel. It was agreed that from May 1943 some restrictions were to be put on service concessionary travel, but it was confirmed that the reduced fare arrangement for boys attending military schools that had been evacuated to remote areas should continue. A year later in 1944, the growing number of service personnel travelling continued to be of concern to the REC, who were aware that the forthcoming D-Day invasion preparations would further increase the military freight traffic. Certain restrictions were applied in March 1944 including restrictions to leave intended to help contain travel over the Easter period. Restrictions were also placed on the servicemen's families too, in 1944 the wives and dependents were restricted to only three journeys during the summer.

Chapter 10

Time to Take a Holiday

The British determination to celebrate a holiday is obvious to the most casual spectator.

England's Hour, Vera Brittain 1940

For many years following the Second World War the popular belief was that during the conflict everybody in Britain gallantly worked together in a united effort to defeat the enemy. Writers such as Angus Calder described the dedication and travails of the wartime civilian population in his book *The People's War* which was published in 1969. It was this author however who twenty years later set out a revised view of wartime behaviour with the publication of another book, *The Myth of the Blitz*. The historiographic thrust of Calder's 1991 book is not to deny the events in the same way that a 'holocaust denier' might pervert facts, but by using what information is freely available, he asserts that the public's understanding of the events has been largely germinated by wartime propaganda and patriotic sentiment. He confronts the populist vision of a nation in which every loyal citizen gallantly contributed to the war effort and stoically accepted all the deprivations – a mythical population that would surely never have undertaken any 'unnecessary' railway journeys. Such journeys would have been the opposite to the blind acceptance of government-imposed restrictions that were absolutely necessary to produce the unified all-out effort required to win the war. While it has been shown that arguably much of the travel by service personnel might be deemed unnecessary, any extra travel by the civilian population was largely reasonable and necessary due to the wartime circumstances.

Except, that is, for holiday travel. Taking long railway journeys for a holiday during the war might be seen as an indicator that the public were not always prepared to patriotically fall into line with the wartime government's propaganda. The push against any restriction in the taking of holidays came from those hard at work in the factories and fields. During the war, all those of working age had to register for employment and then endure the very long working weeks for arguably inadequate remuneration.

Throughout the war period the civilian population appeared to never lose its desire to travel away from the drudgery of the workplace during the bank holidays or to spend a week or two at the popular holiday resorts such as Blackpool. In the first months of the war the government did not make any direct attempts to restrict 'unnecessary' holiday travel. The railways were on the side of the public as they attempted to maintain as near as possible a 'business as usual' service for their passengers – and this included holiday traffic – despite the pressures from the government to reduce the number of services. Initially the REC decreed in September 1939 that the 1940 editions of the railways' holiday guides would not be published in 1940; nonetheless in December 1939, the LNER announced that it did intend to issue its 1940 edition of its *Holiday Handbook*. Similarly, the LMSR was to continue with the publication of its *Holidays by the LMS* and its companion guide promoting the joys of a holiday at the Scottish resorts that it connected by rail. The GWR too proposed to publish its *Holiday Haunts* in 1940.

The government's view on this subject was voiced by the minister of transport, Captain Euan Wallace, who in 1940 readily understood the need for workers to take holidays and announced that the railways should provide services in wartime on condition that they were 'as far as possible compatible with their performance duty'. Thomas Levey MP, the Conservative member for Elland in Yorkshire, queried this rather vague message and questioned Euan Wallace in the House of Commons on 10 April 1940. He wanted to know if the railways were to provide excursion trains with cheap fares during the forthcoming summer season. The minister would not give a direct answer, but clearly stated that while in wartime precedence had to be given to the movement of government and other essential traffic, the railways should endeavour to maintain the ordinary passenger traffic as far as was possible. He reiterated his view that the government recognised the importance of workers being able to enjoy leisure and recreation and that the intention was that the railways could provide the cheaper travel facilities providing that this would not interfere with the railways' essential wartime duties. Not receiving an explicit confirmation that excursion travel was to be made available to the public during the forthcoming summer, the MP for Elland seemed to imply that within the sub-text of the minister's reply was the hint that there would not necessarily be any cheap excursion trains that summer. Under pressure Captain Wallace responded by stating that he 'hoped' that such facilities would be provided.

Despite the ministry's apparent lack of any precise policy on leisure travel, the railways remained very keen to provide a holiday service during the summer of 1940. The Ministry of Transport and the REC had discussions about the provision of additional trains to enable the public to travel to coastal resorts for their annual summer holidays. The REC believed that the public desire to enjoy a seaside holiday would best be met by providing a number of additional trains to be run between selected industrial areas and the pleasure resorts which were most conveniently situated from the railway point of view. It was proposed that, as far as was possible, mid-week trains would be run where they could be justified by the expected volume of traffic. These additional holiday trains would be advertised locally with full details as to the fares to be charged. The REC proposed that the tickets should cost the holidaymaker not less than what would be the single fare for a double journey. By 17 May 1940, the railway companies had made their full preparations to begin an advertising campaign intended to promote the series of holiday trains at reduced fares. The campaign was to use posters at stations, to distribute handbills and to place announcements in local newspapers. It was also hoped to enlist the support of positive editorial comment in the local newspapers. The only concession to the war situation was that any advertising in the press must be subject to the limitations of space in the newspapers and magazines. Starting in June and continuing into September an ambitious programme of additional trains was proposed by the GWR, LMSR and LNER on Sundays from London and many provincial stations. The SR, meanwhile, were to provide additional trains on Tuesdays, Wednesdays and Thursdays from its London termini.

Meanwhile, as the railway companies made their preparations for what was hoped to be a busy summer of holiday services, the railways had to provide services for the first significant holiday period following the ice-stricken Christmas of 1939 which was the Easter holiday in March 1940. Notwithstanding the heavy pressure on their services, the railway companies were able to provide an augmented programme of passenger trains to cater for those travelling during the holiday period. Easter in 1940 occurred on the earliest possible date in the year for the festival, but this proved to be no disincentive to the public to travel as they were rewarded by better than average fine weather. Despite the perceived national gloom and trepidation, the numbers of those travelling at Easter created a volume of traffic which exceeded the forecasts of the many pessimists. Thousands of London residents left the city for short breaks in the country or at the coastal regions while many of the recently evacuated civil servants travelled home to London in the opposite direction for the holiday break away from their new workplaces at Bath, Harrogate, North Wales, Torquay, Southport and many other locations. The favourite resorts for the holidaymakers were Paignton, Torquay, Bournemouth and Brighton. The LMSR had record bookings for travel from Euston, for not only were the receipts higher than for the previous Easter, but the actual increase was also twice that which had been recorded in 1938. It ran 385 additional trains on Thursday, 21 March for the civilian holidaymakers in addition to the 109 special leave trains which it provided for the forces. The busiest period was on the morning of Good Friday 22 March when the bulk of the passengers were boarding the holiday trains which were destined to run to Lancashire and Scotland, and also to the ports at Holyhead and Heysham for connections to the sailings across the Irish Sea to Eire and Northern Ireland.

There was a similar story on the GWR when services that had been suspended at the outbreak of war were, as they had been for the previous Christmas holiday, temporarily restored. The GWR declared that traffic was even heavier than in peacetime and on Good Friday every booking office window at Paddington station was open as there was so many passengers queuing to buy their tickets. On the LNER too, a number of train services which had recently been withdrawn were temporarily reinstated and, added to these, more supplementary trains were provided for the Easter holidaymakers. The travel agents, Thomas Cook and Son, noted that as holiday traffic to the continent was no longer possible, those who would have taken a holiday abroad now booked tickets to English resorts instead.

This brief period of holiday joy proved to be just another unfortunate facet of the 'phoney war'. With what we now know about the history of the Second World War, the railways' excursion plans for the summer of 1940 now appear to have been over-optimistic, even possibly somewhat naïve. On 10 May 1940, the German army began the invasion of the Low Countries leading to the surrender of the Dutch government only four days later. With the increasing threat of invasion, the government did more than just plead with the populace to forgo their Whitsun holiday by remaining at work and avoiding all unnecessary travel, it enlisted the assistance of King George VI who issued a Royal proclamation cancelling the bank holiday.

Unfortunately, this drastic measure did not result in the elimination of all of the holiday travel that had been planned in May 1940. The answer to the question that this was due to the monarch's plea being made too late for it to filter through to most of the population or that there was mass disobedience is uncertain. Despite the government's orders, at Blackpool the entertainment providers and boarding-houses claimed to be quietly satisfied by the influx of visitors during the 'cancelled' Whitsun holiday. This was despite the late withdrawal of the advertised 126 extra trains that the LMSR had scheduled. Some of the hotels and boarding-houses did receive telegrams from compliant would-be holidaymakers, but it was claimed that these were relatively few in number and many of the resulting vacancies were filled by those who had arrived in the resort without pre-booking any accommodation. The town and its visitors made the best of the situation as the promenade and the sands were described as being crowded with visitors. The normal scheduled passenger trains were run as usual but due to the number of passengers wishing to return home, particularly by the LMSR trains to Manchester, the passengers had to be what was euphemistically described by the railway as 'regulated', that is passengers were left behind when the overfull trains left on Monday evening. Those who had to stay in Blackpool for an extra night had to obtain supplementary ration tickets which were available at the town's Central Station.

Further south along the Lancashire coast at Lytham some reduction in the number of visitors was experienced but the holiday atmosphere was maintained. As it had been in Blackpool, much of the cancelled accommodation was filled by visitors who had made late decisions to come for a short holiday in the town. The usual open-air and indoor band concerts were well attended. Bathers took to the sea at St Annes and boating was popular on Fairhaven Lake. The locality is associated with golf and over the Whitsun period many visitors arrived to enjoy a game on the golf courses. No noticeable reduction in road transport was observed, so given that it was a holiday weekend it would seem that much of the available petrol rations were put to good use to convey visitors either by motor coach or by their own personal cars to Lytham. At Southport, a town served by both the LMSR and the Cheshire Lines Committee – a railway owned jointly by the LMSR and the LNER – the local corporation carried out its planned programme of special holiday events. For the first time a pierhead concert was held which proved to be very successful and was well attended. A large party of 250 visitors who had planned to travel to Southport from North Wales cancelled their accommodation but some civil servants who had been evacuated to the town due to the war decided not to return home for a short break and consequently filled many of the vacant rooms in the boarding-houses.

On the other side of the country at Scarborough, all of the holiday attractions continued as planned. The numbers of visitors however were reduced by thirty per cent down to the level that would be expected during a 'normal' summer weekend. The town had been doubly affected by both the decision to abandon the Whitsun holiday in many of the West Riding towns and the cancellation of the extra trains that the LNER had originally proposed to provide. Despite the increase in car ownership that had occurred during the 1930s, relatively few holidaymakers would have arrived at Scarborough by car, but it was noted that the number of visitors arriving by car for either a half or full-day visit was described as 'considerable' but it was conceded that there had been a smaller number than expected.

The fortunes of the Lake District were mixed. The hotels in Windermere and Ambleside were inundated with cancellation telegrams. The uncertainty as to the number of train or bus services that were to be provided into the area was the reason given why the many day trippers arrived either by car or charabanc. It was reported that those who intended to have either camping or cycling holidays had often started out on their holiday before the government issued its order and they had continued with their plans as if nothing was amiss.

Despite the mix of outcomes at the northern resorts, the true realities of the war had begun to strike home, and the government was pleased that so many people had responded to the plea to cancel their Whitsun holiday. But worse for intending holidaymakers, the government went even further by insisting that the public should forgo *any* annual holiday they were planning for the summer. In later years of the war the general mood of the public was to insist that they all fully deserved to be able to take holidays but given the grave international situation in May 1940 a large proportion of the public did patriotically respect the pleas not to travel. To further dissuade holiday traffic and maintain vital production in the factories the government decreed that the 1940 August bank holiday was to be cancelled, and the railways obliged by agreeing to operate only the normal Sunday and Monday timetables. Later in July, with the nation under the threat of imminent invasion, the original defence area order issued on 20 June 1940 which had originally consisted of only the twenty-five-mile coastal strip from the Wash to the eastern border of Sussex, was extended to include the holiday resorts of Brighton, Shoreham, Worthing, Littlehampton, Bognor and Selsey and further west as far as Portsmouth and included the Isle of Wight.

After the Dunkirk evacuation, the government's appeal to abandon annual holidays for the duration of the war was intended to divert transport resources away from leisure travel towards the movement of troops, the production of war materials – munitions and weapons – and the ever-present requirement to convey the nation's coal supplies. For the railways any decision to avoid or curtail the huge numbers of people who wished to take a seaside holiday in August might appear as a welcome relief as their routes were already severely overburdened with the abnormal traffic due to the war. The government proposed anybody wishing to take a break from work should arrange to take long weekend breaks and if this coupled with rosters of rest periods for staff this would keep in constant operation all of the essential units of industry. Additionally, the manufacturing companies should be encouraged to arrange for their staff to take staggered holidays – a notion that the railway companies had long advocated.

Consequently, despite the government's exhortations, many workers and their families believed that after their strenuous wartime efforts in the factories and elsewhere they deserved a good holiday and were prepared to tolerate the crowded trains. Some of the public were unconvinced of the need to restrict travel as it could be observed that the overcrowding was not universal and often trains had empty seats. Furthermore, it was to be proved that holiday passenger numbers were lower than pre-war and some of the trains were less crowded than had been predicted by contemporary press coverage. Despite the government's pleas to abandon holidays, the REC aligned themselves with this growing belief that to maintain personal health and workplace efficiency a holiday away from home was necessary and justified and it was reasonable during the stressful war period to expect more people to want to take holidays away from their home and workplace. The government however launched what it saw as a compromise and launched its 'holidays-at-home' strategy. Following government encouragement, it was hoped that the populace would avoid any travel to seaside resorts and take time off work to enjoy the delights that their local areas could offer. Newsreels showing crowds of happy families sunbathing in municipal parks or enjoying jumping into the local lido were soon to be shown in the cinemas.

The Easter bank holiday in 1941 was observed quietly in London. The call to 'stay at home' was generally obeyed, although some Londoners made short journeys to either visit friends or relatively near-by attractions. The centre of London became a magnet for those living on the outskirts of the capital as the West End pavements were crowded with people visiting the cinemas and often queuing for places in the restaurants. Those who approved of the holidays-at-home appeal saw London as a good example of what was possible. Observers noted that in the capital throngs of local people partaking of this 'new manner' of holiday enjoyed what the capital city had to offer them rather than travelling away by train to country districts and seaside towns. London Zoo had 10,000 visitors but the Victoria and Albert Museum (the only museum that remained open during the war) had only 1,400 visitors. At Stamford Bridge 7,500 spectators watched a football match between Chelsea and Arsenal.

In North Wales at Easter 1941 the holidays-at-home campaign had a lesser effect as trains to Rhyl, Llandudno and Colwyn Bay were full as were the hotels and boarding houses at these resorts. Many of the visitors to the area however were parents who were using their holiday time to visit evacuated children, either those who had been part of the government scheme or those who had made their own private arrangements. Also arriving from the south were family groups taking the opportunity to travel up from London to visit relatives who were civil servants now outposted at towns along the North Wales coast. At Southport the local residents were surprised by the volume of visitors, particularly the large number arriving by train. Over 15,000 visitors arrived at the LMSR station, and these included 10,000 from Merseyside. Given the proximity of the Liverpool conurbation to Southport these journeys might be included in the 'holidays-at-home' category. But others travelled from further afield, from Manchester, Rochdale, Wigan and Preston.

Despite some of Manchester's citizens departing for Southport by train, generally the population of Manchester remained at home over the holiday period. The railway stations were described as being crowded with passengers, but these were mainly servicemen or their families rather than those leaving the city for a short holiday. No concessions were made by the railway for those wishing to make a journey for a day trip or short holiday, and many train services were withdrawn. The general consensus held by the Manchester residents was that to make a train journey to their favourite venue, Blackpool, was more trouble than it was worth. Only what was described as 'business' express trains to destinations such as London or Birmingham were supplemented by the provision of duplicate trains when necessary.

When summer arrived, the public were less inclined to comply with the government's wish that holidays should be abandoned. Those who wished to take a holiday at the coast would have been encouraged to learn that the coastal 'defence areas' were being very slightly reduced. On 25 March 1941 it again became possible to visit the south coast west of Peacehaven which opened up Brighton and Littlehampton to visitors. The ban had been reduced to only include a coastal strip five miles in depth along the Norfolk, Suffolk and Essex coastline, the whole of Kent (except for a few inland Rural and Urban Districts), and some of the Sussex coast. To remind the public about the defence area rules, on 29 May the minister of home security issued a statement aimed at any intending holiday makers which clearly stated that they must not overlook the ban which permitted only those who had business in these areas were allowed to enter. The message to the public clearly reaffirmed that visits for a holiday or other recreational trips were not permitted and that anyone entering the defence area must carry their identity card with them.

Reducing the coastal defence area was not to be taken as the green light for more holiday traffic as a memorandum dated June 1941 from Gilbert Szlumper made it very clear. The REC were reminded by Szlumper that it was official government policy that the public must be exhorted to refrain from travelling away from home for their annual holiday. The exceptions to this edict were for any of the war workers who wished to travel to visit their evacuated families. Szlumper in his memorandum informed the REC that the Ministry of Information was to produce a poster with the slogan: 'Please Avoid Travelling – HOLIDAY AT HOME – Goods Transport Must Come First in wartime'. He had been asked to find out from the REC if they thought that such a poster would be effective in curtailing passenger traffic. Rather coldly, the REC, who by then was well aware that curtailing passenger numbers was a difficult task, replied that they did not believe that such a poster would be effective, but nonetheless they would exhibit it if requested to do so.

Despite the intervention by Szlumper, it was obvious that the railways were to continue with what they saw as their statutory duty which was to match passenger demand with appropriate service provision as the holidaymakers transferred their allegiance away from the banned south coast resorts for those in the southwest of England.

The SR and GWR gained business with additional holidaymakers travelling to their resorts in Dorset, Devon and Cornwall. Similarly, those in the north eschewed the south coast beaches, travelling instead to resorts in the northwest such as Morecambe and Blackpool. Such was the increase in traffic to these areas that extra trains had to be run. The railway companies often resorted to running what was at the time the standard practice of providing 'duplicate' trains, resulting in a single service in the count of passenger trains advertised in the public timetables but actually run as two or more separate trains to cope with the overwhelming demand by the holidaymakers. Those following railway operations were able to observe that this 'duplication' of services was taking place after the holidaying public had been prohibited from travel into the restricted areas on the south coast.

Examples of duplication that were noted included the activities of the LMSR in the north-west when on Saturday 21 June it ran a total of seventy-one extra trains, a number of which were overcrowded, for example the 8.42am Manchester Victoria to Blackpool with 1,800 passengers on the train. A similarly overcrowded 8.42am Halifax to Blackpool left with 1,500 passengers, both of these trains were composed of fourteen coaches. A week later the SR ran eight additional Saturday extras to Bournemouth and the West Country – all of which were overcrowded. On the same day, the GWR ran twelve extra trains to the West from Paddington, and these included the Cornish Riviera Express which ran as five separate trains, the fifth of which carried 900 passengers. In an attempt to provide extra seating, the REC proposed the withdrawal of all the catering vehicles which would provide extra compartment coaches with between fifty and sixty extra seats. Withdrawal of the few in number Sleeping Car services was not recommended however since it was suspected that passengers would simply transfer to day services thus aggravating overcrowding on these trains. But the railways were having difficulties in operating so many trains; amongst their issues was the shortage of precious locomotive coal. The REC accepted the idea of vouchers for workers to visit their evacuated families following the Blitz; stating that it was not possible to run special excursions for war workers taking their week's holiday.

Meanwhile the evacuees were not to be forgotten by the railway companies and the local authorities. Despite that, earlier in the year in March, the REC had decreed that weekly holiday season tickets would not be issued in 1941, in July, it was announced that special vouchers for reduced rate return tickets with an eight-day validity were to be issued for those who wished to spend their week's summer holiday with members of their families who had been evacuated. This scheme, which arguably was not contrary to the policy that only workers visiting evacuated families should travel for a holiday, was to run until the end of September. The vouchers for the tickets were to be made available to anybody who was entitled under the existing arrangements for cheap travel to visit evacuated relatives. The only condition to be applied was that the applicant had to show evidence that they had booked accommodation for themselves at the holiday destination.

Also in July the Ministry of War Transport announced on Tuesday 29 July that the movement of freight traffic would continue throughout the holiday without interruption. The public seem to have had little care for the ministry's intentions, and it was reported that notwithstanding exhortations by both the railway companies and the government that in the national interest they must abstain from all unnecessary travel, passenger movements during the August bank holiday period were described as 'relatively heavy'. This was despite the newspaper advertisements that had appealed to the public to avoid unnecessary travel. Posters and press advertisements had included the text: 'If you are taking the day off on August bank holiday either "stay put" or go where your own legs will carry you'. The public were informed that they should not expect any special travel facilities. The government propaganda message intended for those who were tempted to travel by train that August was to not hinder the war effort as the goods traffic on the railways was more important than the passenger traffic. Also, the message to anyone who thought that they could travel by car rather than by train, the simple message to them was 'don't waste petrol'.

The following summer, 1942, the government seems to have realised that no matter what, many hard-working war workers were desperate for a holiday. In its ongoing appeal to the public's patriotic duty and in an effort to reduce the demand on the railways, throughout the year the ministries of labour and information continued to promote the 'holidays at home' policy. The government recognised the necessity to ensure that every hard-working factory worker who was engaged in essential war work was able to have a summer holiday but at the same time there was the necessity to keep as many people off the railways as was possible. Part of the Ministry of Labour's propaganda that unnecessary railway travel handicapped the war effort was to cite instances where essential workers, after queuing patiently at a station, were unable to travel on the train as it had to depart full of passengers making, apparently, unnecessary journeys. To carry out the difficult and not very popular policy of holidays-at-home, local authorities and other organisations were requested to organise a variety of events in their towns. The Ministry of Labour would assist by coordinating efforts if required in the efforts to encourage the populace not to travel away for their annual holiday.

Not every local authority was happy with the policy. The clerk of Barnoldswick council was not convinced that the population of this small market town in Yorkshire could be tempted away from the holiday resorts. He regretted that the railway companies were continuing to run excursion trains and it would be an unfortunate waste of public money if the town was to organise events and only a very few people attended. In respect of the 'holidays-at-home' policy, John Rhys Davies, the member of parliament for Westhoughton – which is four miles southwest of Bolton – asked the parliamentary secretary to the Ministry of War Transport if he would like to spend his holiday in Bolton or Manchester when Blackpool was only 40 miles away by train?

In line with the government's policy and despite many misgivings, many of the local authorities did accept the government's challenge and organised events to tempt residents away from the fun and frolics to be enjoyed at the seaside resorts. It was hoped that the local lidos and parks would prove a substitute for the sea and the beaches. In Harrogate where there were many staff working in the town for the RAF and outposted government departments, a three-week programme of events was organised during August 1942. Thousands of the Spa town's residents and others from the surrounding area were entertained by watching or partaking in a big athletic meeting held on the Harrogate cricket club's ground; an event which was promoted as a 'victory gardens show' held in the car parking area of the Royal Hall; a road-walking event, or a children's pet show which had over 800 entries. There was also a 'salvage drive' which accumulated a mile of unwanted books. Unwanted publications which were donated to the mile of books laid out through the streets included old council agendas, mystery novels, theological works and street directories. The athletic event was organised by the Hospital Sportsman's Effort Committee and was deemed to be the most ambitious of the stay-at-home season. At the conclusion of the events the mayor, Ernest Schofield, concluded that the three-week event had been successful and that he had not received a single complaint from either a resident or a visitor.

Not all workers were prepared to accept the pleas not to travel by train and enjoy your holiday at home. One objection to the holidays-at-home was that families separated by evacuation would naturally wish to spend their summer holidays together. The Ministry of Labour's advice was that a worker whose family had moved to a safer part of the country should travel to the reception area and the family holiday spent at that location.

In July 1942 critical questions were asked by the MPs in parliament who believed that more should be done to restrict railway travel and requested details about any measures being taken to prevent unnecessary travel. The parliamentary secretary to the ministry of war transport, Sir Arthur Salter (the MP for Ormskirk), replied to such concerns by informing the House of Commons that the strategy at the time was to rely simply on appeals to the public to refrain from any unnecessary travel, especially long-distance travel. To discourage travel he stated that a large number of cheap fares had been cancelled and others had been restricted to allow travel over a comparatively short distance. He asserted that only a limited number of passenger trains were run, and he assured the House that these did not impede essential freight movements and that in no circumstances would this limit be exceeded.

Following this answer Sir Arthur was further questioned when he was asked if he was aware that there was widespread concern following newspaper reports that additional trains were being provided for holiday travel which was resulting in railway stations becoming overcrowded with holiday visitors to popular resorts. He responded by agreeing that some extra trains had been provided but only on the strict understanding that they would not in any way impede the movement of essential freight operations. Another MP enquired as to what instructions had been given to the railway companies in respect to the provision of extra or duplicate trains for holidaymakers and was it fair to those who had sacrificed their annual holiday and following instructions had stayed at home where they continued to suffer the effects of the shortage of domestic coal. Sir Arthur answered by saying that it was a matter of balance, the relatively small amount of coal used in the locomotives could be weighed against the considerable advantage not only to the enjoyment but also the overall health of those who travelled by train to the holiday resorts. It was noted that this went against previous statements from the ministry in respect to permitting the railway companies to provide additional trains, so, had this decision been reversed? Sir Arthur, somewhat cornered by the intense questioning, explained to the House that there had been some relaxation of the rules but to a very limited extent and, as he had explained, on condition that essential freight traffic was not hindered. The debate in the House of Commons moved on to discuss the possible travel arrangements for the wake weeks and town holidays that were a feature of the large industrial towns when whole communities would leave together for the annual break from the drudgery of the factories. Annually extra trains were run to accommodate the short-term peak in demand for holiday travel over relatively short distances. The ministry announced that under no circumstances should any more trains be run by the railways to meet this demand than had been run the previous summer.

As in 1941, with the 1942 August bank holiday approaching, as part of the 'holidays at home' campaign, the Ministry of War Transport made use of the newspapers and on the BBC radio to appeal to the public to refrain from travelling by train during the holiday period. These attempts to reduce holiday traffic proved to be even less successful than had been the similar attempts to dissuade the public to travel during the previous Easter and Christmas holidays. On the first day of the holiday weekend, 1 August, there were dangerous crushes and overcrowding at the GWR's Paddington station – the principal route to the unrestricted resorts in the west. Given the travel restrictions to many of the resorts in the south-east of England, to many observers of railway operations it came as no surprise that anybody who did not share the government inspired patriot sentiment that holidays should be spent at home would make the simple choice and flock westwards. The *Railway Gazette*, irritated by the government's interference in railway operations, opined that had the railways been left to manage their own business instead of being dictated to by those without any railway experience, the obvious desire to travel westward would have been foreseen and suitable provision provided. At King's Cross, Liverpool Street, Waterloo and Victoria the government propaganda seems to have had a limited success, the passenger numbers were reported as being less than on a normal Saturday preceding a Bank Holiday and many trains were not fully loaded.

On 23 February 1943 Ernest Bevin, the Labour MP and prominent trade unionist whom Churchill had appointed as the minister of labour and national service in the wartime cabinet, when speaking in a debate on the mobility of labour in the House of Commons, made his views on holiday travel very clear. He hoped that everybody would be encouraged not to travel. This was because the forthcoming months were to be vital for the movement of the armed forces and munitions. He told the members of parliament that a government policy on holidays would shortly be forthcoming but stated that anxious as so many parents were to visit their children who were scattered across the land, he reminded them that the one great help that they could give to the national war effort during the following year was to simply 'stay put'. Other members of parliament listening to Bevin were concerned that it was not just parents who were suffering from enforced separation due to the war. There were also concerns about the welfare of female war workers, mainly young unmarried women, who had been transferred away from their home locations to work in factories engaged in war related industries, in particular the manufacture of munitions. They too needed an opportunity to meet family members, often their parents. Mr (later Sir) Oliver Simmonds, the MP for Birmingham Duddeston, was deeply concerned about the plight of the hundreds of women working in his constituency who were separated by great distances from their homes. Understandably these women, he said, felt that they too were entitled to travel home to enjoy a prolonged period with their families in their home locality.

Despite Bevin's hint that a firm policy on holiday travel was soon to be announced, no clear ruling as to exactly what this might be was to emerge. The various government ministries appeared to have been in conflict respecting this issue. The Ministry of War Transport announced that there would not be any extra trains provided during the summer. Ernest Bevin, despite his lack of favour for any holidays to be taken away from home, nonetheless made the case for the staggering of holidays. This would have assisted the railways by reducing the traffic peaks. The Ministry of Health sent out circulars to all of the local authorities urging them to put plans in hand. The opinion of many was that any potential holidaymaker had to make up their own mind whether or not he or she was justified travelling by train to a holiday destination. The *Railway Gazette* commented on an article in the *Manchester Guardian* pointing out that more elaborate plans were being made for holidays-at-home and at the same time additional trains continued to take workers on holiday to the seaside, commenting that these trains were not strictly excursion trains but many in the industrial north were very glad that they were still available.

The holiday prospects for 1943 did however look brighter for on 1 March the 'defence area' ban on leisure and holiday traffic was partially lifted and the coastal areas from the Wash to the Thames estuary, between Hastings and Littlehampton and the whole of the Isle of Wight, became accessible again. All that remained barred to the holidaying public was the coast of Kent and East Sussex. This welcome relaxation immediately created a problem for the LMSR. The railway immediately became aware that the intensity of the passenger traffic to Southend and intermediate stations was rapidly approaching peacetime levels. The volume of passengers on the trains was such that many of the war workers who regularly used this line were being crowded out. The REC had argued that any system of 'limited travel' would be impractical and difficult to administer but faced with the overcrowding on the Southend route local LMSR staff used their own initiative and worked out a system which allowed the many passengers holding either season or workmen's tickets the certainty of accommodation on their regular trains. This was achieved, following an urgent census at each of the stations, by a limitation on the number of 'ordinary' bookings to be made at each of the stations. Once any of the stations reached its predetermined quota of sales no more were issued.

In the summer of 1943, the government's pleas to forgo holiday travel were blatantly ignored by a public which had after years of wartime fear and deprivation become tired and frustrated by the monotony of work in the wartime factories and offices. There was a pre-war demand for holiday travel without the provision of addition trains. On Saturday, 24 July 1943, the weekend before the traditional August bank holiday, the 1.25am night train to Ilfracombe departed leaving 1,500 passengers disappointed on the Waterloo station concourse. On Friday 30 July the SR ran a relief train for the 1.25pm departure and the following day a queue began to form for this same train at 3am. The Ilfracombe train would have been used by holidaymakers to many Devon destinations, but those going all the way to north Devon resorts had great difficulties in finding accommodation, some desperate individuals walked as far as Combe Martin and resorted to sleeping in hammocks strung from the branches of trees in an orchard. The local food officer in Ilfracombe confirmed that there were sufficient quantities of 'staple foods' for the influx of visitors. All of the London termini had to manage what appeared to the railway officials as a mass exodus from the capital while thousands were returning to London to spend their holiday time at their pre-war addresses. At Paddington the GWR had to erect barriers at the start of the bank holiday exodus to control the crowds wishing to travel by night trains to the west. Queues for the night trains to Cornwall and South Wales started to form early in the evening.

In North Wales it was reported that thousands of passengers arrived by early trains on Saturday to enjoy a short holiday in Llandudno, Colwyn Bay and Rhyl but the torrent of arrivals eased up later in the day. Despite many of the holidaymakers having the foresight to bring with them their own food, considerable strain was placed on the local catering and food shops. At Conway, not only were the pubs 'dry' on Sundays as required by law, they were also 'dry' the whole of the weekend due to the shortage of beer. Many of the visitors to North Wales travelled by train from Liverpool. The LMSR maintained that they were very busy but not overwhelmed by the crowds at either Exchange (for the Blackpool coast) or Lime Street (for North Wales) stations. Such was the desire to be able to board what were to become packed trains bound for North Wales that queues formed early for the scheduled departure, for example on the Friday a queue started to form at 4.30am for a 7.20am service. Meanwhile trains from Lime Street to Euston were described as leaving full 'as usual'. Generally, across the north of England, it was reported that what the press called 'holiday invasions' resulted in visitor numbers being the highest of the war years and at some resorts these rivalled pre-war figures.

Despite all the government and local authority encouragement, the REC Publicity Control Committee on 14 October 1943 expressed little surprise at what they deemed as the failure of the government's 'Holidays at Home' campaign. Noting the exceptional holiday traffic during the traditional August bank holiday period, they acknowledged that too many people, particularly those in the North, had dutifully forsaken their week away at a remote holiday destination but instead took trips daily out by train to more local attractions, negating completely the aim of reducing rail travel. In the Scottish city of Perth, while the population appeared to outwardly accept the holiday-at-home concept, nonetheless rather than travel a great distance to a seaside resort, they travelled only as far as Dundee. While there was a holiday atmosphere in the city of Perth with all of the shops closed, because the local ice rink had been closed for the duration of war, many young people boarded the LMSR train to journey 18 miles to Dundee to enjoy the Dundee-Angus ice rink. At the same meeting the committee considered the likely policy for holiday travel in 1944. The Ministry of War Transport was expected to take the lead by requesting that holidays be staggered so as to avoid unmanageable peaks in passenger traffic. The committee's analysis of the situation was that it would be reasonable to expect more people wanting to take holidays away from home and workplace. The committee members also accepted the growing belief that if personal health and workplace efficiency was to be maintained, a holiday away from home was necessary and justified. Note the acceptance of the word 'necessary'. In the winter months early in 1944, just as the public's thoughts began to look forward to warming days on a beach, the Ministry of War Transport informed the REC that due to the uncertainty as to what conditions might prevail in the coming year, regretfully they would not authorise any additional trains to be scheduled into the forthcoming summer timetables. Furthermore, neither would they authorise the running of special trains in connection with important works or town holidays. The promise to review the situation in the spring of 1944 was reported to the passenger traffic subcommittee on 5 January 1944. More bad news for those with the reasonable and simple wish to enjoy a break from the wartime drudgery was received at the next meeting of the subcommittee when it was reported that it would not be practical in the current circumstances to run the same trains as had been run during the summer of 1943.

The 'current circumstances' were the need to build up supplies of munitions, to transfer military equipment from manufacturing base or port of import to the receiving military bases, and to convey troops which were being reinforced by the influx of American soldiers – all to make preparation for the anticipated invasion of the European mainland in 1944. The code-name for this operation was 'Bolero'. Passenger trains, particularly if they were transporting 'unpatriotic' workers to enjoy a holiday by the sea, had no place in this clandestine operation.

Chapter 11

Towards Victory

If in those spring days of 1944 some observer from another planet had been perched high in the air with a bird's eye view of the south and south-west of England, it would soon have occurred to him that something vast and strange and, as far as could be, secret was going on.

Bernard Darwin *War on the Line* 1946

As the war progressed, ever more pressure was placed on the railways and the public to reduce passenger travel. The top-secret Operation Bolero was a two year long preparation for the allied invasion of Europe during which time the nation's inland transport (predominantly the railways although there was also much road traffic) had to transport across the country all of the ingredients for a concerted all-out military campaign. There was a steady build-up of military traffic, both in personnel, equipment and munitions activity, prior to the invasion of Europe which would take place in June 1944 – D-Day.

In addition to the military build-up and the spread of military activity, government and private organisations had continued to relocate their businesses away from London. Since the beginning of the war, as well as several government departments, many of the private companies moved office staff out of London. These included the Standard Telegraph and Cable Company who relocated staff to Leicester, and Sankey-Seldon who moved their staff to Tadworth and Oxford. The railways also moved staff away from London – at the outbreak of war the SR established an office and control centre in Dorking, a much safer location than the central London offices at Waterloo station. The SR board continued to have its meetings in Waterloo until the offices were bombed and the meetings were held across the river at the Charing Cross Hotel. The GWR did the same by moving to Aldermaston in Berkshire and the National Union of Railwayman also went to another small town which was in the 1940s in the same county, Wallingford.

Many cultural and educational establishments had also relocated away from the danger areas during the war creating further passenger traffic for the railways. These included the Slade School of Art which relocated to the Ashmolean Museum in Oxford. At the start of the war the theatres had been closed but the decision was soon reversed as it was understood that they could perform a morale-boosting service. Following bomb damage in the cities, many theatrical companies moved to the safety of the provinces. Other companies toured during the war including the Old Vic and Sadler's Wells who entertained civilians, war workers and service personnel on leave by travelling to locations such as northern industrial towns and Welsh mining villages. In 1944, this increase in 'theatrical' traffic was noted by the REC, who claimed to have no difficulty in accommodating these large groups in reserved compartments. The BBC did already have a presence in North Wales since 1935, but during the war BBC Bangor hosted the corporation's variety department. Perhaps the most iconic production from the studios in North Wales was ITMA ('It's That Man Again') which was broadcast from the city from 1940 until 1943.

In December 1940 the MOF expanded its operations by making the decision to establish what it described as its 'war room' facility in the Colwyn Bay locality. The chief purpose of the new war room was to act as the centre for the collection of information and the passing forward of the instructions for action to be taken on the reports received. The war room took on the responsibility for the collection and dissemination of reports from all sources in respect of the direct and indirect effects of enemy action which impacted upon the work of the Ministry of Food. A war diary of air raid incidents was to be used to collate reports on damages to food warehouses and other locations that dealt with food manufacture, supply or distribution. It was also charged with receiving and acting upon any messages containing what was described as 'key points'. For example, any message containing 'fish' or 'fruit and vegetables' would be passed on by teleprinter to the Oxford office. Any reports appertaining to other commodities such as 'dried fruits', 'eggs', or 'flour and cereals' were to be telephoned to the various offices spread across North Wales. The main war room was built in the basement of the Colwyn Bay Hotel, with a back-up room provided at the former school at Rydal. The war room also had a potential other role as a national control centre should there be an enemy invasion and a direct communications link was provided to the western command headquarters.

These relocations of important business and strategically important government offices resulted in more passenger traffic on the railways. Recognising the natural wish for all transferred workers, whether employed by government departments or private companies, to visit their families, the Ministry of Labour announced a 'cheap travel for transferred workers' scheme on 30 April 1942. This enabled transferred workers, subject to some conditions, to visit their homes by paying only 7/6 for the return ticket. The scheme was to be suspended during the winter months (from 15 September) as the need to restrict passenger travel was more acute in the winter to safeguard the flow of coal traffic. A later modification which appreciated the need for labour to harvest crops in the summer permitted agricultural workers whose homes were in Northern Ireland or Eire to travel on the scheme in the winter months.

As the war progressed and the nation, with the assistance of its American allies, duly prepared for the massive assault on mainland Europe on D-Day in June 1944. This created the need for many discrete production centres to be established in the provinces to provide the hardware. Many of these factories were Royal Ordnance Factories (ROF) while others were the result of massive expansion and diversification of existing privately owned manufacturing companies.

Often these private companies would set up production away from their traditional locations in urban locations and move out into the countryside to 'safer' locations.

The many civilian workers who had been moved away from their homes to work in these remote factories, as well as travelling home occasionally by rail, were often provided with special trains to take them to work and return them at the end of their shifts. For example, in April 1944 the REC gave approval for a special train for 300 workers to convey them from their wartime works in Coventry and Birmingham to Barnoldswick in the West Riding of Yorkshire. This part of England had become the host to companies such as electrical component manufacturers and car makers, including Rover, who converted former cotton mills for their wartime activities. At Barnoldswick the early jet engine 'W2' was developed by Rover to Frank Whittle's design. In 1943 it was decided that the Rolls-Royce company would step in and take over the Rover factories to produce the RB23 Welland jet engine. The first jet engine to be both designed and built from 1944 at Barnoldswick was the RB41 'Nene.'

Due to the increasing military traffic, it became all too evident that the railways' ability to provide adequate passenger services was becoming more difficult. The passengers' travel experience was further deteriorating, travel by train had been almost 'business-as-usual' in 1939 but was incrementally becoming more difficult. The chronic shortage of locomotives was mainly due to the railway workshops having to concentrate on non-railway production such as aircraft, tanks, and munitions. The record levels of traffic associated with Operation Bolero had greatly increased train loads and further aggravated the situation. The increased hours the engines were used in service and the inferior fuel that had been used was a factor in the increase in the number of repairs which the railways had been unable to carry out due to not being able to obtain sufficient labour in their running and repair sheds. Consequently, there was an ever-growing number of locomotives in the sidings awaiting repair. Many of the railways' freight locomotives had been sent to France with the BEF in 1939/40 but these had either been destroyed or had been left on the other side of the Channel after the German onslaught in 1940 so locomotives were delivered to Britain from America. These were the USATC class S160 which had been built in the USA by ALCO and Lima in 1942 and 1943 and shipped to South Wales. The intention was that these very foreign looking engines would be used in Europe after the planned invasion but in the meantime, under the guise of simply 'running in' the locomotives, they were put to good use by the railways who were becoming short of serviceable locomotives. The GWR gratefully received 174 locomotives, the LNER 168, the LMSR 50 and the SR 6, a total of only 398 of the expected 800 shipped were to be put to good use on British railways. The second batch of locomotives arrived in Britain but were held in store at the GWR Ebbw Junction depot ready for use in Europe. The 'loaned' American locomotives running on British railways were due to be sent to Europe so at the end of March 1944 the railways had to withdraw them from service so that they could be prepared for their intended role. All of these engines had to be put into top running order by the railway workshops before shipment, and this requirement was a further handicap for the railways struggling to attend to the necessary repairs to their own locomotives.

The railway workshops' war-related work resulted in a substantial reduction in the number of new engines being built. This dearth of new locomotives necessitated many older locomotives being kept in service long after they had reached the end of their expected economic life, and the maintenance of these ancient assets had consequently become a heavy task. Nonetheless, some new locomotive construction did take place, and not just by repeating the building of existing types but also a few new engines were built to new designs which were arguably more suitable for the wartime conditions. The LNER built the first of its Class B1 4-6-0s which it described as being their 'standard general utility' locomotive and thus suitable for war duties.

Production was not rapid, despite the immediate need for modern mixed traffic locomotives; only the first 10 were built during the war between 1942 and 1944. Post-war production soared to a final total of over 400. Between 1942 and 1945 the SR built 20 of its Merchant Navy Pacific locomotives which can only be described as express locomotives, but the railway insisted that they were 'mixed traffic', justifying their construction during the war. The SR did however produce 40 of their 'austerity' Q1 0-6-0s which were ideal for wartime freight traffic and their stark appearance was the polar opposite to the elegant Merchant Navy locomotives.

There was also a serious shortage of passenger vehicles for since the outbreak of war a large number had been destroyed and several thousand damaged. Almost 1,000 carriages had been converted for use as ambulance trains and many of these had been sent overseas. Other carriages were being used at certain locations to provide temporary accommodation for transferred industrial workers. The shortage of labour and materials had prevented the construction of new vehicles during the war and the available stock in 1946 was several thousand coaches less than at the outbreak of war. This rendered it necessary to keep the remaining stock in traffic for excessively long periods without repair and this caused a steady deterioration in their general condition. The REC accepted that the incidence of passenger traffic and shortage of passenger vehicles was not identical for each of the four main companies but nevertheless overcrowding was general on all systems during the summer months. It will be noted that the REC implied that it was the holiday traffic in the summer months that was the tipping point resulting in overcrowded trains, suggesting that this was not a problem outside of the holiday season. In 1944 the public perception that the war was now nearing the end was one of the factors which caused many more people than in 1943 to wish to travel for holiday purposes. The public, knowing little about Operation Bolero, craved normality and many sports events still being run despite wartime austerity. For example, the 1944 cup final was held at Wembley on

Saturday, 15 March. This was however an unofficial event organised as a replacement for the suspended FA cup and was won by Charlton Athletic, beating Chelsea 3-1. The government allowed the match to take place, but the railways were not permitted to provide any extra trains. Charlton Athletic were however not the only winners, the FA earned £26,000 of which almost half, £12,000, was transferred to the government's coffers as entertainment tax. Horse racing was also continuing to a limited extent, but no special trains were permitted for travel to the horse racing fixtures, so all racegoers were forced to use the normal services. This resulted in acute overcrowding in the trains and many racegoers were left stranded at the stations as full trains departed. In April 1944 the government delivered another blow to horse racing when it barred the railways from conveying horses by rail to the race meetings.

Facilities at the stations were beginning to suffer after almost five years of war. There was some criticism in the press about the poor service that was being provided in the railway station buffets which included the allegation that 'the scene within a railway buffet is dismal and horrible'. A response came in a letter to the *Railway Gazette* from a worker in one of the station buffets who claimed that a railway buffet attendant's day was both trying and strenuous and was especially so since the withdrawal of restaurant cars made the public dependent on station buffets for refreshments. She agreed that some of the premises were due for reconstruction which, but for the war, doubtless would have already been undertaken, but a number of railway refreshment rooms had been modernised in recent years. She also agreed that a brightly lit buffet was very attractive, but fuel had to be saved so lighting was being kept to a minimum. It had been suggested that 'the tea is never ready', but the attendant maintained that many of the customers were so argumentative that even if the tea was ready to be served before the complainer entered the room, he would probably protest that his tea was 'stewed'. She understood that at many busy junction stations the tea was always ready, particularly just before the arrival of a train from which 200 to 300 passengers may besiege the rooms. It frequently happened that several busy trains would follow each other into the station at very short intervals, and the buffet staff would then endeavour to serve everyone, so often in these circumstances, the counters might sometimes have been not as clean as the staff would like them, but this was dealt with immediately things quietened down. The attendant declared that it was most unfair to complain when they all did their best to put what really mattered first – that was to provide passengers with something to eat and drink. On the general matter of slowness of service, she claimed that it was not always appreciated that the Ministry of Food required the girl serving behind the counter to keep a record of every cup of tea, every bun, meat pie, sandwich or other item she sells, so as to enable the inevitable government form to be filled up. Without the production of that form, no replacement of supplies was ever authorised. The attendants would often have a much clearer idea of time available for catching a connection than the traveller, and frequently knew that the customer who declared that he had only two minutes to consume his drink would actually have a full ten minutes to enjoy his drink before his train was due to leave. The buffet staff did not want to make any excuse that their wages were poor – because often the wage packet contained twice the money compared with before the war. The final riposte from the attendant was to say that the women serving in the railway buffets had a particularly harassing and tiring job to perform and 90 per cent of the travelling public were appreciative of the manner in which their work was done, and they were as resentful as she was of the recent attacks in the press.

In January 1944 the REC and government were aware that, despite their propaganda output, passenger numbers continued to rise. The REC were concerned that the situation on both the main lines and cross-country routes would become 'more acute than experienced in 1943'. Consequently, the REC insisted that it was becoming even more necessary for the government to make arrangements to stagger workers' holidays. In February 1944, the Ministry of War Transport, in the full knowledge that huge demands were already being placed upon the railways and that these were soon to be increased as D–Day approached, was naturally concerned that passenger trains might hinder the all–important military traffic associated with Operation Bolero and stipulated that the number of passenger trains to be run during the summer of 1944 must not exceed the number that had been provided in 1943. In fact, the ministry insisted that the number might have to be reduced. The REC offered their suggestions, proposing a curtailment of both service travel and 'business' journeys by government department staff, and both of these were carried out to a limited degree at critical times. A partial revival of the 'permit to travel' idea re–emerged with the suggestion that civilians could only travel after signing a declaration that their travel was essential – an idea not accepted by the government.

The REC passenger subcommittee predicted that weekend travel was likely to be particularly difficult during the coming year especially that to the main holiday resorts, and they conceded that, in the circumstances, the railways should not offer improved services outside the usual holiday peak as they might not be able to fulfil these services. Nonetheless the REC passenger subcommittee predicted an increase in passenger journeys and feared that this would make travelling conditions even worse for the public unless they could be persuaded to take their holidays earlier or later in the summer. The prime motive for the proposal to stagger war workers' holidays was to keep production going during the summer months, albeit with fewer operatives, rather than the usual complete shutdowns of factories for two weeks. This policy obviously had of course a knock–on advantage to the railways. In 1943 the Ministry of War Transport had issued a report admitting that the attempt to stagger holidays as had been advocated by the minister for labour Ernest Bevin had not been successful. Consequently, an urgent request came from the government that a 'renewed effort' must be made to spread the holiday periods in the coming summer of 1944.

The primary cause for so much concern about passenger numbers was the impact that passenger trains would have on the Allied invasion of Europe. It would soon be necessary to make drastic cuts in passengers to allow the unrestricted passage of troops with their equipment to the secret embarkation ports. Details of what was likely to be necessary could not be made public and to manage passengers' expectations the concept of a 'stand to' was developed. The REC proposed that the public should be informed that due to the pressures being put on the railway services it could not be guaranteed that all of the services to be shown in the new 1944 summer timetables would be run. Furthermore, trains were likely to be cancelled at short notice. The Ministry of War transport informed the REC that it had no objection to the wording 'cancelled until further notice' being used when trains had to be suddenly withdrawn. The military authorities were nervous about too much information being distributed to the public and requested that any such lists of cancellations of trains should only be posted at the stations affected. Nonetheless in May 1944 authority was given for press release concerning the withdrawal of eighteen LMSR and LNER services as these were well away from the main military activity. Also, authority was given to run special trains for school and college vacations in the summer of 1944 on condition that the trains did not interfere with essential freight or passenger traffic (and it was not stated but this would include any military traffic) and that the running was provisional and liable to cancellation. To further reduce passenger traffic during the critical summer months, during the six-month period April until September, the number of vouchers issued for visits to evacuees would be reduced from each month to one every other month.

From the perspective of our age when 'social media' can spread news around the world in a few seconds, it seems strange that such information indirectly linked to secret military activities should be made public. Such changes would only have been made at the very last minute and the Allies had been fooling the enemy into believing that the attack would be via the Straits of Dover. The railways helped in this subterfuge by transporting decoy materials for spreading about the Kent countryside, one SR driver was surprised how easy his locomotive coped with a very long train of covered wagons until he peeped under the tarpaulin to discover that the 'tanks' were actually made of cardboard.

With Easter 1944 approaching and, in theory at least, the public being unaware of the stress being imposed on the railways by Operation Bolero, in January 1944 the REC took stock of the situation and made plans for the holiday timetables. Good Friday 7 April was to be treated as a normal working day; on Easter Saturday a normal Saturday service was to be provided without any of the usual bank holiday extra services; a normal Sunday service was to be provided on Easter Sunday and Easter Monday, usually a bank holiday, the normal weekday service would be run without any bank holiday extra trains. To deter holidaymakers and avoid overcrowding on the trains, adjustments were to be made to the concessionary fares that were still available to certain groups of travellers. The long-standing workmen's ticket would be available as normal. The issue of tickets for organised parties of young people travelling to camps and rallies was withdrawn for the holiday period unless they were provided for parties of military or air force cadets travelling to training locations. Commercial travellers' week-end tickets would not have their validity extended to include Good Friday and Easter Monday. The reduced rate tickets for relatives visiting refugees (and that included those displaced due to the bombing) were to be suspended from Thursday, 6 April until Tuesday, 11 April. The REC requested that the managers of workers of staff at evacuated government departments – and others whose place of work had been transferred – must restrict their approval of leave between 6 April and 11 April, whether the employee was to travel either at their own or at government expense. War production workers and members of the fire brigades, civil defence units and police reserve units who had been transferred to work away from home must not be issued with vouchers for travel during the same holiday period. With school holidays in mind, the amount of luggage and bicycles belonging to children or students returning home from the dispersed boarding schools or university colleges must be kept to a minimum. The REC stated that such items, often sent as 'passenger luggage in advance', were clogging up many stations and an appeal was made to schools and colleges to contact the local stations for advice. The availability of one type of concessionary ticket was not going to be an issue since Lord Leathers had succeeded in his desire to ban the cheap day return ticket which would have been much used over the Easter holiday period. The withdrawal of this facility had reduced leisure rail travel as anticipated but with unintended consequences – severe overcrowding on the buses in the Croydon area. As a final deathblow to the remaining restaurant car services, the REC announced that after the usual bank holiday withdrawal of the dining cars, they would not be reinstated after the Easter holiday period.

Despite the 'is your journey really necessary?' strictures from the government and reports about overcrowded trains, there was still those for whom a railway journey was a thrilling adventure. One of those was a schoolboy who travelled from Waterloo to Padstow in north Devon without any complaints of overcrowding or blocked corridors – or even filthy dirty locomotives. It can be assumed that his journey was outside of the peak holiday period, but he may have been returning to boarding school after a school holiday. He wrote a long letter to his father which was later published in the SR's staff magazine. No date was given for this adventure but from what information was provided it was sometime between late 1942 and 1944. The boy described how his train of eleven carriages left Waterloo at 10.55am which was the wartime departure time for the 'Atlantic Coast Express'. Hauling the train was one of the SR's Lord Nelson class 4-6-0s, *Sir Martin Frobisher*. The train first ran surprisingly slow to Queen's Road, and then even slower as it passed Loco Junction which was the access to the huge Nine Elms motive power depot. A possible explanation for such a slow speed may have been temporary speed limits since a considerable amount of damage had been wrought upon this section of the line during the recent Blitz.

Steaming sedately through Clapham Junction, passing the carriage-washing shed the boy saw what he describes as 'an ugly old 4-6-0 Paddlebox' on a short goods train. A London and South Western Drummond 4-4-0 was also to be spotted propelling a rake of coaches through the washing plant and the boy was able – despite the shortage of staff in the locomotive sheds – to report that the locomotive looked 'very smart'. Once Clapham Junction had been passed at 11.7am, the speed increased as far as Woking. Using the wheel-tap counting method the young traveller estimated that the train was moving along at a steady speed of 55mph as it passed through Wimbledon and later reached 60mph at Surbiton. At Wimbledon they passed another train bound for Waterloo 'tearing by' hauled by one of the new 'Merchant Navy' class locomotives.

The train arrived in Woking station at 11.30am. Here, in the local goods yard, an H15 4-6-0 and a new 'utility' Q1 0-6-0 were engaged in shunting activities. The boy noticed at Woking a train of flat trucks loaded with what he described as 'caravans' – hardly a wartime necessity, but they might have been intended as temporary accommodation or office trailers for the military. A real treat was in store for the young railway enthusiast for as the train passed through Brookwood a 'simply perfect' ancient Adams 0-4-2 was spotted shunting in the goods yard. Again, despite the locomotive's age and the wartime conditions this locomotive was also described as being 'very smart'.

The train arrived at Basingstoke at noon. Another Lord Nelson 4-6-0 was seen here which tore through the station at an estimated speed of at least 70mph. The boy claimed that his train was later subjected to a speed restriction at Worting Junction where the west of England and Southampton lines diverge. He was under the impression that, despite the wartime speed restrictions, his train's speed was reduced to 70mph. The countryside near Andover was described as 'boring', but near Thruxton aerodrome there was some excitement – a plane was seen towing a glider. This airfield had been an RAF base between 1940 and 1946 and the troop carrying Horsa gliders were at this site, and many of these which became surplus to requirements remained there until they were scrapped in 1945. Probably what the boy saw was a (secret) training flight in preparation for D–Day. At Andover the young traveller was 'amazed' by the number of sidings, and he spotted some GWR locomotives in the yard.

Salisbury was reached at 12.39pm. If this was a correct timing – and there is no reason to assume that the lad was mistaken as his letter was published by the Southern Railway – this was only 26 minutes longer than the non–stop 1962 schedule and this trip had included two stops at Woking and Basingstoke. This means that the overall average speed for the journey including stops was 48mph, not bad when wartime trains had supposedly been officially substantially 'decelerated'. At Salisbury two coaches were removed and one of the new Merchant Navy class locomotives, 21C7 *Aberdeen Commonwealth*, replaced the Lord Nelson locomotive. After enjoying seeing a variety of steam locomotives around the station, just before leaving the city at 12.45, another express train was seen, this time a fifteen carriage express with 21C4 *Cunard White Star* leading. The boy described this locomotive as a 'marvellous sight', and despite the austere wartime plain black livery, the engine's paint and motion work was gleaming. The boy's train was held by a signal check in a cutting just outside Salisbury, then restarted with an ease that impressed the young enthusiast for it moved across the bridge spanning the river Nadder without 'a sound nor a puff from the engine'. It was a steady run to Templecombe where passing above the Somerset and Dorset Joint Railway afforded a view of one of the S & D 2–8–0s. The boy wrote that he was impressed by the way that 21C7 accelerated the train up Crewkerne bank, the speed never falling below 45mph.

Beyond Templecombe, the train passed through the beautiful Devon countryside, it was a bright sunny day with the hint of a heat haze clinging to the hilltops. The foot of Honiton bank was reached at 2.1pm, where speed had to be kept down to 25mph due to ongoing permanent way repairs. *Aberdeen Commonwealth* climbed the bank without any effort at all such that at the top of the incline the engine had steam to spare with a spurt of steam lifting off the safety valves – this blowing off of steam at the top of the bank was the only sound that could be heard. The boy remarked that the King Arthur locomotives previously used on this line would have noisily reduced speed to 15–20mph. *Aberdeen Commonwealth* had a relatively easy task with only nine carriages as one of the reasons given to authorise the building of the Merchant Navy locomotives in wartime was that at locations such as Honiton bank it would be possible to lift fifteen coaches unassisted up the incline. The same locomotives could, and often would, be used on long freight trains on the route to Exeter. The more 'wartime' locomotives, the much lighter Q1 locomotives, never ventured west of Basingstoke.

At Sidmouth Junction four coaches were taken off, destined for Sidmouth and Exmouth, and the train duly arrived at Exeter Central at 2.28pm – only 33 minutes slower than the 1962 schedule. There was much to see at Exeter Central, the passengers on the train were at last able to see 21C7 for the first time as it made its way back to Exmouth Junction on one of the centre lines. This locomotive appeared that day to be more in keeping with wartime expectations as it was very dirty, but nonetheless still a fine sight.

The train continued with an SR 2-6-0 in charge, easily 'freewheeling' down the bank to Exeter St. Davids where a GWR west country express hauled by a Castle class 4-6-0 was passed. Back on SR lines Okehampton was reached, where the Plymouth portion was detached, and complicated shunting manoeuvres were carried out to place a horsebox behind the engine. The now much shorter train trundled through the lush Devon scenery to arrive at Egloskerry station which that day was engulfed in smoke from large grass fires. At Delabole the station appeared to be deserted, as no work could be seen to be taking place in the quarries. The horsebox which had inflicted the delay to the train at Okehampton was taken off at St Kew Highway station – costing several more minutes.

But the train seemed to be making up time as it raced towards Wadebridge, taking the tight curves on the way at speeds of between 35 and 40mph. On this section the first views of the Camel estuary were glimpsed. There was little railway activity to be seen at Wadebridge station, only a GWR tank engine taking water. The tide was half out and the low water in the Camel estuary was host to many seabirds. Padstow was hidden by a heat haze but came into view after a slow crossing of the girder bridge. Arrival into Padstow station was at the scheduled time of 6.30pm, just 50 minutes longer than the post–war schedule.

As part of Operation Bolero all of the armaments, aeroplanes, munitions and the countless sundry military stores items had to be supplied to various locations in the south of England. Much of the equipment and consumables of war were deposited, perhaps less discreetly than would have been liked, in multiple dumps spread across many rail heads in southern England. The stores and equipment were in danger of overwhelming the larger railheads such as Eastleigh so were distributed to relatively minor stations and this traffic had to take precedence over the usual goods traffic at peaceful locations such as Andover, Brockenhurst, Christchurch, Winchester or Lyndhurst Road deep in the New Forest. The build-up of troops spread right into the west country. As far west as Westward Ho! on the north Devon coast the Army's amphibious warfare centre was located and during the lead-up to D-Day, British troops were stationed nearby on the north side of the river Torridge, and a mass of American troops on the other side. During their training period the servicemen from both nations would travel off to Exeter and beyond from the SR stations at Bideford or Instow, often crowding into the trains and blocking the corridors.

With the imminent Allied invasion of Europe, the government and REC propaganda became more serious. Now there was no place for humour, as new posters adopted a distinctly strident note. On the

'Is Your Journey Really Necessary?' poster the benign middle-aged couple and their dog standing in front of the booking office window pondering as to what they should do was replaced by a fully armed soldier brandishing his rifle, effectively barring access to the railway's booking clerk. A new poster primarily aimed at those who were considering taking the train to a seaside resort that summer was issued by the REC and had the stark, brisk message printed in bold letters, 'Do not Travel'. The *Railway Magazine* promoted the same message on the front cover of their July/August 1944 edition and reinforced this with an illustration of a railway semaphore signal in the 'stop' position. This edition of the magazine would have been delivered to subscribers in June at the time when the invasion was taking place. This intrusion into the world of railway enthusiasm was not universally well received by the readership. One correspondent showed his disdain in the next issue and possibly summed up the public's attitude to being branded 'unpatriotic' in respect to holiday travel when he wrote, 'One can get a lot of propaganda at the railway stations and in the daily press – do let us keep clear of it in the *Railway Magazine.*'

D-Day arrived on 6 June when Allied troops of the 21st Army Group commanded by General Montgomery made the surprise crossing of the English Channel to land in Normandy, and not, as the Allies had led the Nazi Generals to expect, making the shorter crossing using the Straits of Dover. Anybody who resented the young British and American troops crowding onto trains for leisure journeys at subsidised ticket prices in the months before D-Day should consider that during the first fifteen days of combat in Normandy during June 1944, 40,000 Allied soldiers were either killed, wounded or listed as 'missing'.

Despite the extra railway traffic prior to D-Day, the month after the invasion proved to be even busier, in fact the busiest so far during the war. The railways ran a staggering total of 17,500 additional troop and equipment trains – an increase of 33 per cent compared to the military traffic during May. These trains had to be run without interrupting other essential traffic such as the 4,000 coal trains and the 25,000 trains which carried war workers to remote factories engaged in war production.

Despite the progress in France and the opening up of holiday beaches, for the SR at least the worst aspect of the war, the damage from enemy action, continued with the V1 and V2 attacks. The SR along with the rest of southeast England began to suffer the effects of first the German V1 flying bombs – the 'doodlebugs' and later the V2 missiles. The 'V' stood for *Vergeltungswaffen* meaning 'retaliatory weapon' or 'reprisal weapon', relating to the German point of view that these weapons were in response to the massive RAF and USAAF bombings of the large civilian populations of Germany. For passengers in the south this made an unwelcome return to the bleak days of unplanned diversions and the subsequent irritating delays. Both of the V weapons held their individual terrors for the civilian population: the doodlebugs first announced their arrival by the throbbing noise from their primitive ram-jet engines and then, following its cut off, there would be incredible tension while those below waited to find out exactly where it was to land; and the V2s came with a different class of terror, travelling faster than the speed of sound, they arrived without any noise warning whatsoever.

The Southern Electric lines suffered considerable damage from the V1 doodlebugs at various locations including structural damage to Victoria, Wimbledon and Falconwood stations and to bridges at Merstham and Peckham Rye. The station at Falconwood was destroyed on 31 August 1944. Unfortunately, passing through the station were both of the high voltage cables to Dartford which were also damaged. This resulted in severe disruption of the electric passenger services to Dartford by all three routes. On the very last day of the V1 attacks the bridge at Peckham Rye carrying the SR's Catford loop over the former South London line was so badly damaged that it had to be taken down and replaced by a temporary military style trestle bridge. Services on both lines had to be cancelled but the SR was able to take full advantage of its extensive suburban network and many Victoria trains were diverted to Holborn Viaduct. Hampton Court Junction suffered the effects of a V2 rocket and in Bermondsey a bridge carrying the South London lines across Southwark Park Road was destroyed, necessitating the construction of another temporary trestle bridge.

For many clerical staff working in London the need to travel by train for a holiday well away from the daily horror of the flying bombs pounding the capital grew stronger. When the August bank holiday weekend arrived what was described as an 'invasion' took place as thousands arrived before dawn on the Friday for trains to Devon, Cornwall and Bournemouth. The 1.25am train from Waterloo to the west country was packed with passengers, leaving 900 more to wait in a queue for an extra train provided at 10.50am. They were joined by others who left on a train at 12.50pm. Trains leaving Victoria for resorts still technically part of the defence area had empty seats, but it was reported that many holidaymakers intended to disobey the ban. At Manchester Victoria, bookings for Blackpool were less than previous weeks and two long special trains ran with empty seats. The LMSR at Liverpool expected a rush of passengers who were hoping to leave early and avoid the crush, but they were surprised by the low numbers of people arriving at Liverpool Exchange which they described as being less than for the week before; indeed there were more passengers returning from their holiday.

With potential passengers still clamouring for a well-earned holiday, the REC was concerned that it would not be possible to meet all of their holiday needs in 1945. Their difficulties were being further hampered by the restrictions imposed by the minister of war transport which were intended to ensure that there would be no interference with the working of essential traffic. The GWR claimed that their passenger traffic during the week preceding Christmas in 1944 had exceeded all of the previous records and, although the ministry had prohibited the railway from running more long-distance trains on any one day than were run on an ordinary weekday in December 1943, they actually carried on the heaviest day, Friday, 23 December, 26,000 more passengers from Paddington on long distance trains than on the peak day of the previous Christmas period. In circumstances such as these it proved inevitable that many passengers suffered considerable inconvenience and delays. This inability to provide an adequate service for all passengers was the cause for genuine regret by the GWR management.

Nonetheless on Monday, 5 February the LNER were able to introduce a number of improved East Anglian services to and from Liverpool Street. These included trains to Yarmouth (South Town) and Lowestoft (Central) – these extra trains were run in the evenings. The railway hoped that these improvements to their East Anglia service would alleviate overcrowding caused by the lifting of the coastal defence area ban and would also meet the local demands for a better business service so far as the existing circumstances permitted.

In March 1945 the REC issued an announcement which endorsed the government's recent statement insisting that the staggering of holidays would be even more necessary during the coming summer due not only to the railway transport point of view, but also for the benefit of those travelling for a holiday as well as being advantageous for the proprietors of seaside and holiday accommodation and for those who were responsible for local entertainments and amenities. Despite the known advantages, the REC in another report noted that while these advantages were obvious, it was unfortunate that the efforts that it had made to encourage the widespread adoption of staggered holidays both before and during the war had achieved very little success. There were various reasons for the failure of the scheme which included the need to take into account the school holidays together with the conflicting interests of the many different industries. It was noted however that a major difficulty was the common practice of groups of workers, and often whole towns where there was a predominate local industry – to all take their holidays together. The concept of 'town

holidays' was understood by the REC, and this had been explained by
a committee which had been established by the Ministry of Labour
in 1939 to investigate issues relating to workers' holidays, and their
brief included investigation into any effects which were likely to arise
from the expected increase in those receiving holidays with pay. From
a railway point of view, a more extensive adoption of the staggered
holidays principle which was before the war highly desirable was then
a matter of vital importance. The REC insisted that should there not
be any material progress made, holidaymakers were likely to experience
serious discomfort if they chose to travel at weekends during the 1945
summer months.

On 7 May 1945 Germany surrendered and on 8 May the nation
celebrated VE day. On 23 May Churchill resigned as prime minister
and ran a caretaker administration prior to a general election held
on 5 July. This ushered in a Labour government with the stated aim
of nationalizing the railways. The REC however remained in overall
charge of the railways until the creation of British Railways on
1 January 1948 – a new era had begun.

The many problems facing the railways during the war years were
explained from the GWR point of view in its annual report for 1944/45.
The other three railway company annual reports told a similar story.
The GWR stated that 60 million passenger journeys had been made
in 1944 which was a 64 per cent increase compared to the last full
year of peace in 1938. While the railway's passengers travelled greater
distances, the total passenger train mileage was 10 million miles which
was 23 per cent less than in 1938. The railway had to give priority to
what was deemed essential traffic which was carried successfully despite
the general shortage of locomotives and staff. During the war the GWR
claimed to have been prevented from providing what it deemed to be
an adequate or satisfactory service due to the unprecedented passenger
traffic. To accommodate the extra passengers, most GWR trains had
to be strengthened with additional coaches, and the resulting heavier
loads not only imposed a severe strain on the locomotives but also

affected adversely the general timekeeping of the trains. In many cases the provision of additional coaches made the trains too long to be dealt with at the existing platforms without drawing up a second time, and as many of the long-distance trains were generally overcrowded, they could not be dealt with by the limited, and often inexperienced, station staff within the scheduled time normally allowed. The GWR attributed most of its difficulties in working passenger services to the general shortage of labour.

So, was travel by train as bad as that described in the introduction to this book? All of the elements of the statement were to some extent accurate but not necessarily universal or applicable to the whole war period. Was railway travel three times as expensive? It is difficult to make a precise judgement on this, but the government were always insistent that prices must not rise in order to ration travel, but only as necessary to cover extra costs. The cumulative inflation across the war years was about 50 per cent. This is, of course, much less than the 'three times' quoted, but not many passengers paid the 'full fare' as most who had to travel due to the exigencies of the war travelled at reduced rate – or free – at the government's expense. For those whose travel was not essential, previously available cheap tickets such as the cheap day returns were withdrawn. Therefore the 'three times' is appropriate but only applicable to those such as the lady from Cranleigh who were making purely optional journeys to do 'shopping' in London using cheap day return tickets.

With many more passengers travelling on fewer trains, it is obvious that at times trains would be very crowded. This does not mean however that trains were 'always' overcrowded. The traffic surveys which are on record do show very full trains, but these were taken on known busy services to assess the practicability of proposals such as a permit or limited train arrangement. There is no indication that these were necessarily 'typical' services and as many of them were 'relief' trains it can be judged that the companies were very good at matching capacity demand. The recorded 25 per cent average increase in passengers on any single train has to be seen in the context that trains had extra carriages attached which would have accommodated the additional passengers. Also, at a time when many local passenger trains were run as much for the conveyance of mail and milk within the attached vans, such trains running in rural areas had plenty of extra seating capacity.

It has been shown that most of the 'overcrowding' was due to service personnel so the likelihood of finding a severely overcrowded train was related to the route on which you were travelling. One correspondent commented that trains travelling up to Yorkshire were 'always' full of servicemen and their kit while his local trains in leafy Surrey were not crowded. The complaints that reached parliament about overcrowding on the main line north of King's Cross resulted in the provision of special leave trains which included buffet cars manned by NAAFI staff. These special trains would have relieved the chronic overcrowding on the public trains.

The removal of seat reservations would have simplified administration at a time when clerical labour was short, but it was always possible for groups to reserve whole compartments. There was a wide list of groups eligible, ranging from theatrical groups to parties of seamen whose ships had been sunk in the Atlantic and had been rescued and were on their way home. The railways fought hard to keep their dining cars running in the trains and on-train catering survived two attempts to have them all banned. The railways fought back, and some restaurant services remained, the final demise however was more to do with the shortage of staff, the lack of crockery and linen due to pilfering and shortages of food. Yes, trains were often cancelled or were delayed, but it would seem that this was usually during air raids or during the 'stand to' in preparation just before or after D-Day.

Holiday trains during the war were often overcrowded, but these were relatively few days throughout the year and many 'weary war workers' were more than happy to cram themselves into a train (and at times risk being left behind at a resort due to a full return train) if it meant a break from the monotony of life working hard on war work in a dreary northern town for a day or two by the sea at Blackpool. Furthermore, if anybody remembers travelling to the Isle of Wight by train on a summer Saturday in the 1950s, they will tell you a good tale about peacetime crowded holiday train travel! We need to be very careful of the careless use of the word 'always.' Perhaps 'sometimes', 'often' or 'occasionally' might be more appropriate. If a war worker who always had to scramble to get onto trains on his way to or return from the once-a-year holiday in Blackpool, he might well believe that trains were 'always' full. More regular travellers might feel that trains were 'sometimes' full. One difficulty with the word 'always' is that it is often used to describe one or more well remembered bad travel experiences while the more frequent and boring ordinary journeys are forgotten. With this in mind it is interesting that after the Women's Institute report on neglect of evacuees, the LCC's conclusion was that while the reports were true, these were reported while the more usual satisfactory care went completely unnoticed.

During the Second World War many who travelled on British railways had compelling personal needs to travel and these needs were often amplified by the stressful situation that they found themselves in during the war. Many of the railway journeys made by the civilian population were strictly not 'necessary' journeys, but many might be alternatively classified as 'reasonable' journeys. Part of the perceived wartime mythology is that the British public – working in unison to defeat the enemy – loyally and patriotically followed government instructions at all times. They would never, surely, have undertaken any unnecessary wartime travel. While it s not possible to fully understand each passenger's purely individual motivation to travel or their degree of patriotism in respect to travel, many thousands of people who were not necessarily regular peace-time travellers during the war acquired new reasons to travel which were directly attributable to the exigencies of war and their journeys might be described as reasonable if not strictly necessary. For any personal non-business railway journeys the travellers had to address the moral issue of choosing between the national war effort and any genuine and understandable family commitment. The dilemma was to decide if it was 'necessary' for them to undertake visits to see evacuated children; or to take part in family reunions for those separated by the war – some of whom might be grieving or suffering poor mental health due to the strains of wartime; or if they were service personnel to make extra visits home given that they might soon be posted to a war zone and be killed.

Despite the massive increase in passengers on the trains during the war, it is probable that, despite the critics, campaigns such as 'is your journey really necessary' were successful in reducing passenger numbers. It is likely therefore that, housewives such as the lady from Cranleigh might abandon their regular 'shopping' in London and perhaps venture only to local shops and the businessman journeying to Birmingham might travel less often and fit in two or even three meetings into a single day to cut down on rail travel. The REC minutes do not show that business travel remained at pre-war levels, only that a large proportion 'remained', implying a noticeable reduction. They also conceded that the level of first-class travel had fallen compared with pre-war days, but this had been offset by Government first-class business travel. Many of the population in the 1940s were likely to have taken the issue of patriotism very seriously and obligingly accepted the government's instructions without question however inconvenient or distressing were the consequences. For these people, they exhibited the opposite of the 'myth' described by Calder. But any reduction in passenger numbers due to publicity was more than offset by all the new and compelling reasons for people to travel that have been described. Some of these potential passengers may have been dissuaded by the 'Is Your Journey Really Necessary' campaign but there were mixed messages from the government – do not travel but we will pay half of your rail fare to visit your child who has been evacuated.

Throughout the war there was conflict between the government and the REC. The government were adamant that the railways should take steps to reduce passenger travel but could not offer any practical solutions. But 'doing nothing' did in a sense resolve the situation, the railways continued to accept 'the traffic that presents itself' but gave priority to military traffic when necessary – even if that involved some overcrowding and some extra-long train journeys due to delays. Any constraint on passenger travel was an anathema to the railway companies and the public – if they thought that they had a good reason to do so – were always prepared to travel notwithstanding the overcrowded trains or the government's anti-travel propaganda.

Bibliography

ABERNETHY, Simon Thomas, *Gender, and Commuting in Greater London, 1880 – 1940* unpublished dissertation submitted for the degree of Doctor of Philosophy. July 2015 University of Cambridge Faculty of History.

ADDISON, Paul and CRANG, Jeremy A. *Listening to Britain*. The Bodley Head, London, 2010.

BAKER, Norman, 'A More Even Playing Field – Sport During and after the War' in *Millions Like Us* edited by Hayes, Nick and Hill, Jeff. Liverpool University Press, Liverpool, 1999.

BISHOP, Alan and BENNET Y Aleksandra (Ed). *Vera Brittain's Diary 1939-1945*. Victor Gollancz Ltd, London, 1989.

BROOKSBANK, B.W.L. *London War Damage*. Capital Transport, London, 2007.

CALDER, Angus. *The People's War*. Pimlico, London, 1969.

CALDER, Angus. *The Myth of the Blitz*. Pimlico, London, 1992.

DARWIN, Bernard. *War on the Line*. Southern Railway, London, 1946.

ELLIOT, Sir John. *On and Off the Rails*. George Allen and Unwin, London, 1982.

GARDINIER, Juliet. *Wartime Britain 1939 – 1945*. Review, London, 2005.

HAYES, Nick and HILL, Jeff (Editors). *Millions Like Us*. Liverpool University Press, Liverpool, 1999.

HEARTFIELD, James. *Unpatriotic History of the Second World War*. Zero Books, Alresford, 2012.

KING, John. *Gilbert Szlumper and Leo Amery of the Southern Railway*. Pen and Sword, Barnsley, 2018.

KNOX, Collie. *The Un-beaten Track*. Cassel and Company, London, 1944.

MARSH, James. *A 1940s Childhood*. The History Press, Stroud, 2014.

MCLAINE, Ian. *Ministry of Morale*. George Allen and Unwin, London, 1979.

MOODY, G.T. *Southern Electric*. Ian Allan, London, 1958.

POOLEY, Colin G. and Turnbull, Jean. *The Journey to Work: A Century Of Change*. Area, 1999.

REYNOLDS, David. *Britain, The Two World Wars and The Problem of Narrative: Public Memory, National History and European Identity. The Historical Journal Manuscript* ID HJ-2016-005.R2, Cambridge University Press, Cambridge, 2016.

SLADEN, Chris. 'Wartime Holidays and the "Myth of the Blitz"'. *Journal of Contemporary History*. Sage, London, 2002.

SLADEN, Chris. 'Holidays at Home in the Second World War'. *Journal of Contemporary History*. Sage, London, 2002.

SLADEN, Chris. 'Wartime Holidays and the "Myth of the Blitz"'. *Cultural and Social History*, Vol. 2 No. 2, 2005.

SMITH, Harold L. *Britain in the Second World War*. Manchester University Press, Manchester, 1996.

TODMAN, Daniel, *Britain's War - Into Battle 1937 -1941*. Penguin Random House, London, 2017.

WATTS, D.C.H., 'Evaluating British Railway Poster Advertising: London & North Eastern Railway Between the Wars', *Journal of Transport History*, Vol. 25, Issue 2, 2004.

YASS, Marion. *This Is Your War*. HMSO, London,1983.

Records held at The National Archives:
ADM 1/12832 Courier service London to Bath
ADM 116/3769 Evacuation of Admiralty departments
AIR 2/6135 Addison report, Harrogate staffing
AIR 28/340 Operation record books

AIR 29/490 Air Crewe holding units

AIR 2/4505 Evacuation of Air Ministry staff to Harrogate

AN 2/158 Accommodation for Railway Executive

AN2 /14 Extract from minutes of meeting of the passenger superintendents subcommittee

TNA AN2/3 Government use of railway workshops

AN2/722 Reduction of passenger travel 1941: Inland Transport War
Council

AN 2/732 REC traffic estimates

AN2/989 Provision of soap and towels on trains

AN 3/1 5 Railway Executive Committee (REC) full committee minutes

AN 3/15 REC Coaching (Passenger) subcommittee minutes

AN 3/16 REC Coaching (Passenger) subcommittee minutes AN
3/18 REC Coaching (Passenger) Subcommittee minutes

AN 3/33 REC M&EE subcommittee

AN 3/48 REC catering subcommittee AN 3/51 REC Publicity
Control Subcommittee minutes AN 3/54/31 REC Suggestions
from Readers of *The People* Newspaper

AVIA 15/3624 Ministry of Aircraft Production files

CAB 65/9/2 War Cabinet minutes 3 September 1940

CAB 66/17/46 Control of railways

CAB 65/19/6 Future of the railways

CAB 67/1/35 Diversion of Shipping, 12 October 1939

CAB 67/5/16 The Coal Situation, March 1940 CAB 67/5/16
Transport of Coal, 23 December 1940

CAB 67/8/70 Financial arrangements with the railways 21 October
1940

CAB 123/69 Lord President's files.

HW 64/52 Transport at Bletchley Park

HW 64/73 Recruitment at Bletchley Park

HW 64/70 Staffing conditions Bletchley Park

MAF 127/43 Establishment of war room

MAF 127/52 Treasury report on MAF at Colwyn Bay

RAIL 645/118 Southern Railway Officers' Conference Meetings
RAIL 645/119 Southern Railway Officers' Conference Meetings
RG 23 Social Survey – Getting to Work

London Metropolitan Archives
LMA LCC/EO/WAR/01/001 History of evacuation
LMA LCC/EO/WAR/1/54 LCC evacuation files
LMA LCC/EO/WAR/1/55 LCC evacuation files
Mass Observation:
Six Railway Posters 29 October 1939

Periodicals:
All 1939/45 editions of:
Railway Gazette
Railway Magazine
Southern Railway Staff Magazine
London and North Eastern Railway staff magazine
Great Western Railway staff magazine

Also,
Backtrack January 2016: The Cold War Part 1 Dr. Malcolm Timperley

National and Regional Newspapers
Aberdeen Press and Journal
Arbroath Guide
Barnoldswick and Earby Times
Bath Chronical and Weekly Gazette
Belfast Telegraph
Daily Herald
Daily Mirror
Harrogate Herald
Hartlepool Northern Daily Mail
The Manchester Guardian

Mid-Sussex Times
News and Journal (Aberdeen)
The Evening Telegraph
The Observer
The Scotsman
The Shields Evening News
South Yorkshire Times and Mexborough and Swinton Times
Sussex Agricultural Express
The Times
Western Daily Press and Bristol Mirror
Western Morning News

Internet Sources
britishairways.com
Bath.co.uk/history
bbc.co.uk/history/ww2peopleswar/stories
bath-heritage.co.uk
Catherine Pitt thebathmagazine.co.uk
Derrick Grady,bbc.co.uk/history/ww2peopleswar/stories
From the archive.exploringsurreypast
gazettelive.co.uk/news
history.blog.gov.uk
historyextra.com
kingswood.bath.sch.uk
madeinpreston.co.uk
military-history.fandom.com
Malcolm Neesam thestrayferret.co.uk
massobs.org.uk/mass-observation-1937-1950s
newenglishartclub.co.uk/news/june-berry-studying-art-1940s
rafcommands.com/forum
rafmuseum.org.uk
rhyljournal.co.uk/news//17871308.fascinating-stories-second-
    world-war-evacuation

somersetlive.co.uk/news/somerset-news/remembering-bath-blitz
staybehinds.com
Ukweatherworld.uk (accessed February 2016 – this site is now defunct)
wartimememoriesproject.com

Parliamentary Reports
Hansard

Index

A

Adison,? (Report on conditions
for outposted staff at
Harrogate) 104/5
Admiralty 32–36
Agricultural workers 167
Air Ministry 37–39, 103–105,
109
Air raid Precautions Bill 17
Air raid precautions/
warnings 13, 16, 17, 20,
25–27, 30, 33, 37, 48, 87,
101, 114, 123, 137, 143,
144, 150, 151, 153, 235, 256
Anderson, Sir John 16, 19, 31,
35, 130, 160, 165
Ashfield, Lord 169–173
Attlee, Clement 14, 164

B

Bath 32–36, 81–103, 199, 215
Bath Mayor, Adrian Hopkins 35
BBC Bangor 235
BEF (British Expeditionary
Force) 14, 43, 125, 127
Berkeley Square House 37

Bevin, Ernest 15, 229/30, 242
Bletchley Park 204–211
Blitz 94, 141–152
Buffet Cars 51/2, 55, 116, 121,
135, 182/3, 193/4
Burgin, Leslie MP 44–46
Business travel 50, 53, 56, 71,
84, 98, 104, 106, 113, 117,
120, 130/1, 166/7, 169,
180–182, 211, 221, 234,
236, 242, 253, 258

C

Chamberlain, Neville 17
Christmas Holiday traffic
60–62, 66, 111, 147, 151/2,
188/9, 215/6, 228, 252/3
Churchill, Winston 15, 34, 106,
141
Civil Defence 186, 190, 191,
244
Coal traffic 49, 50, 70, 71, 79,
121, 157/8, 161, 173, 221,
227, 236, 251
Colwyn Bay 108–111, 142, 180,
221, 231, 235/6

Committee of Imperial Defence 45
Commuter traffic 20, 43, 51,
    55, 60, 98, 113, 130, 140,
    142/3, 154

D
D-day 103, 174, 211, 234, 236
Defence Areas 130/1, 177, 221,
    242, 247, 249, 249, 258
Down Street 13
Duncan, Sir Andrew Rae 70
Dunkirk 125/6, 130

E
Easter holiday traffic 166, 174,
    211, 215, 216, 220, 221,
    228, 244/5
Elliot, John 159, 173
Evacuees (children) 17-24,
    81-97, 122-132, 221, 258
Evacuees (government staff)
    35-38, 98-106, 108-121,
    215, 218, 245
Evacuees (individuals) 88, 97,
    147, 156, 167/8, 224

F
Freight traffic 12, 15, 26, 44/5,
    47-49, 57, 64, 74, 81, 134,
    136, 154, 155-157, 159,
    160-162, 165/6, 169, 183/4,
    186, 211, 222, 225/5,
    227/8, 238/9, 243, 248/9

G
General Post Office (GPO) 37,
    68, 106, 181
Goods traffic – see freight traffic
Gresley Sir Nigel 14, 152
GWR (Great Western Railway)
    12, 20, 22, 29, 32, 34, 35, 42,
    53/4, 58, 61/2, 89, 90/1,
    93, 99, 100, 103, 116/7, 119,
    120, 124, 140, 143/4, 151,
    154, 161, 169, 178, 180, 182,
    188, 193, 196, 213/4, 216,
    223, 228, 231, 235, 238, 246,
    248, 250, 252-255

H
Harrogate 37-40, 103-106, 109,
    142, 199, 215, 226
'Holidays-at-home'
    campaign 220-221
Home Guard 100-102, 131,
    186, 190, 191
Hyndley, Lord 70

K
Kent and East Sussex Light
    Railway 12

L
Land Army 167
LCC (London County Council)
    18, 19, 21-23, 81-85, 87-90,
    94-97, 123/4, 130, 257

Leathers, Viscount 163,
    164/5,180, 183, 245
Lighting during blackout
    (on trains) 113-116, 135/6,
    138/9, 145
Lighting during blackout (on
    railway land) 137/8
LMSR (London Midland &
    Scottish Railway) 12, 20,
    23, 32, 40, 42, 54-58, 61,
    66, 92, 114-118, 120/1,
    124, 133, 136, 139, 147,
    149-152, 154, 158, 176,
    180-183, 186, 193-195,
    197, 204, 207, 209, 210,
    213, 215, 217, 218, 221,
    230, 232, 237, 243, 252
LNER (London & North
    Eastern Railway) 12, 14,
    20, 23, 25, 26, 37, 40, 42,
    54-57, 60, 66, 76, 92, 93,
    104, 112, 115-117, 120,
    121, 124, 133, 139, 145,
    151-154, 157/8, 167, 178,
    181, 183/4, 192, 194, 198,
    208, 213/4, 216, 218, 238,
    243, 253
Locomotives (all) 12, 41/2, 49,
    51, 68, 121, 128, 138, 152,
    180, 184, 237-239
  LNER A4 4-6-2 152
  LNER B1 4-6-0 238/9

SR Merchant Navy 4-6-2
    239, 246/7
SR Q1 0-6-0 239, 246, 248
USATC class S160 238
LPTB (London Passenger
    Transport Board) 12, 13,
    27, 72, 116, 157/8, 169,
    189, 190

M
Maxwell, Somerset MP 17
Middlesborough station air
    raid 153
Milne, Sir James 53, 161
Ministry of Aircraft Production
    37/8, 103, 106, 108, 181
Ministry of Health 18, 23, 84,
    87, 95/6, 121/2, 230
Ministry of Transport 11,
    26/7, 31, 45, 84, 89, 90, 93,
    118/9, 128/9, 132/3, 160,
    163, 192, 214
Ministry of War Transport 11,
    163, 170, 173, 175, 179,
    198, 200, 224/5, 227/8,
    230, 232/3, 242/3
Ministry of Works 109
MO (Mass Observation) 17-80,
    175
MOF (Ministry of Food)
    108-111, 235
Missenden, Eustace 14, 128

N

National Air Communications
   Service 105/106
National Union of
   Railwayman 235
Noel-Baker, Phillip MP 175,
   195/6

O

Old Vic theatre 235
Operation Bolero 174, 234, 237,
   239, 242, 244, 249

P

Paddington station air raid 143
Passenger numbers/
   overcrowding surveys 119,
   177, 178/9, 195–199
Pick, Frank 27
Piggott, Sir Henry 209
Private schools 32, 33, 103,168,
   206, 211, 245
Pullman 51, 60, 116, 120, 182

R

RAF 38, 39
(REC) Railway Executive
   Committee 12–15, 19–21,
   24–28, 40–42, 45, 47, 49,
   50–54, 57, 60, 63/4, 70–73,
   77/8, 80/1, 84/5, 105/6,
   112/3, 117–119, 121, 127,
132–134, 142, 155, 157,
   159, 160–170, 172/3,
   175/6, 179, 184, 189,
   191,197, 200/1, 203/4,
   209, 211, 213, 215, 220,
   222–224, 230, 232/3,
   235, 237, 239, 241,
   243–245, 249, 250, 253/4,
   258/9
Restaurant cars 51/52, 54,
   55–57, 60, 61, 116–118, 121,
   134/5, 139, 148, 178–184,
   193/4, 240, 245, 256
ROF (Royal Ordnance
   Factories) 236
Rover car company 237
Royal Artillery's Coast Gunnery
   School 108

S

Sadler's Wells ballet 235
Sankey-Seldon 234
Service personnel travel
   39, 40, 134, 159, 167,
   171, 181, 185, 186–203,
   211
Slade School of Art 235
Slater,? (Report on conditions
   for outposted staff at
   Colwyn Bay) 109, 110
Sleeping Cars 54, 61, 115, 121,
   181, 194/5, 203, 224

SR (Southern Railway) 12, 14,
        21/2, 23, 28, 32, 41/2,
        50-54, 58, 60-62, 67-71,
        90, 93, 112-116, 121,
        124-128, 130, 136, 139,
        140, 142-145, 149, 151/2,
        154, 157-159, 177-179,
        182, 188/9, 193, 196,
        198/9, 214, 221, 223,
        231, 234, 238, 239,
        244-249, 251
Standard Telegraph and Cable
        Company 234
'Stand to' period 243, 256
'Square Deal' campaign 45, 47,
        155
Station buffets 133, 240/1,
        257
Szlumper, Gilbert 14, 22, 132,
        142, 163, 222/3

T
Temple, Richmond 74, 176
Tenth Report from the Select
        Committee on National
        Expenditure Session
        1940–1941 159

Timetables (wartime emergency)
        20-25, 39, 41-43, 49, 50,
        53-57, 60/1, 89, 91, 103,
        112, 117, 122, 125, 132,
        139, 146, 147, 151, 158,
        179, 184, 219, 223, 243

V
V1 raids 251
V2 rockets 251/2
Viant, Samuel MP 195

W
WAAF (Women's Auxiliary Air
        Force) 106-108
Wallace, Euan MP 45, 62, 85,
        88, 113, 213
War workers 158, 222-225, 229,
        230, 235, 242, 251, 256
Wedgwood, Sir Ralph 152, 164
Whitsun holiday traffic 125,
        182, 216-218
Wood, Sir Kingsley 38
Wood, Sir William 176

Y
York station air raid 152